Race Results

Hollywood vs. the Supreme Court
Ten Decades of Racial Decisions and Film

by Eileen C. Moore

COOL
TITLES

TITLES

Published by
Cool Titles
439 N. Canon Dr., Suite 200
Beverly Hills, CA 90210
www.cooltitles.com

The Library of Congress Cataloging-in-Publication Data Applied For

Eileen C. Moore—
Race Results: Hollywood vs. the Supreme Court - Ten Decades of Racial Decisions and Film

p.   cm
ISBN-13: 978-1-935270-00-3
1. Social History   2. Film & Video/General   3. Civil Rights   I. Title
November 2009

Printed in the United States of America

1 3 5 7 9 10 8 6 4 2

Book editing and design by Lisa Wysocky, White Horse Enterprises, Inc.

For interviews or information regarding special discounts for bulk purchases, please contact us at
njohnson@jjllplaw.com

Distribution to the Trade: Pathways Book Service, www.pathwaybook.com, pbs@pathwaybook.com
1-800-345-6665

Editor's Note:
Original quotations have been left in their original form,
regardless of punctuation, spelling or grammar.

Acknowledgements

In the past, I have noticed how some authors go on and on thanking people, and I've wondered if it's a lot of nonsense. Not at all. I found I had to work hard to limit my thanks here to the small number of people who strongly influenced and encouraged me, and just give a group thank you to the many who engaged in discussions and debate that permitted me to ponder and expand kernels of ideas.

At the University of Virginia, Professor Michael Klarman painted a portrait of the America of the 1950s, which started me on my quest of wondering how this great country of ours could have permitted black people to be treated as second and third class citizens. Professor Earl Dudley ignited a fire under me to pursue the crazy idea I had of looking to both the United States Supreme Court and Hollywood for answers.

In the 1990s, while I was still a trial judge on the Superior Court, a lawyer named Neville Johnson tried a case in my courtroom. Years later, I ran into him and his then wife-to-be, Cindy Macho, at a Bar event. He was intrigued enough about my project that he asked to see a copy of my abandoned manuscript. I can say unequivocally there would be no book without Nev. He is a caring person who wants to leave this world in a better condition than how he found it. Because of Nev, I picked it up again and turned it from a thesis into a book.

Nev introduced me to Lisa Wysocky, my editor. Between Lisa and Cindy, now Cindy Johnson, I feel I have a support team brimming with great ideas, hard work and inspiration. They each strongly believe in what I have done.

Finally, and perhaps most importantly, I must thank my husband, Michael Fields, for his constant patience and feedback. He could always be counted on to bounce off ideas and give me a forthright reaction.

Who knows what will happen with the book from here? To quote Yogi Berra, "It's tough to make predictions, especially about the future." But a lot of people have made it a pleasant journey.

Table of Contents

Preface

RACE RESULTS WAS ORIGINALLY WRITTEN as my thesis when I was pursuing my Masters degree at the University of Virginia, which I received in 2004. The three-year program was offered to thirty Supreme Court and Court of Appeal justices from around the country. We stayed at the University of Virginia-Charlottesville (UVA) for six weeks during the summers and submitted a thesis for the degree.

It was an interesting place to find myself. Many of the professors were ten or twenty years younger than the students. Each had both a Juris Doctorate and a PhD in another field. One might suspect such a program to be trivial. Not so. No appellate judge wants to look less than scholarly. And with such learned persons at the front of the classroom, it was a genuine challenge to survive in class. It was much like being back in college. While we did not have the same kind of worry we had back when, such as paying off school loans, getting a job or passing the bar exam, the pressure was on nonetheless. Many a night, I got very little sleep because I was up studying.

The thesis professor pointed out that students usually have to write about an issue litigants drag before the courts. But we were in a unique position to write about something we wanted to write about. He told us to select a topic that would keep us awake at night. My first selection was to write how California's Code of Civil Procedure violates the Separation of Powers doctrine. After selecting that topic, however, I was able to achieve my first full night's sleep since starting the program, and I realized that topic was just too boring.

In our Constitutional Law class, Professor Michael Klarman was in the process of taking us through many Supreme Court cases. He spent quite a bit of time on *Brown v. Board of Education*, the 1954 case that found racial segregation in America's public schools to be unconstitutional. One night in my dorm bed, I started to ponder about that time in America. I became caught up in thinking how good, decent people could permit a system of apartheid to exist in a country dedicated to democracy for all. That's when I thought about two incidents in my own home.

I was a little girl in 1954, the year the *Brown* decision was handed down. I was the third of five children and another baby was on the way. My aunt and grandmother needed to come live with us for financial reasons. Our home at 5712 N. Lambert Street in the Germantown section of Philadelphia had three small bedrooms and one bathroom, so it soon became obvious that we needed to move somewhere that had more space for ten people to live. My parents found a home in Roxborough, another section of Philadelphia. Unfortunately, the first sale of our Lambert Street home fell through. The next offer came from would-be purchasers who were black.

In such a small house it's hard not to hear your parents talking, even when you don't quite understand what is happening. Lambert Street had no black families. My parents knew if they sold their house to a black family, every one else's property values would immediately decline, so they held onto the Lambert Street property until a white buyer appeared. I remember my father saying something to the effect of, "I can't do that to my neighbors." As I recall, it was nine months later that the house sold to a white family.

Meanwhile, since my parents had already purchased the home in Roxborough, they were saddled with two mortgage payments. To say this had to have been a financial strain is putting it lightly; by today's standards, we were poor.

Around 1959, my sister got married. Without a car or even a driver's license my mother rarely went out alone, except to walk to the supermarket. But because of the imminent wedding, she took the bus to downtown Philadelphia to purchase her mother-of-the-bride dress. I still remember the dress: black taffeta with embroidered rust/gold designs.

While she was downtown, she stopped at Woolworth's for a sandwich. She sat at the counter and had her order filled right away. Then a black man sat down next to her. He made his selection promptly and waited for service, but the white man behind the counter ignored the black man. Eventually, and without saying a word, the black man got up and left. Mother left, too, without finishing her lunch. When Mother came home, she was sobbing. It was obvious she felt shame because she said more than once, "I just didn't know what to do."

So in 2002, when I had to select my thesis topic, I found myself wondering what sort of information people such as my parents, and most of our parents and grandparents, were receiving about African Americans:

- Why weren't people marching in the streets decades earlier than they actually did?
- Why was my father afraid of letting his white neighbors down?
- Why didn't my mother know what to say to the man behind the counter?

I wondered who was sending out messages. Of course, the United States Supreme Court, the highest court in the land, was the first institution that came to mind. Who else, I thought, was directly or indirectly providing information about race to the American people? Then the Hollywood movie industry came to mind.

How perfect, I thought. The Court, is often considered the most conservative in the country, and Hollywood has always been perceived as being quite liberal. I devised the idea of comparing the two, decade-by-decade, to see just what legal and cultural messages each was sending to the American people. The idea was very exciting, especially as I had no idea where my comparisons would take me.

Introduction

RACE ISSUES INVOLVING THOSE OF African heritage have been plaguing America since the first footstep onto Plymouth Rock. How could a nation so deeply committed to democracy and equality for all, as the United States of America has always proclaimed itself to be, permit a system of racial apartheid?

Slavery may be long gone, but racial issues are still on our forefront. In 2007, we saw the exoneration of three lacrosse players from Duke University after they were falsely, and very publicly, charged with sexually assaulting an African American woman. That was the same week radio shock jock Don Imus was publicly decried for making derogatory remarks about black women athletes from Dartmouth. The very next week, *60 Minutes* ran a segment about black rock stars who support a form of noninvolvement by discouraging members of the black community from cooperating with the police, even when they are victims of crimes.

How did we get to this point?

The decisions of the United States Supreme Court shape and reflect the changing values of American society. The products of the American motion picture industry also both reflect and shape these values. So parallels may be drawn between decisions of our Supreme Court and expressions of popular culture as shown in motion pictures during the same period. Combined, the two identify changing attitudes toward African Americans and their place in society decade-by-decade.

Critics accuse the United States Supreme Court of accommodating racism in cases involving discrimination against African Americans.[1] Accusations have also been launched against Hollywood[2] to the effect that the movie industry perpetuated the plight of blacks in America, either by directly encouraging racism or by reinforcing stereotypes through deliberateness or insensitivity. Hollywood had a habit of casting the Negro actor either as a clown, a fool, lowly and contented, or as vicious and depraved.[3] As recently as 1995, there was a protest against racial insensitivity and discrimination toward African Americans outside the Oscar awards ceremony.[4] In contrast, George Clooney made remarks at the 2006 Academy Awards about how courageous the film industry has been in tackling difficult topics.

The United States Supreme Court had several opportunities to follow newly enacted laws and shape the recently passed Fourteenth Amendment, which was intended to secure and protect the right to be free from discrimination in the exercise of both state and federal rights.

How black Americans fared before the highest court in the land compared to how they were treated in the movies is the focus here. But to place matters into perspective, a look at what was going on in the country before there ever was a Hollywood is a must.

Shortly after the Civil War, the United States Supreme Court had several opportunities to follow newly enacted laws and shape the recently passed Fourteenth Amendment, which was intended to secure and protect the right to be free from discrimination in the exercise of both state and federal rights. Instead, time and again, the Court ignored the people the amendments were supposed to protect, and chose to protect property and business over civil rights. Without any help from the Court, newly freed slaves were greeted into their free status with repression that was sometimes worse than slavery, instead of the freedom they expected. The bruised South, buoyed with power when it became obvious the new amendments could be circumvented, installed rigid and terrifying laws known as Black Codes to control African Americans.

Meanwhile, as the nineteenth turned into the twentieth century, a handful of immigrants founded the motion picture business. The American film industry created an image of America out of its founders' idealism, a vision so powerful it ultimately shaped the myths, values, traditions and archetypes of America itself. This country soon came to be defined, in large part, by its movies. Its founders actually created the American Dream.[5] The original movie moguls wanted to be more American than Americans. They loved this country. Famous film producer Louis B. Mayer, who eventually headed the Republican Party in California, was so patriotic he took his new country's birthday as his own.[6] But, from what immigrants saw at the time movies started, there was no room in the American dream, or in traditional American values, for American blacks.

One of the earliest filmmakers, however, was not an immigrant at all. Born in Kentucky in 1875, David Llewelyn Wark Griffith pioneered film techniques such as the close-up, cross-cutting, fade-in and fade-out, and was one of the founders of United Artists.[7] D.W. Griffith grew up during Reconstruction, which likely provided him with the types of experiences that drove him to adapt the novel of a raving racist, Thomas Dixon, for his first epic in 1915, *The Birth of a Nation*. Griffith was awarded a special Academy Award in 1935 "for his distinguished creative achievements as director and producer, and his invaluable initiative and contributions to the progress of the motion picture arts."[8]

From their inception, movies provided education as well as amusement. It was D.W. Griffith who started the "message movie." Griffith's films were part of the progressive movement during the decade and a half before World War I. As the art became more sophisticated and advanced, Griffith yearned to make epics with increased artistic independence.[9]

Griffith's 1915 blockbuster, *The Birth of a Nation*, hit the country by storm. It portrayed blacks as being simplistically divided into two types. The good kind was happy and content serving whites. The bad kind wanted to intermarry and brutalize whites. This movie set the racial tone for immigrant moviemakers to follow. Upon hearing of criticism about his movie, Griffith professed surprise that anyone would accuse him of disliking blacks. He defended himself by saying, "That is like saying I am against children."[10]

Other Hollywood moviemakers were also not shy about moralizing in movies. Louis B. Mayer and Adolph Zukor, both said to be paternalistic by nature, freely planted moral lessons and transmitted values.[11] Mayer is supposed to have been so concerned with conveying traditional American values that he was once seen holding Mickey Rooney by the lapels and shouting, "You're Andy Hardy. You're the United States. You're the stars and stripes. Behave yourself. You're a symbol." Zukor, who headed Paramount, envisioned movies as a source of intellectual elevation.[12] That's why Warner Brothers' films seemed to have a mission. They were pegged with a vague, underdog liberalism.

Jack Warner once told a reporter that pictures play an all-important part in the cultural and educational development of the world.[13] *Fortune* reported that Harry Warner had two major interests: business and morals.[14] The motto of Warner Bros. Studio was, "Combining good picture-making with good citizenship."[15] For years Columbia Pictures, headed by self-styled moralist Harry Cohn, produced one smart "moral comedy" after another.[16] Lessons about the evils management inflict upon

For decades there was no room for blacks in America's expanding notion of liberty and equality, and there were few lessons on racial tolerance.

labor, the horrors of war, the importance of accepting foreign cultures into American life, and the value of freedom were injected in liberal doses by moviemakers.

But for decades there was no room for blacks in America's expanding notion of liberty and equality, and there were few lessons on racial tolerance. In films, blacks were cast as buffoons or as being evil. White audiences confirmed their beliefs about blacks at their neighborhood theater. Negroes fortified their inferiority complexes at separate theaters. The theme of white virtue always triumphing over black vice in films was so commonplace, NAACP[17] author Loren Miller lamented its effects in the early 1930s. He had been in a "Negro movie house" when the scene depicted a beautiful blond heroine in the clutches of savage Africans. Just as hope was ebbing away, she was saved. Miller said that ordinary Negro working people burst into wild applause as she was rescued. "Obviously those spectators were quite unconscious of the fact that they were giving their stamp of approval to a definite pattern of racial relationships in which they are always depicted as the lesser breed."[18] Hollywood was seemingly oblivious to the abomination of race discrimination in its products.

Unequal treatment of blacks in America became so deeply imbedded in the American psyche, that when the United States Supreme Court finally decided to interpret cases according to the spirit and intent of the founders of the Fourteenth Amendment, it was too little and too late. Racial beliefs about differences between blacks and whites had been completely inducted into the American way of life.

It took a combination of circumstances to jump-start white Americans into the reality of what "democracy" was doing to their black countrymen. The most shocking impact to the national consciousness was World War II. As the world watched what bullies with power could do to the weak, Americans began to wake up and come to grips with what they were doing in their own backyard.

The earliest American film studied for this book that had black adults mingling among mainstream whites as equals was made in 1945, eighty years after slavery ended, and the scene was only a few seconds long. Shocking though it was to Americans, World War II was still not enough to shake people into racial change. Despite the Court's valiant effort at school integration in 1954, the white majority was not ready to consider significant change until the 1960s when blacks, frustrated with the slow wheels of justice, took matters into their own hands. On national television, blacks told the emperor he wore no clothes. For all the world to see, white American home grown bullies were seen beating peaceful black protesters. Shocked television viewers watched as fire hoses and German Shepherds were turned on black children. Finally, most white Americans began to comprehend the extent of the black bondage that existed under the stars and stripes.

Had the United States Supreme Court done its job earlier, when the Abolitionist Movement with books such as Uncle Tom's Cabin and underground railroads had already primed the American psyche for acceptance, blacks probably could have insinuated themselves into mainstream America decades earlier.

Had the United States Supreme Court done its job earlier, when the Abolitionist Movement with books such as *Uncle Tom's Cabin* and underground railroads had already primed the American psyche for acceptance, blacks probably could have insinuated themselves into mainstream America decades earlier. Martin Luther King, Jr. once remarked that while a court can declare rights, it cannot deliver them.[19] Even when the country's laws were finally racially neutral, the minds of its people were still closed to anything but racial difference and segregation.

When blacks were finally able to get the South's boot off their jugulars and vote in meaningful numbers, they amassed their own political power, and accomplished critical advances on their own. Had the Court acted sooner, blacks probably could have made their achievements earlier. When the timing is right, public perception and sentiment can be turned around within a brief period. Witness the significant change in attitudes about slavery that took place in the North less than a decade after the Abolitionist Movement started. Militant abolitionists dated from the early 1830s, and within ten years, a younger generation in the North took the morality of abolition for granted.[20] Because the Court was remiss in its job, by not interpreting the Constitution—and later the Fourteenth Amendment—the way its founders intended, Hollywood, perhaps unwittingly, added insult and injury to blacks by imbedding an idealized version of racism into the American subconscious.

Ironically, even though both the post-Civil War Supreme Court and early filmmakers reflected what they saw in America's racial landscape, they shaped, and often imbedded, segregation and bigotry into America's soul. Movies kept prejudice alive, even sometimes whipping it up, and made the breakdown of racial chauvinism more difficult. The Supreme Court wasted decades of reform by applying newly passed Constitutional Amendments to property and contract rights, instead of allowing blacks to benefit from them, as was intended.

But, as the twentieth century progressed, the two institutions parted ways. The movie industry persisted in its negative portrayals of blacks while the United States Supreme Court, often because of the legal creativity and insistence of the NAACP, pressed Congress and the states to apply the law on a racially equal basis.

When the Civil Rights Movement reached the majority of Americans, however, even Hollywood produced films that portrayed blacks realistically and sympathetically. But the halcyon days of the 1960s did not prove profitable at the box office because of the competitive combination of television and moves to the suburbs. When faced with reflecting African Americans in American society, versus using them as a means of drawing Americans back to the movies by negatively portraying blacks, the movie industry took the low road. Raunchy sex and violent scenes were used as the backdrop for most black actors from around 1970 until the end of the twentieth century. Movie after movie depicted black actors as lowlifes, prostitutes, violent criminals and drug abusers.

The Supreme Court, often considered one of the most conservative institutions in the country, took a different course than Hollywood. The Court led up to its landmark decision in the 1954 case of *Brown v. Board of Education* for decades. Once the Court committed itself to eliminating legal protections for a segregated American society, it never veered off that track. The justices, whether nominated by Republican or Democratic presidents, committed themselves to ridding the country's laws of discrimination. Thus, the institution frequently criticized for being too slow and resistant to change, the United States Supreme Court, pressed toward equal rights for African Americans. After the first few decades of the twentieth century and throughout the rest of the century, the United States Supreme Court was consistently more progressive than Hollywood in its treatment of African Americans.

On the other hand, the film industry committed itself to its bottom line. Equality, humanity and basic fairness toward blacks were mostly ignored. The American institution most often branded as being too liberal, Hollywood, was actually quite backward with its negative, and often racist, portrayals of blacks in its movies.

The Process

SO HOW DID I COME to my conclusions? And how did I choose which movies and court decisions to review to get to those conclusions? I knew right away that I wanted to include only those movies and decisions that affected the mindset and perception of the majority of Americans, for these were what shaped the thoughts and actions of generations of our citizens.

Much has been written about black genre films,[21] which usually have a black producer, director or writer and speak to black audiences, but they were not the movies that were seen by most white Americans. Nor were they likely to shape white public opinion. For the most part these films are brilliant, but, because their message was from blacks to blacks, most were not used for comparison here. Instead, popular films seen by the majority are discussed, so as to examine messages about race that were sent by the mainstream movie industry. This demonstrates what Hollywood was telling white audiences about blacks.

Deciding which movies to include was not easy. There were many movies before 1915, but that year has been selected as the one to begin film research for a number of reasons. There were many changes in the film industry around that time. Editorial techniques in film making had reached a certain sophistication.[22] Nickelodeons tailed off and movie palaces grew in neighborhoods. Around that time producers were yearning for increased middle class respectability to lure more people to the movies.[23] And, perhaps most significantly, 1915 was the year *The Birth of a Nation* was released to movie theaters.

To incorporate the most popular and influential movies, four categories are covered. The first three categories were chosen to include an element of objectivity to the selection process. The fourth category is purely subjective. First are Academy Award winners for Best Picture of the Year; second are the American Film Institute's Top 100 American Films; third are films of acclaimed and popular director Alfred Hitchcock[24] because his films span several decades; and, fourth, a category which could be called miscellaneous, will include other films that appear to be relevant.

We start with a general background account about African Americans managing their lives post slavery. Then, for each decade of the twentieth century, and the first decade of the present century, there is information on racial circumstances in America, a description of significant Supreme Court cases that deal with race, and a racial analysis of films. At the end of each decade there is a wrap-up that includes the racial implications of the legal decisions and the movies of that decade. Finally, both legal cases and movies from a broader perspective are reviewed.

The front page of on an 1857 issue of Frank Leslie's Illustrated Newspaper covered the Dred Scott case where the United States Supreme Court ruled that a slave who entered a non-slave state could not therefore gain freedom. The decision increased anti-slavery feeling in the North, and lead to America's Civil War. (Photo by MPI/Getty Images)

General Background

AMERICAN RACIAL ARRANGEMENTS ARE UNIQUE and have resulted in highly visible, yet numerically inferior, black groups that often have been ostracized from the larger white group.[25] Author and civil rights reporter Marshall Frady said that as early as Thomas Jefferson, there was recognition of the basic fundamental crisis faced by this republic, that of racial schism and "that the American political adventure, conceived in such brave hope and largeness of idea, may have also held from its very inception, when the first black man in chains set his foot on the continent's shores, the seeds of its undoing."[26]

African slaves were brought to this country centuries ago mainly to pick cotton.[27] Practical though their intentions were, early Americans were well aware of the abomination of slavery. During the revolution, Jefferson blamed slavery on King George, accusing him of waging a cruel war against human nature by violating its most sacred rights of life and liberty in bringing people from a distant land into "an assemblage of horrors in another hemisphere."[28] Instead of inserting such an accusation into the Declaration of Independence, as was first considered, compromises were made to induce South Carolina into participating in the union. That's why words were included in the Constitution that barred congressional prohibition of slavery.[29] Another provision discussed the return of runaway slaves. "No Person held to Service of Labour in one State, under the Laws thereof, escaping into another, shall, in Consequence of any Law or Regulation therein, be discharged from such Service or Labour, but shall be delivered upon Claim of the Party to whom such Service or Labor may be due."[30]

Slavery was based on fear. Every African American in the slave states was subject to random terror—beatings of all kinds, mutilation, sale to another master, marriages broken up, children sold down the river. By law, the slaves could not read or write.[31] During America's early years, a code of silence governed the country's approach to slavery. Instead of speaking honestly about slavery, our founders masked the deeper issue by discussing the slavery system as if it were a bland but tedious governmental detail. For example, John Adams wrote in a letter to Thomas Jefferson, "I hope some good natured way or another will be found out to untie this very intricate knot."[32]

The Abolitionist Movement

While the government remained inept at abolishing slavery, private individuals actively protested its existence with a very vocal abolitionist movement. William Lloyd Garrison began publishing the *Liberator* in 1831. Its front page motto read, "I am earnest—I will not equivocate—I will not excuse—I will not retreat a single inch—*and I will be heard*." Garrison depended on moral persuasion to battle slavery in the United States.

By the end of the 1830's a younger generation took the morality of abolition for granted, and began to take up anti-slavery positions and exercise influence against slavery. Historian Paul Johnson claims this was the beginning of liberal humanitarianism in the United States. An underground railroad assisted runaway slaves to free soil. Northern legislatures passed laws that made it difficult to enforce the Fugitive Slave Act, and slave-hunters became increasingly unpopular. On July 4, 1854, Garrison burned a copy of the Constitution with the words, "So perish all compromises with tyranny."[33]

Remarkable for its political influence was a book published in 1852, *Uncle Tom's Cabin*, by a Connecticut woman, Harriet Beecher Stowe. It sold ten thousand copies the first week, and three hundred thousand copies by the end of the year. In Britain it sold 1,200,000 copies the first year. Black servants and abolitionist literature provided her information about slavery. Angry Southerners challenged its authenticity, so the author and her family combed newspaper clippings and reports of actual cases. The real cruelties and injustices were far worse than Stowe's fictional account. Some thought it the greatest novel ever written, and it was translated into forty languages. Novelties such as statues, toys, games, handkerchiefs, wallpaper, cutlery and plates were made from the story of Eliza, Tom, Eva, Topsy and the other book characters. "Uncle Tom" is considered one of the most successful propaganda tracts of all

Many legal scholars consider the Dred Scott decision to be the worst ever rendered by the Supreme Court.

time, and some believed Mrs. Stowe was responsible for Lincoln's election.[34]

In 1856 the United States Supreme Court handed down *Scott v. Sanford*, 60 S.C. 393, popularly known as "The Dred Scott case." The opinion, written by Chief Justice Roger Taney, a southerner, said that slaves, while they could be citizens of individual states, were not citizens of the United States; that Congress did not have the power under the Constitution to forbid slavery in the territories; and, furthermore, that slaves were property protected by the United States Constitution.

Taney, part of the agricultural aristocracy of the South, was very protective of the property of his own kind. One law professor said of him, " . . . Taney is [to be] damned for a cantankerous if not malevolent divisiveness that, except for Lincoln and the force of arms, might have rent the nation permanently asunder."[35] Many legal scholars consider the Dred Scott decision to be the worst ever rendered by the Supreme Court. It triggered violent reaction and irreconcilable partisan passions. The North and South soon moved toward civil war.[36]

Meanwhile, slaves prayed for liberty. African American scholar W.E.B. DuBois said that "few men ever worshiped freedom with half such unquestioning faith as did the American Negro for two centuries. To him so far as he thought and dreamed, slavery was indeed the sum of all villainies, the cause of all sorrows, the root of all prejudice; Emancipation was the key to a promised land of sweeter beauty that ever stretched before the eyes of wearied Israelites. In song and exaltation swelled one refrain—liberty . . . ."[37]

One chant heard in slave quarters went: "Oh freedom! Oh freedom! Oh freedom over me! Before I'll be a slave, I'll be buried in my grave, and go home to my Lord and be free."[38]

The End of Slavery

Eventually the prayers of the slaves were heard, and a war was fought over their freedom. Historian Arthur Bestor says the Civil War was, in a subtle sense, a constitutional crisis. The Union

Roger Brooke Taney (1777-1864) circa 1825. This American politician and jurist was Chief Justice of the United States Supreme Court from 1836-64. He is known for his ruling in the Dred Scott case, in which he held that slaves were not United States citizens and could not bring lawsuits into federal courts. (Photo by Hulton Archive/Getty Images)

had often been viewed as nothing more than a compact among sovereign states. With constitutional interpretation, it could be dissolved. Doctrines of strict versus loose construction of the Constitution were pitted against each other. Constitutional theories about slavery developed around economic issues, since the economic life of many regions of the South depended upon the labor slavery provided.[39]

Yet the non-economic aspects of slavery were what made the issue so inflammatory. The institution of slavery also provided a social order for the races. Some evidence of this can be seen in the 1860 census, which revealed that more than half the slaves in the nation were held in bondage outside the boundaries of the original Union.[40]

The Civil War officially ended slavery. Educator and former slave Booker T. Washington later related how he found out about his emancipation. "The night before the eventful day, word was sent to the slave quarters to the effect that something unusual was going to take place at the big house the next morning. There was little, if any, sleep that night. All was excitement and expectancy. Early the next morning, word was sent to all the slaves, old and young, to gather at the house. In company with my mother, brother and sister, and a large number of other slaves, I went to the master's house. All of our master's family were either standing or seated on the veranda of the house where they could see what was to take place and hear what was said. . . . The most distinct thing that I now recall in connection with the scene was that some man, who seemed to be a stranger, a United States officer, I presumed, made a little speech, and then read a rather long paper. The Emancipation Proclamation, I think. After the reading, we were told that we were all free, and could go when and where we pleased. My mother, who was standing by my side, leaned over and kissed her children, while tears of joy ran down her cheeks."[41]

After the Civil War, a Union commander in Virginia remarked that most southern whites wished to reduce blacks to a condition that would give the former masters all the benefits of slavery, but none of the responsibilities. He said he thought it would be dangerous to leave the freedmen to the care of state legislatures.[42] The Thirteenth Amendment to the United States Constitution (which prohibited slavery), the Fourteenth Amendment (intended to guarantee federal and state constitutional rights for all), and the Fifteenth Amendment, (which gave the right to vote to all citizens regardless of race), were passed and ratified as attempts to assure a smooth transition for the freedmen.[43] Proponents of the Fourteenth Amendment wanted a specific mandate of color blindness, but their proposals were rejected, and non-specific language was the most they were able to achieve. While there was a commitment in the North to end slavery and allow blacks to have the rights to hold property, have access to the courts, and enter into contracts, it was not sufficiently strong enough to

The Thirteenth Amendment to the United States Constitution (which prohibited slavery), the Fourteenth Amendment (intended to guarantee federal and state constitutional rights for all), and the Fifteenth Amendment, (which gave the right to vote to all citizens regardless of race), were passed and ratified as attempts to assure a smooth transition for the freedmen.

induce black enfranchisement, legalize interracial marriage or integrate schools.[44]

Reconstruction

Ulysses S. Grant was President during most of the Reconstruction period. In his annual message to Congress in December 1874, Grant said, "Treat the Negro as a citizen and a voter, as he is and must remain, and soon parties will be divided not on the color line but on principle. Then we shall have no complaint of sectional interference."[45] The last federal troops left the South in 1877.[46] Grant's appeal was ignored and the Union commander's fears proved to be true. As soon as the northern troops were gone, oppressive laws against African Americans, known as black codes, were passed throughout the defeated South.[47]

In 1866, the Ku Klux Klan was founded in Tennessee. Historian Stephen Ambrose says the KKK was a continuation of the war, an attempt from Southern planters to maintain at least a part of what they had enjoyed before the war.[48]

Within a few years, the Ku Klux Klan was at the height of its activity—bands of men whose purpose was to regulate the conduct of black people, with the express goal of preventing blacks from exercising any influence in politics. They corresponded somewhat with the patrollers from slavery days, who were bands of white men organized for the purpose of regulating the conduct of the slaves at night. Essentially, they prevented slaves from going from one plantation to another without passes, and kept slaves from holding any kind of meeting without permission, and without the presence of at least one white man. Booker T. Washington said, "Like the patrollers, the 'Ku Klux' operated almost wholly at night. They were, however, more cruel than the patrollers. Their main objects in the main were to crush the political aspirations of the Negroes, but they did not confine themselves to this, because school houses and churches were burned by them, and many innocent persons were made to suffer."[49]

During the entire Reconstruction period, from about 1867 to 1878, former slaves throughout the South looked to the federal government for help. "I had the feeling," said Booker T. Washington, "that it was cruelly wrong of the central government, at the beginning of our freedom, to fail to make some provision for the general education of our people, in addition to what the states might do, so that the people would be better prepared for the duties of citizenship. . . . I had the feeling that mistakes were being made, and that things could not remain in the condition they were in then very long. I felt that the Reconstruction policy, so far as it related to my race, was in a large measure on a false foundation, was artificial and forced. In many cases, it seemed to me, that the ignorance of my race was being used as a tool to help white men into office. That there was an element in the North that wanted to punish the southern white men by forcing the Negroes into positions over the heads of the southern whites. I felt that the Negro would be the one to suffer for this in the end. Besides, the general political agitation drew the attention of our people away from the more fundamental matters of perfecting themselves in the industries at their doors, and in securing property. . . . I saw colored men who were members of the state legislatures and county offices who, in some cases, could not read or write, and whose morals were as weak as their education. . . . More and more I am convinced that the final solution of the political end of our race problem would be for each state that finds it necessary to change the law bearing upon the franchise to make the law apply with absolute honesty, without opportunity for double-dealing or evasion, to both races alike. Any other course, my daily observation in the South convinces me, would be unjust to the Negro, unjust to the white man, and unfair to the rest of the states in the union, and will be, like slavery, a sin that, at some time, we shall have to pay for."[50]

Jim Crow

Jim Crow was a term used in popular minstrel shows of the nineteenth century. The minstrel shows featured white actors who wore black-faced make-up and danced to the refrain, "Jump Jim Crow." That refrain was also used to refer to post-Civil War segregation laws, the black codes. Blacks in many states were soon restricted to Jim Crow drinking fountains, railroad cars, theater sections, hospitals and schools.[51] New vagrancy laws provided ominous supplementary controls.[52]

Reality Was Less Than Ideal

The reality of the Jim Crow South was a far cry from the loose promises that had been made to the freedmen. They expected property and political power. It had long been the more or less expressed theory of the North that the chief problems of emancipation might be settled by establishing the slaves on the forfeited lands of their masters, a sort of poetic justice said some.

The celebrated Field Order Number 15 stated all islands from Charlestown south, the abandoned rice fields along the rivers for thirty miles back from the sea, and the country bordering the St. John's river, Florida, were reserved for the settlement of Negroes who were set free by the war. The property was to be placed in the hands of the Freedmen's Bureau for lease and sale to ex-slaves in forty-acre tracts.[53]

The ideal of liberty demanded powerful means, and idea of the Fifteenth Amendment was to give the freedman freedom.

The ideal of liberty demanded powerful means, and idea of the Fifteenth Amendment was to give the freedman freedom. The ballot he had once looked upon as a visible sign of freedom, he now regarded as the means of gaining and perfecting the liberty that the war had partially endowed him. "And why not?" asked DuBois in "The Souls of Black Folk." "Had not votes made war and emancipated millions? He simply wishes to make it possible for a man to be both a Negro and an American without being cursed and spit upon by his fellows, without having the doors of opportunity closed roughly in his face."[54]

DuBois pointed out that many dreams were shattered. One day the commissioner of the Freedmen's Bureau told the freedmen their land was not theirs. There was a mistake somewhere. Not a single southern legislature stood ready to admit an African American, under any conditions, to the polls. DuBois wrote, "There was scarcely a white man in the South who did not honestly regard emancipation as a crime, and its practical nullification as a duty."[55]

A race feud was beginning. Throughout the rural South, black farmers were peons, bound by law and custom to an economic slavery from which the only escape was death or the penitentiary. As soon as the crop was ready, the merchant took possession of it, sold it, paid the landowner his rent, subtracted bills for supplies, and if there was anything left, as was not always the case, he handed it over to the black serf. The result was continued bankruptcy of the tenant. Once in debt, it was not easy for an entire race to emerge. If the African American escaped, a white sheriff could be counted upon to return him to the master, since the black man was always in debt.[56]

The police system of the south was primarily designed to control black men, and tacitly assumed that every white man was a member of the police. The first and almost universal device was to use the courts as a means of re-enslaving the blacks. It was not a question of crime, but one of color that settled a man's conviction on almost any charge.

In this way, W.E.B. DuBois said African Americans came to look upon courts as instruments of injustice and oppression, and upon those convicted in them as martyrs and victims. When the real black criminal appeared, and instead of petty stealing and vagrancy, was guilty of robbery, burglary, murder and rape, there was a curious effect. Blacks refused to believe the evidence of white witnesses or the fairness of white juries. So the greatest deterrent to crime, the opinion of one's own social cast, was lost, and the criminal was looked upon as crucified rather than hanged.[57]

The police system of the south was primarily designed to control black men, and tacitly assumed that every white man was a member of the police.

Existing Separately

Education in the South was horrid for whites, but much worse for blacks. Of every five dollars spent on public schools in Georgia, white schools got four dollars, and black schools one. Inferior education notwithstanding, it was the lack of social interaction that prevented the races from understanding each other. While there was daily intermingling of the two worlds, there was almost no community of intellectual life or transference where the thoughts and feelings of one race came into direct contact and sympathy with the thoughts and feelings of the other. There was little or no intellectual commerce. They went to separate churches. They lived in separate sections. They were separated at public gatherings. They traveled separately. They read different papers and books.

DuBois lamented that "[i]n a world where it means so much to take a man by the hand and sit beside him, to look frankly into his eyes and feel his heart beating with red blood. In a world where a social cigar or a cup of tea together means more than legislative halls and magazine articles and speeches, one can imagine the consequences of such utter absence of social amenities between strange races."[58]

Blacks developed their own culture by combining their African heritage with their American experience, according to DuBois. He said the black preacher became a unique personality: he was a leader, a politician, an orator, a boss, an intriguer, an idealist. Black religious music, with its rhythmic melody and touching cadences was an original and beautiful expression of human life and longing. "It," he said, "became the one true expression of a people's sorrow, despair and hope."[59]

The African American church, with its characteristic African character, became the social heart of black life in the United States. Churches were the hubs of entertainment, culture and lectures. Strangers were introduced. Jobs were found. Money was collected and churches became centers of immense and far-reaching power.[60]

No Friends Here

In 1873 the United States Supreme Court demonstrated it could not be counted as a friend to the freedmen when it almost succumbed to the business-backed interpretation of the due process clause of the Fourteenth Amendment. The Louisiana Legislature, some say because its members were bribed,[61] awarded one company a twenty-five-year monopoly of the slaughterhouse business in New Orleans, a move that could be considered the type of health measure state legislatures usually pass. But, competing slaughterhouses hired former Supreme Court justice Joseph Campbell to plead they had been deprived of property without due process of law.[62] Due process is the idea that the government must respect all legal rights owed to a person that are stated by law. The Court dealt a fatal blow to part of the Fourteenth Amendment in *The Slaughterhouse Cases*, 83 U.S. 36, by making a close textual reading, which is a careful interpretation of a brief passage of text. In effect, the Court deleted the privileges and immunities clause of the Fourteenth Amendment, which says that no State can make or enforce any law that reduces the privileges or immunities of citizens of the United States, from the Constitution.

Of every five dollars spent on public schools in Georgia, white schools got four dollars, and black schools one.

The *Slaughterhouse* ruling emasculated one of the three main clauses of Section One of the Fourteenth Amendment, and narrowed the scope of the amendment's protection.[63] As a result, the freedmen were left to the law of the particular state of residence for protections of privileges and immunities within a state. Blacks who lived in states that passed black codes were not likely to find protection against race discrimination under their own state constitutions.

In 1876 the Court held in *United States v. Cruikshank*, 92 U.S. 542, in a case that involved the massacre of more than one hundred black men, that the indictments of the white defendants were deficient because they did not allege a denial of federal rights of the black men. The Court ruled the rights of due process and equal protection in the Fourteenth Amendment limited actions by states, and not by individuals, and concluded that any punishment of the white men for the murders must lie with the state of Louisiana.

In *Strauder v. West Virginia*, 100 U.S. 303, the Court held in 1880 a statute that expressly limited jury service to white males violated the Fourteenth Amendment's Equal Protection Clause. But advantages to this ruling were negated by the Court's holding in *Virginia v. Rives*, 100 U.S. 313, that absence of black men from juries, no matter how complete, systematic or obvious, was not a violation of the Fourteenth Amendment. So successful exclusion of black men from juries depended upon selecting a jury commissioner who was willing to claim with a straight face that the jury pool included all eligible persons.

In 1896 the Supreme Court gave the federal government's seal of approval to segregation. In *Plessy v. Ferguson*, 163 U.S. 537, the Court upheld a Louisiana statute that

Successful exclusion of black men from juries depended upon selecting a jury commissioner who was willing to claim with a straight face that the jury pool included all eligible persons.

required "separate but equal" accommodations for the races when traveling on railroads. The dispute arose as a test case to challenge a Jim Crow law. The challenge had support from the railroad officials, who objected to the increased costs of supplying separate cars.

Hoping to strike down the law, the Citizens' Committee of New Orleans recruited a black man named Homer Plessy. On June 7, 1892, Plessy bought a first-class ticket for a commuter train, sat down in the car for white riders and the conductor asked whether he was a colored man. Plessy was arrested when he said he was not.

Here, the Court interpreted the Thirteenth Amendment to apply only to actions whose purpose was to reintroduce slavery itself. The case also held the statute did not violate the Fourteenth Amendment's requirement that all citizens had the right to equal protection under the law. The main point was that laws that required separation of the races did not suggest that one race was inferior to another. By analogy, the opinion linked transportation with education, and gave the Court's approval to segregated schools as well. A sole dissenter, John Marshall Harlan, argued the Thirteenth Amendment restricted not only slavery, but badges of slavery.[64]

Intent Versus Application

Modern historians can still find solid evidence that racial segregation was the original understanding of the framers of the Fourteenth Amendment. Michael Klarman wrote: "To circumvent that evidence, it is necessary either to reject originalism as one's theory of constitutional interpretation or to focus one's originalist lens at a higher level of generality, attending to the Framers' general conceptions of equality rather than to their views about the permissibility of particular social practices."[65]

The Constitution had been amended in 1866 to assure national powers over persons and property in the States in an effort prevent race discrimination. The Fourteenth Amendment was supposed to secure and protect a constitutional right to be free from discrimination in the exercise of one's state or federal.[66] The amendment was crammed down the craw of the defeated South, since no state was allowed re-admission to the Union until it ratified it.

In the middle of one of the five sections of the amendment are the words, "nor shall any state deprive any person of life, liberty, or property, without due process of law." The phrase was copied from the Fifth Amendment,[67] which forbids the *federal* government from making such deprivations. As originally written, the Fifth Amendment meant that no one suspected of a crime could be hanged, jailed or fined without fair, legal treatment before and after trial.[68] But Supreme Court justices who were committed to protecting wealth twisted the due process clause of the Fourteenth Amendment, and the clause came to mean something quite different than the equivalent words in the Fifth Amendment.

Over a thousand Supreme Court decisions have since revolved around the due process clause of the Fourteenth Amendment, and they have rarely dealt with African Americans accused of a crime. Instead, cases deal with corporations who claimed through their lawyers that some state law, which taxed or regulated their business activities in some way, deprived them of property without due process. Each legislator who had a hand in putting the Fourteenth Amendment into the Constitution thought he was helping insure the civil rights of the freedmen. Author Fred Rodell wrote that the legislators "had no notion that he was sheltering corporate and other businesses, way into the indefinite future, from vexatious state regulations. . . ."[69]

The Supreme Court dealt one more blow to blacks in *Allgeyer v. Louisiana*, 165 U.S.578, in 1897 by emasculating another phrase of the Fourteenth Amendment that was meant to protect them. It followed the corporate version of the due process clause of the Fourteenth Amendment and held that it guaranteed the right to enter into lawful contracts and protected liberty to contract. Ignoring the intent and purpose of the post-war amendments, the Supreme Court time and again protected property, while leaving the freedmen to fend for themselves.

In *Williams v. Mississippi*, 170 U.S. 213, decided in 1898, an all-white grand jury indicted African American Henry Williams for murder and an all-white petit jury convicted him and sentenced him to be hanged. Williams argued a violation of the Equal Protection Clause of the Fourteenth Amendment because blacks had been excluded from jury service. The Supreme Court held in 1898 the statute, which kept blacks off juries, was fair. It found legislative intent was irrelevant, even though blacks were kept from serving on Mississippi juries by a statute that provided that only qualified voters could serve on juries. The twist was that another statute limited the number of black voters by requiring both literacy and a poll tax. What was important, said Justice Joseph McKenna for the court, was there was no indication the law was administered in an unequal manner. After this ruling, other southern states followed Mississippi's lead. Poll taxes, literacy tests and white-only primary elections effectively kept southern blacks from voting.[70]

Of the three big phrases in the Fourteenth Amendment, which were held out as protection of black Americans after they had been freed from slavery (the privileges and immunities clause, the due process clause and the Equal Protection Clause) only

Poll taxes, literacy tests and white-only primary elections effectively kept southern blacks from voting.

Plessy's "separate but equal" interpretation of the Equal Protection Clause left any hope for African Americans as the end of the century loomed near. Rodell remarked that the South "latched onto the 'separate' and laughed off the 'equal'"[71] did not seem to bother the Supreme Court. In 1899 the Court refused to enforce the "equal" part of the "separate but equal" doctrine it approved in *Plessy v. Ferguson*. In *Cumming v. Richmond County Board of Education*, 175 U.S. 528, the Court invoked a nearly impossible standard for African Americans parents who sued when Augusta, Georgia's first high school for blacks was closed for lack of funds. For the Court, Justice Harlan wrote the plaintiffs had to prove the school board was motivated solely by "hostility to the colored population because of their race."[72]

A New Century

The legend above the portal to the United States Supreme Court reads "Equal Justice Under Law." As the nineteenth slid into the twentieth century, former slaves and their descendants had little reason to rely on those words.

Meanwhile, there was a diminishing commitment in the North for racial equality. One factor was that the preceding decade saw a massive migration of southern blacks to the North. Another was concern among Northerners about the dilution of the country with strong immigration from southern and eastern Europe. America's imperialist adventures in annexing Hawaii and acquiring Puerto Rico and the Philippines was, to a certain extent, justified on racial terms. It was considered to be manifest destiny and the "white man's burden."[73]

While touring Europe in 1899, Booker T. Washington met Justices Harlan and Fuller at a reception at the American Embassy in Paris.[74] Chief Justice Melville Fuller, who as an Illinois legislator led the opposition to Lincoln's Emancipation,[75] was on the side of the majority in *Plessy*. John Marshall Harlan, a former slave holder,[76] was the lone dissenting justice in *Plessy*. And Booker T. Washington was a former slave. What were the three men thinking as they sipped their champagne?

By now, intrepid Midwesterners had settled in a place close to Los Angeles, about twelve miles from the Pacific Ocean. Coyotes, skunks and rabbits roamed freely. The place was christened in remembrance of Illinois's holly bushes. Hollywood was born.[77]

1901-1910
Racial Framework

AT THE BEGINNING OF THE twentieth century, W.E.B. DuBois feared that God was about to punish America for its race complications.[78] Blacks in many states were restricted to Jim Crow drinking fountains, railroad cars, theater sections, hospitals and schools.[79] By 1904, the average number of blacks lynched annually exceeded one hundred, becoming in some communities a perverse form of entertainment for white families."[80]

As blacks migrated from the South, they settled in various cities along the way north. Thoroughgood[81] Marshall, and his wife, Annie, settled in Baltimore. They opened a small grocery store, and Annie Marshall objected when the electric company decided to install a light pole in the middle of the sidewalk in front of the store. Day after day, Annie Marshall sat on a kitchen chair on the spot the company wanted to put the pole. Eventually the workmen left. Years later their grandson, Thurgood Marshall, would remark that Grandma Annie may have had the first successful sit-down strike in Maryland.[82] The year after Thurgood Marshall was born in 1908, the National Association for the Advancement of Colored People, the NAACP, for which Thurgood would become the chief legal counsel, was founded.[83]

Many Southern states used every trick in the book to keep blacks away from the polls, and those who wanted to vote had to go through an obstacle course.[84] During this decade, the Supreme Court did not seem particularly interested that very few blacks voted. In *Giles v. Harris*, 180 U.S. 475, 1903, Justice Oliver Wendell Holmes refused relief in a voting rights case involving five thousand blacks from Montgomery County, Alabama, and called it a political question. Holmes, finding the charge to be incredulous, wrote the case, "imports that the great mass of the white population intends to keep the blacks from voting."

Many Southern states used every trick in the book to keep blacks away from the polls, and those who wanted to vote had to go through an obstacle course.

Another blow against an interpretation of the Fourteenth Amendment favorable to blacks by the Court occurred in 1905. Favoring property rights over personal rights, the Court held in *Lochner v. New York*, 198 U.S. 45, that a New York statute that provided that no employee shall work in a bakery more than sixty hours a week or ten hours a day was unconstitutional. At the time it was common for journeymen bakers to work more than one hundred hours a week in bakeries located in squalid cellars in tenement houses. The dampness, combined with unsanitary conditions, extremes of hot and cold, and constant exposure to flour dust, was thought to be harmful to the health of the bakers. The shorter hours provided in the statute were seen as a way to extend fairness to workers who were in no position to bargain for themselves.[85]

In striking down the New York statute intended to protect workers, the Court continued the parameters set in *Allgeyer v. Louisiana* regarding the Fourteenth Amendment's constitutional protection and protected employers instead. While there is debate regarding the precise intentions of the framers of the post-Civil War amendments, it is clear no one intended the Fourteenth Amendment should be used to protect employers' rights to enter into employment contracts. The *Lochner* opinion states: "The general right to make a contract in relation to his business is part of the liberty of the individual protected by the Fourteenth Amendment of the Federal Constitution. Under that provision no State can deprive any person of life, liberty or property without due process of law."

In 1908 in *Berea College v. Kentucky*, 211 U.S. 45, the Court again considered the constitutionality of racial integration. A Kentucky statute forbade interracial instruction at all schools and colleges in the state. Berea College had been founded in 1855 as a college for Appalachian whites and former slaves. Berea, and Maryville College in Tennessee, were the only integrated institutions of higher education in the South.[86] Considering *Lochner's* protection of property and contract rights, this had to present a difficult question for the Court. Why shouldn't a private institution be able to integrate its student body? The Court effectively ducked the constitutional issue by hold-

Movies, rudimentary though they were, satisfied some of the cultural and social needs of immigrants.

ing that because Berea College was a corporation under a state charter, restrictions could be imposed upon it under a state statute.

The Supreme Court cited *Plessy* in *Chiles v. Chesapeake and Ohio Railway Company*, 218 U.S. 71, 1910, finding a Kentucky statute forcing a black interstate passenger who paid for a first class ticket into a "colored" section of the train once he entered Kentucky, to be reasonable. They said the law reflected the general sentiment of the community.

In racial matters involving segregation, disenfranchisement, jury service and separate but equal standards, the Supreme Court continually found the "Constitution was sufficiently malleable to accommodate southern white racial practices."[87]

Meanwhile, movies, rudimentary though they were, satisfied some of the cultural and social needs of the immigrants. Early movies were known as Nickelodeons. They cost a nickel and the hundreds of movies made for them were silent, which was an advantage. Most of the people who watched them did not speak English.[88] Neal Gabler says Nickelodeons served as a democratizing force, and created a sense of cultural identity and unity with America. They were an art the immigrants could call their own.[89] During the next decade, the rest of America would grow to love the movies as well.

1911-1920
Racial Framework

DURING THIS DECADE, LIFE BEGAN to change a little for some blacks. At this time, most African Americans still lived in the South and worked under sharecropper contracts on farms. They were completely dependent on white landowners, just as they had been during slavery. The landowner usually gave them supplies, then took half their crop. The sharecroppers were perennially in debt to the plantation store.[90] But blacks began leaving the backwaters and settled in cities such as Richmond, Baltimore, St. Louis, Louisville, and others. As a result, numerous cities passed segregation ordinances designed to keep the races apart.[91] Life in the cities, if freer than the rural South, was not close to equal for the races. The Deep South states of Mississippi, South Carolina, and Louisiana did not have a single four-year black public high school in rural or urban areas.[92]

An off-handed remark by a newspaper publisher about a tragic criminal case in Georgia in 1915 might best describe the racial context in the South during this decade. A young woman employee at a pencil factory was murdered. No one knew who did it, but suspicion quickly fell on two people: a black janitor and the factory's white owner—who was Jewish. The ambitious district attorney schemed with the publisher, who advised to go for the owner. "We can lynch a nigger anytime, but when do we get a chance to hang a Yankee Jew?"[93]

Life in the cities, if freer than the rural South, was not close to equal for the races.

An NAACP report published in 1919 stated that during the previous thirty years, there was an average of one hundred mob lynchings a year.[94] Historian Lawrence M. Friedman wrote of an incident that involved Brock Henley, who was identified by a white woman as the man who assaulted and robbed her. The woman's husband led a crowd to the jail where the black man was incarcerated. They sawed through the steel bars, seized Henley and hung him, as well as another black man, in broad daylight. Their bodies were so riddled with holes and burned, that they were beyond

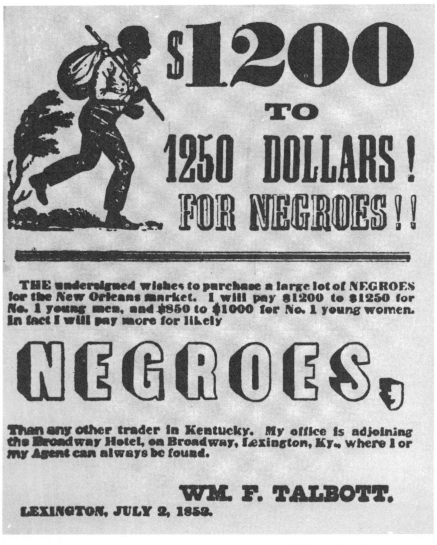

A July 2, 1853 advertisement posted by slave trader William F. Talbott of Lexington, Kentucky, who wanted to buy "Negroes" for $1200 to $1250 for the New Orleans Market. (Photo by Hulton Archive/Getty Images)

recognition. The woman thanked the crowd, and told them she had not known she had so many friends. The coroner's verdict was that the death was at the hands, "'of a mob composed of unknown persons.'"[95]

President Woodrow Wilson enjoyed telling "darkey" stories in dialect to his cabinet, primarily composed of white Southerners, at the White House. During the early years of his administration, the Post Office began segregating its clerks by color. The Treasury Department segregated its toilets. The Civil Service Commission began to require photographs with job applications, and then hired along racial lines. Despite winning reelection in 1916, because he kept America out of the war, Wilson had America in the war six months later, justifying intervention on human rights principles.[96]

Expectations of blacks and whites were different after the war, during which many black troops fought bravely despite inadequate training.

Almost 400,000 black Americans performed service in World War I. Black clergy led bond drives, and blacks contributed over two hundred fifty million dollars in Liberty Loan drives. Yet throughout the war, the United States military remained completely segregated, with blacks assigned to menial jobs. W.E.B. DuBois urged his fellow African Americans, "Let us not hesitate. Let us, while this war lasts, forget our special grievances and close ranks shoulder to shoulder with our white fellow citizens and the allied nations that are fighting for democracy. First your country, then your Rights!"[97]

Expectations of blacks and whites were different after the war, during which many black troops fought bravely despite inadequate training. Returning black veterans, who had experienced more equal treatment in France, were unwilling to submit to pre-war indignities and restraints. "Make way for democracy," declared DuBois. But it was around this time that the "First Great Migration" took many African Americans north and west, and the nation's booming war industry collapsed, resulting in a severe shortage of jobs. White America wanted a return to "normalcy," and lashed out at blacks, leftists, unionists and foreigners they believed threatened law and order. The revived Ku Klux Klan expanded to over one hundred thousand members nationwide. One of the worst periods of interracial violence in American history occurred in the summer of 1919 when black hopes and white fears collided.[98]

1911-1920
The Supreme Court

DESPITE THE RACIAL CONTEXT OF the times, the Supreme Court gave some heed to the interests of black Americans during this decade. Four prominent groups of cases were decided. One involved peonage legislation, or laws that coerced primarily black labor. The second involved accommodations and facilities. Another concerned grandfather clauses and the Fifteenth Amendment. And lastly, there was an integrated neighborhood case.[99]

Early in the twentieth century, black farm worker Lonzo Bailey signed a contract to work as a farmhand for the Riverside Company at the rate of twelve dollars a month. The company advanced him fifteen dollars. He worked throughout January and part of February 1908 for a total of five weeks and then stopped working. An Alabama statute, which did not mention that it was aimed at black workers, made it a crime to quit after entering an employment contract, without paying back an advance in pay. He was convicted of the crime of defrauding his employer in Montgomery, Alabama, and was ordered to return the fifteen dollars and pay an additional fine of thirty dollars. If he could not pay, he was to be confined at hard labor.

Bailey argued the purpose of the law was to make poor blacks virtual serfs by tying them to the land, under threat of being sentenced to a chain gang. In *Bailey v.*

Alabama, 219 U.S. 231, issued in 1911, the Court cited the Federal Peonage Act of 1867 and the Thirteenth Amendment, which forbids involuntary servitude except to punish a crime, to invalidate the Alabama statute. Despite a dissent from Justice Oliver Wendell Holmes, the Court found the statute formed a type of peonage, or compulsory service to pay debts.

A few years later, the Court in *United States v. Reynolds*, 235 U.S. 133, 1914, struck down another Alabama statute, which criminalized breach of surety agreements under which private parties paid fines to release criminals from jail in exchange for labor, on the same basis as *Bailey.* A surety is a person who agrees to be responsible for the debt or obligation of another. It is also security against loss or damage, or for the fulfillment of an obligation, such as the payment of a debt.

An Oklahoma statute was also invalidated by the Supreme Court. The law authorized railroads to exclude passengers in luxury compartments according to race, rather than providing separate but equal facilities. In *McCabe v. Atchison, Topeka & Sante Fe Railroad Co.*, 235 U.S. 151, 1914, the Court said the exclusion violated the Fourteenth Amendment, despite an unequal demand for such accommodations among the races.[100]

In 1915 there was finally some indication from the high court that there would be relief for African Americans in voting rights cases.

In 1915 there was finally some indication from the high court that there would be relief for African Americans in voting rights cases. Oklahoma's statute had a grandfather clause, which allowed anyone to register to vote if he or family members had been eligible to vote in 1867, or just before the Fifteenth Amendment, which gave the right to vote to all citizens, was ratified. Justice White, abandoning the intent requirement from *Williams v. Mississippi*, 1898, and the effect requirement from *Harris v. Giles*, 1903, wrote that the statute was a violation of the Fifteenth Amendment's right to vote.

One modern historian, Lawrence M. Friedman, sees the case, *Guinn v. United States*, 238 U.S. 347, 1915, as a signal of change from above, but says he does not think it made any difference what the Supreme Court did at that point. According to Friedman, "it meant little or nothing in practice. The Court had no power to enforce its decision, to affect what happened on the ground, at the tolling booths and registries, and in the humid southern climate of general repression."[101]

Whether or not the Supreme Court gave its blessing to integrated neighborhoods in 1917 is open to question. In *Buchanan v. Warley*, 245 U.S. 60, 1917, the Court invalidated a Louisville, Kentucky ordinance that segregated neighborhood blocks by race on the ground it interfered with property rights protected by the due process clause

. . . there were private contracts, conspiracies among real estate agents, few real estate loans available to blacks from banks, and threats of violence, all for the purpose of segregating neighborhoods.

of the Fourteenth Amendment. The case was decided in the midst of the *Lochner* era when the Court's commitment to property and contract rights was at its highest. In the opinion, the Court said a white man should not be denied the right to dispose of his property solely because there was a black purchaser. After all, during this time in America, there were private contracts, conspiracies among real estate agents, few real estate loans available to blacks from banks, and threats of violence, all for the purpose of segregating neighborhoods. So it is highly unlikely the Court's holding was intended to benefit African Americans.

A lawyer hired by the NAACP argued the *Buchanan* case. Moorfield Storey contended the due process clause of the Fourteenth Amendment prevented local governments from interfering with property rights without due process of law.[102] It looks as though the organization was attempting to beat the white man at his own game. That is, even if they had to argue the Fourteenth Amendment protected the constitutional right of "liberty to contract" of the white property owner, they were able to get the result they wanted, integration of a neighborhood.

1911-1920
Hollywood

MILD THOUGH THE SUPREME COURT'S rally for African Americans was during this decade, there was no equivalent move in Hollywood, where blacks were portrayed with utter disrespect and contempt. Urban audiences at movie theatres were as new as the technology. Many of the recent immigrants carried no baggage of racial lore and were receptive to the cinema's silent communication with them. Immigrants were loyal movie patrons.[103] No doubt they learned much of their racial lessons at their neighborhood theaters. And *The Birth of a Nation* (1915, AFI's #44) was college level racism.

There is a scene from a Hitler propaganda film that shows hundreds of rats running by the camera. The film is often shown in documentaries about the Nazis. The depiction of Jews being compared to rats is similar to what *The Birth of a Nation* does to blacks over more than three grueling hours. Words such as scandalous, outrageous, depraved, salacious, horrible, appalling and disgraceful are not sufficient either. It was painful to watch this movie.

The NAACP tried to stop the film. First, they sent pamphlets to small towns across America with lists of pending state censor bills. Then they directly attacked it with censorship arguments. A little success was achieved when they tied their argument to anti-riot ordinances. For the most part, the NAACP came head to head with the First Amendment. They brought the film before the National Board of Review, a private body created by producers to give films respectability, but the screening before the Board was interrupted by wild applause. When the NAACP tried to have large portions of the movie cut, they managed only a few deletions. They had little success in pressuring legislatures, and were met with an unprecedented advertising campaign by its distributor, Epoch Corporation. Many angry blacks protested its opening.[104] Rabbi Stephen S. Wise joined W.E.B. DuBois in picketing Griffith's film, which Wise called an "incredibly foul and loathsome libel on a race of human beings."[105]

> *There is no doubt* **The Birth of a Nation** *was intended to convey a message.*

The biggest obstacle blacks faced when they tried to stop the film was that it was state-of-the -art. It synthesized all the devices, technology, artistry, advances and developments of the cinema to date. It was exciting for audiences to watch the action of horsemen storming through fields and realistic battlefield scenes.[106]

The film is particularly dangerous since it reeks of authenticity. It is similar to documentaries we see today. Several times throughout the lengthy film, a footnote stating "Historical Facsimile" appears on the screen, to demonstrate, for example, that Lincoln actually called for troops to fight in the war, or that General Lee surrendered to General Grant. Posters advertising the film declared "The most realistic and stupendous view of stirring events in the development of our country."[107]

Plus, the movie received public approval from the President of the United States. Woodrow Wilson, who has been described as the most racist president of the twentieth century,[108] agreed that his old school chum, Thomas Dixon (author of the novel upon which the movie was based), could conduct a private showing of *The Birth of a Nation* at the White House. After seeing the film, Wilson remarked, "My only regret is that it is all so terribly true."[109] The film contains several quotes from Wilson, introduced in the text of the silent film as: Excerpts from Woodrow Wilson's *History of the American People*. One Wilson quote displayed on the screen is: "The white men were roused by a mere instinct of self-preservation . . . until at last there had sprung into existence a great Ku Klux Klan, a veritable empire of the South, to protect the Southern country.' WOODROW WILSON"

There is no doubt *The Birth of a Nation* was intended to convey a message. The novel, *The Clansman*, on which the film was based, was converted by Dixon into a stage drama in 1906. The author considered Africans to be below Europeans on the evolutionary scale. Among his accomplishments, Thomas Dixon had been a preacher who pastored the largest church in New York City.[110] At the play's intermission, Dixon would give a speech: "My object is to teach the North, the young North, what it has never known—the awful suffering of the white man during the dreadful recon-struction period. I believe that Almighty God anointed the white men of the South by their suffering during that time . . . to demonstrate to the world that the white man must and shall be supreme."[111]

In *The Birth of a Nation*, Dixon and Griffiths' messages were delivered to the audi-ence silently but clearly. When all was well, blacks were serving whites by doing menial jobs. Whites were smart and in charge. Blacks coveted white women and had to be kept away from them. Whenever a black person interacts with white people in the movie, the actor is actually white in black face. But when blacks are portrayed dancing, eating watermelon or looking particularly evil, they are really black. The only blacks that are not shown as simple and silly are the house servants and the cot-ton field workers, who are displayed as content and happy.

In a scene depicting the South Carolina Legislature during Reconstruction, when there were black members, the camera switches to a session in the House, where one black member takes a swig of whiskey. Another black member takes off his boots and puts dirty feet on top of the desk, while the black member across from him gnaws on a meaty bone. Most blacks are dressed garishly. The matters moved and carried are: "All members must wear shoes."; ". . . all whites must salute negro officers on the streets."; ". . . providing for the intermarriage of blacks and whites." Powerless whites observe from the balcony. As the blacks carried out legislative business, the caption reads, "The helpless white minority."

While contemplating the plight of his people, a former Confederate colonel observes two white children cover themselves with a sheet to scare away four black children. The text says, "An inspiration." The next caption reads: "The result. The Ku Klux Klan, the organization that saved the South from the anarchy of black rule, but not without the shedding of more blood than at Gettysburg, according to Judge Tourgee of the carpet-baggers." Then a screen full of men and their horses, covered with sheets and the emblem of the Confederate flag, looking much like the cross of the Crusaders, with the words: "Their first visit to terrorize a negro disturber and barn burner." and "The new rebellion of the South." Apparently bragging about the honor of the South, the screen reveals, "Over four hundred thousand Ku Klux cos-tumes made by the women of the South and not one trust betrayed."

In another scene, a beautiful, innocent young white girl is in the woods with a basket when she is spotted by a black man, Gus, wearing a Union soldier's cap. She is laughing at a chipmunk in a tree as Gus stalks her. When he approaches the girl, Gus tells her he is a captain and wants to marry her. She runs and screams, and he chases with rage and rape in his eyes. Rather than submit to him, she jumps off a cliff. As she dies, the screen states: "For her who had learned the stern lesson of honor we should not grieve that she found sweeter the *opal gates of death*." Shown as the only institution capable of extracting justice, the Klan tracks Gus down and kills him.

When another white woman is in danger at the hands of a black man, the camera shows columns of Ku Klux Klan riding to her rescue. They gallantly charge through a black mob, shooting and mowing down as many as they can. One can only imagine the emotional level of the film's 1915 audience as the Ku Klux Klan saved the day. After the rescue, the Klan disarms the blacks, and rides through the streets as heroes to adoring white crowds. "Dixie" is played as the next election is held under the watchful eye of the Klan, who does not allow blacks to vote.

1911-1920
Decade Wrap-up

THE UNITED STATES SUPREME COURT reflected the pitiful condition of black Americans during this decade. Legal cases concerned blacks existing in peonage, shunted into inferior segregated accommodations, denied the vote and kept out of white neighborhoods. Hollywood portrayed blacks as devious and dangerous, unless they were kept under tight control by whites. Put the two together, the actual conditions as described in the court cases and the Hollywood portrayals, and whites of the time probably concluded that blacks got what they deserved.

The decisions handed down by the United States Supreme Court during this decade did not seem to make much difference in the daily lives of African Americans. The *Bailey* decision, and other similar cases, changed nothing in the South's labor system. Some southern states made cosmetic changes, but there was no follow through. Blacks continued to be pressed into labor, often herded like cattle to work for little or no wages.[112]

Nonetheless, the Supreme Court applied all three post-Civil War Amendments to the benefit of African Americans. The Court followed the law, but did not stretch it. Although the Court probably did not intend to significantly re-shape the lives of black Americans, it did so indirectly by providing victories that translated into hope for future changes. It is significant that barely fifty years out of slavery, with slavery's

One institution applied the Constitution while the other gave the masses what they wanted, and along the way taught newly-arrived Americans to be bigots.

restrictions on slaves being allowed to read and write, black Americans were able to learn the laws so well. The strategy used in the *Buchanan* case was brilliant. The NAACP lawyers must have known they would lose if they made the black property purchaser the plaintiff, so they found a sympathetic white seller to claim the grievance. While the Court of the times did not always understand the plight of the ordinary white man (much less a black man), it well understood property and contract rights.

The propaganda effect of *The Birth of a Nation* was devastating to African Americans. Author James Baldwin accuses the film of being an elaborate plot for mass murder.[113] The movie left American whites with concepts of two kinds of blacks, the happy, contented and loyal servants to whites; and the frightening, hostile, furious, ambitious ones who wanted to intermarry with whites. Likely, newly arrived immigrants and other northern whites learned and adopted the vengeful southern Reconstruction version of slavery and the Civil War from this exciting, edge-of-your-seat film. So early on, Hollywood shaped white minds to view blacks with antipathy and disrespect.

It is incredulous that the very same year the Supreme Court decided *Guinn v. United States,* involving the black man who was denied his right to vote under an Oklahoma law, Hollywood distributed *The Birth of a Nation.* The Court found the Oklahoma statute to be unconstitutional because of its repugnancy to the Fifteenth Amendment, while Hollywood played the sentimental sounds of "Dixie" to cheering movie house audiences as it portrayed the heroic Ku Klux Klan saving the day by blocking African Americans from the ballot box.

Was Washington, D.C. that far away from Hollywood? It probably was. And in more than just miles. The Court was composed of Eastern, educated, elite men removed from the nation at large, while Hollywood was an assemblage of unrestrained, upwardly mobile entrepreneurs who wanted to make a buck. Each did their job. One institution applied the Constitution while the other gave the masses what they wanted, and along the way taught newly-arrived Americans to be bigots. But, according to author Thomas Cripps, there was one positive result from *The Birth of a Nation.* The movie

Put the two together, the actual conditions as described in the court cases and the Hollywood portrayals, and whites of the time probably concluded that blacks got what they deserved.

provided the first occasion on which black men, long organized into local groups, stretched their muscles across the nation[114] and brought into being an organized national black movement.[115]

This movie poster for director D.W. Griffith's film, The Birth of a Nation, *depicted a robed clansman and a woman riding together on horseback. (Photo by Hulton Archive/Getty Images)*

Zooming In . . .

A Close-up Look at Black Men / White Women

AT FIRST, ONE MIGHT THINK it was guilty consciences that caused white men to be so rabidly fearful of black men who desired white women and chased after them. After all, black men had nothing to do with the light color of many of the slaves.

Some scholars, such as historical author G.M. Fredrickson, are of the opinion that the racist propaganda that black males were ravening beasts lusting after white women rationalized the practice of lynching. That is, white men used the excuse they were protecting their women so they could hang black men.[116]

Fredrickson's view seems more realistic than the guilty conscience theory. Prior to the Civil War, there was some tolerance of relationships between white women and black men, but it may have been minimally tolerated because killing a slave meant destruction of valuable property.[117]

Things changed after the Civil War. No longer was the intentional destruction of property a deterrent to killing blacks, but science provided justification for keeping the races completely separate. During the late nineteenth and early twentieth centuries, eugenics was a popular area of study and provided a framework for arguing in scientific terms that non-whites were inferior to whites.[118]

White supremacy was another rationalization for fearing any kind of miscegenation. Legal, cultural and economic advantages enjoyed by whites over blacks, while

By 1920, virtually every pool in the United States was racially segregated.

still present during Reconstruction, were not as factual as they were when blacks were legally held in bondage. The social link between racial identity and privilege is undeniable. Although slavery was abolished and the Constitution was amended to provide for equality of citizenship, being white, in place of owning blacks, was used to confer privilege in post-Civil War society.[119] Thus it became increasingly important to whites to keep the race pure. A black man with a white wife or a white man with a black wife produced racially ambiguous children and undermined white supremacy.[120]

It is interesting to observe America's experience with public pools. It appears that racial hatred and prejudice was not as much on the minds of Americans as making sure black men did not get too near white women. Municipal pools began opening in the United States in the early 1880s. While pools were segregated along gender lines, blacks and whites commonly swam together without conflict. Black and white men swam together. And, at different times, black and white women swam together.[121]

In 1913, St. Louis built a resort-like pool in Fairgrounds Park and promoted it for use by the whole family. Unlike other pools in St. Louis, for the first time both sexes could swim at the same time. The resort was viewed as being beach-like, and, as was traditional at a beach, men and women played together in the surf and on the beach. However, the resort was strictly segregated along racial lines.[122]

St. Louis officials explained they excluded blacks because whites did not want black men interacting with white women at such an intimate and crowded public place. As one municipal pool after the other integrated along gender lines across the country, each segregated along racial lines. By 1920, virtually every pool in the United States was racially segregated.[123]

Some are of the opinion that America's system of apartheid was an anti-miscegenation tool.[124] Whether the goal of Jim Crow was white supremacy, anti-miscegenation, both, or something else, the United States Supreme Court put its stamp of approval on both Louisiana's separate railroad car law and the whole Jim Crow system when it issued *Plessy v. Ferguson*,[125] in 1896.

Even prior to the Jim Crow system and the *Plessy* case, the Supreme Court endorsed miscegenation statutes when it ruled in the case of *Pace v. Alabama*,[126] in 1883. Alabama's statute provided for greater punishment for adultery between two people of different races than for two people of the same race. When an equal protection argument was made in the case involving a white woman and a black man, the Court said there was no violation of the Fourteenth Amendment because both the black man and the white woman would be equally punished under Alabama's law, even though, had they both been black or both been white, their punishment would have been less.

It was probably the criminal procedure cases that turned the Court around to become more receptive and sensitive to the plight of blacks. All over the South, blacks were being lynched by mobs, and the various states were assisting in state-endorsed lynchings by failing to provide constitutional protections to black defendants. In what became known as the Scottsboro Boys Case, a 1931 incident involving nine young black men falsely accused of raping two white women on a freight train in Alabama, the Court stepped up to the plate. In two opinions, the high court reviewed criminal procedure issues involving the Scottsboro Boys' cases.

All over the South, blacks were being lynched by mobs, and the various states were assisting in state-endorsed lynchings by failing to provide constitutional protections to black defendants.

In 1932, in *Powell v. Alabama*,[127] the Supreme Court reversed the convictions on grounds that Alabama failed to provide adequate assistance of counsel as required by the due process clause of the Fourteenth Amendment. In 1935, the Court, in *Norris v. Alabama*,[128] overturned convictions of defendants Clarence Norris and Haywood Patterson—two of the accused nine—a second time because African Americans were excluded from sitting on the juries in their trials.

Eventually, in 1967, the Supreme Court issued *Loving v. Virginia*.[129] That case held that miscegenation statutes adopted by Virginia to prevent marriages between persons solely on the basis of racial classification violate the equal protection and due process clauses of Fourteenth Amendment.

It was not unusual for films to depict white women being pursued by black men. Much of the plot of 1915's *The Birth of a Nation* revolved around black men stalking and lusting after white women. In fact, even when lust was not involved, early Hollywood films, which portrayed black men as servants to white women, often cast white men in black face instead of using black actors, presumably so the audience would not have to see black men in close proximity to white women. Later Hollywood movies usually did not permit black men to get too intimate with white women on screen. Instead, black men and white women were shown in worker/employer roles such as 1963's *Lilies of the Field* or as buddies or co-workers.

While Eddie Murphy played the part of a cop in *Beverly Hills Cop* (1984), Sylvester Stallone was originally selected for the role. Lisa Eilbacher, a beautiful blonde, played the female lead. She and Murphy are portrayed as platonic buddies in the film. Historian Donald Bogle questions whether the filmmakers feared Murphy's sexuality, and points out, "there is no way Stallone would not have had a movie romance with actress Lisa Eilbacher.[130]

Other films cause the same kind of pondering. In *Murder at 1600* (1997), Wesley Snipes and the beautiful white female lead, Diane Lane, were merely cronies, even when he took her to his apartment and other intimate places. Samuel L. Jackson was placed in the same position in *The Long Kiss Goodnight* (1996), when he and Geena Davis traveled around the country together, spending long periods together in cars, restaurants and hotels.

The film industry often changed the plot of popular novels so that black men and white women were not shown in romantic scenes. In James Patterson's novel *Kiss the Girls*, John Grisham's novel *The Pelican Brief* and Walter Mosley's novel *Devil in a Blue Dress*, the men have love affairs with the women in the books. When Hollywood adapted the books for the screen, it eliminated the love scenes. In *Devil in a Blue Dress* (1995), it is light skinned Jennifer Beals who plays the leading lady who passes for white in the story. Even though in real life and in the part she plays in the film, Beals is partially African American, the film industry was afraid to have Denzel Washington too close to her on screen.

When author Walter Mosley learned the browner Washington could not kiss Beals in *Devil in a Blue Dress* because the studio feared the picture would "lose audiences inAlabama," he said, "Maybe Denzel could *think* about kissing her. He's a good actor."[131]

Besides the deletion of a love affair between a darker man and lighter woman, *Devil*'s story otherwise demonstrates how white men are afraid to have black men near white women. In one scene on the Santa Monica pier, a white woman strikes up a conversation with Denzel Washington's character. A white man witnesses the two speaking, panics, and calls to his friends, "This nigger's trying to pick up on Barbara," at which point the white men attack Washington.

Raiders of the Lost Ark (1981) has a pre-World War II scene in Africa in which a black man holds a white woman while he lustfully touches and smells her hair. A German grabs her, and another states with a wicked look, "If she fails to please me, you may do with her as you wish," as though being ravaged by a black man is the worst fate a white woman could have. That was the same message sent in *The Birth of a Nation*, where the white woman jumped off a cliff rather than submit to a black man.

As late as 2000, *Traffic* apparently intended to inflame the worst fears of parents by having a semi-conscious teenaged white girl strung out on drugs and in bed with a drug-dealing naked and muscular black man. The scene was obviously manufactured by Hollywood since it was not present in the British series, *Traffik*, on which the Hollywood film was based.

What was rabidly feared—the pairing of black men with white women—has come to pass. And you know what? The sky hasn't fallen.

Traffic was not the only time Hollywood tried to fan the flames of fear in its white audiences. Samuel L. Jackson said about his beautiful and scantily clad white girlfriend, Bridget Fonda, in *Jackie Brown* (1997), when he was asked why he kept her around. "Tol' you man, she my fine little surfer gal. She ain't pretty as she used to be and she bitch a whole lot more than she used to. But she white."

Spike Lee's film, *Malcolm X* (1992), provides more fuel for the fire with a statement by Denzel Washington's Malcolm X: "Because so many black women have been raped by the white man, the black man can't wait to get his hands on the white man's prize—the white woman."

Of course, as part of Hollywood's short-lived venture into treating on-screen blacks in a respectful manner during the 1960s, it did sympathetically portray black men in relation to white women. The best example is *To Kill a Mockingbird* (1962) supposedly based on the Scottsboro Boys Case. In the film, black Tom Robinson is compassionately shown as the victim of a scornful, pathetic young white woman when he faces the death penalty after being falsely accused of attacking her.

In the Heat of the Night (1967) shows a black detective efficiently and politely interviewing an attractive white widow without any racial or sexual overtones while the two are alone.

During Reconstruction, there was a derogatory phrase known as the "coffee-colored compromise." In fact, the blending of races may result in exactly that. According to the United States Census Bureau, in 1997 there were 311,000 black/white married couples.[132] So, what was rabidly feared—the pairing of black men with white women—has come to pass. And you know what? The sky hasn't fallen.

1921-1930
Racial Framework

AUTHOR NEAL GABLER WROTE THERE was a cultural division in America in the 1920s. On one side of the cultural divide were white Anglo-Saxon Protestants who clung to a moralistic, traditional way of life, terrified that the influx of immigrants would destroy their values, since non-native Americans couldn't possibly share them.

On the other side were the immigrants and a host of other forces that challenged established values. Immigration, urbanization, mass communication, unionization, professionalization of the middle class, and education all joined ranks to challenge established values. Together, they offered a vast, invigorating alternative to the established American way of life, where the hierarchy was rigid and values unchanging.

Gabler commented that, "One could even say that the social history of America in the 1920s was the story of the combat between these two Americas. One new and ascending; the other old and declining. One smart and sophisticated; the other conservative and respectable."[133]

President Warren Harding died in office in 1923, and "Silent Cal" Calvin Coolidge became President of the United States. Coolidge did very little in the area of civil rights. When forty thousand costumed Klansmen paraded through Washington, D.C. in 1925, one of his comments was, "Biological laws shows us that Nordics deteriorate when mixed with other races."[134]

Herbert Hoover, the 1928 Republican presidential nominee, sought "to drive the negroes out of Republican politics" by supporting "Lily-White" organizations. And, democratic candidate Al Smith of New York toyed with the idea of actively campaigning for black votes. But he arrived in Houston for the Democratic convention shortly after a black lynching and realized New York was different than the rest of the country.[135]

Grins from Aunt Jemima, Uncle Ben and George the Pullman Porter gave assurance to whites that all was well.[136] Congress passed a law allowing mothers and wives of deceased World War I servicemen to travel to France to visit the grave sites of their loved ones. During the Hoover administration, the War Department sent black wives and mothers on separate ships from their white counterparts, explaining "It would seem natural to assume that these mothers and widows would prefer to seek solace in their grief from companions of their own people."[137]

Grins from Aunt Jemima, Uncle Ben and George the Pullman Porter gave assurance to whites that all was well.

Yet even amidst such blatant racism, some blacks managed to succeed. In a manner of speaking. Ossian Sweet was one of them. He left home at age twelve, working as a bellhop, waiter, Pullman porter and jack-of-all trades until he made his way through medical school at Howard University. He saved his money, and in 1925 bought a two-story brick house in an all-white Detroit neighborhood. He moved into his new home under police escort. The next night his neighbors pelted his home with rocks, and then rushed the house. A volley of gunshots issued from inside. A white man was killed and another wounded, and Dr. Sweet was charged with first-degree murder. The NAACP hired famed lawyer Clarence Darrow to defend Sweet, who was not convicted.

Historian Michael J. Klarman points to this case as an example of the difference between northern and southern treatment of blacks who were charged with serious crimes against whites. A black man in the same position as Dr. Sweet would have been convicted in the South.[138] In this case as in others, the African American press recorded it all.[139]

Black music received wide recognition and respectability during this decade. Fred Astaire started his entertainment career as a black-style dancer and emerged into a tie and tails sophisticate. Band leader Paul Whiteman staged a huge concert in 1924, and opened with George Gershwin's *Rhapsody in Blue*. Whiteman always insisted jazz was an all-white invention. The minstrel show, Jim Crow, poked fun at blacks by entertaining in blackface throughout the decade. On Broadway there was an adage: that you started black or ethnic and became steadily whiter and more Waspy as you succeeded.[140]

The 1920s produced a dazzling array of artists and poets from Harlem, known as The Harlem Renaissance.[141] Many strong black figures appeared on the social scene. The black press by this time had matured into a nationwide network capable of reporting on the growing urban black community. City newspapers such as the *Courier* in Pittsburgh and the *Defender* in Chicago grew in popularity with black readers and the use of national black news networks.[142] On January 15, 1929, Michael King was born. He was the son of a Baptist preacher of the same name. When little Mike was five, the elder King changed both their names to Martin Luther.[143] In a few years, young Martin Luther King, Jr. would change the world.

In the meantime, the stock market crash of 1929 sent blacks from bad to worse. Always the last hired and first fired, they were gravely set back with the nation's economic collapse. Within a few years, black unemployment would, in some areas, be 50 percent.[144]

1921-1930
The Supreme Court

DURING THIS DECADE THE SUPREME Court demonstrated its complete approval of keeping the Caucasian race distinguished and separate from other races. Regarding criminal procedure, it drew a firm line at supporting the results of mob-dominated trials. The Court found a nominally private organization to be a state actor, and applied the *Buchanan v. Warley* rationale to find that, yes, a white landlord could rent to black tenants. *Buchanan v. Warley*, was a unanimous Supreme Court decision that addressed racial segregation in residential areas. The Court held that a Louisville, Kentucky ordinance requiring residential segregation based on race violated the Fourteenth Amendment.

In 1790 Congress had declared that free *white* persons were eligible for citizenship. Later, after the Civil War, Congress similarly designated persons of African birth or descent. In the early twentieth century, hundreds of persons of Japanese ancestry had been naturalized, but the practice soon ended.

Takao Ozawa, who was born in Japan, filed his naturalization papers in the territory of Hawaii, after residing in the United States for the previous twenty years. He was a graduate of Berkeley High School and attended the University of California. He had educated his children in American schools. He and his family attended American churches and used the English language in his home. When he was denied citizenship, he went to court. The Supreme Court conceded he was well qualified by character and education to become a United States citizen.

Ozawa argued the term "free white person" that was used in the Naturalization Act of 1790 had been employed specifically to exclude persons of the African race. In 1922 the Supreme Court, in *Ozawa v. United States*, 261 U.S. 204, decided, since Ozawa was a Mongolian and neither a free white person nor of African descent, he did not have the right to naturalization. The Court noted, "Manifestly the test afforded by the mere color of the skin of each individual is impracticable, as that differs greatly among persons of the same race, even among Anglo-Saxons, ranging by imperceptible graduations from the fair blond to the swarthy brunette, the latter being darker than many of the lighter hued persons of the brown or yellow races. Hence to adopt the color test alone would result in a confused overlapping of races and a gradual merging of one into another, without any practical line of separation. . . . the federal and state courts, in an almost unbroken line have held that the words 'white person' were meant to indicate only a person of what is popularly known as the Caucasian race."

The step was really a judicial stomp in that the Court refused to assist the South by sanctioning a form of state assisted lynching.

The Supreme Court further distinguished the white race from Asians in a Mississippi case. Chinese merchant Gong Lum sent his nine-year-old daughter, Martha, to the Rosedale School in Bolivar County. At noon on her first day, October 28, 1924, she was sent home from the public school and prohibited from returning.

Gong Lum appealed the matter to the United States Supreme Court. He argued if there is a danger in association with blacks, "it is a danger from which one race is entitled to protection just the same as another. . . . The white race creates for itself a privilege that it denies to other races; exposes the children of other races to risks and dangers to which it would not expose its own children. This is discrimination."

The decision against Martha was written by Chief Justice Taft in *Gong Lum v. Rice*, 275 U.S. 78, in 1927. "A child of Chinese blood, born in, and a citizen of, the United States, is not denied the equal protection of the laws by being classed by the State among the colored races who are assigned to public schools separate from those provided for the whites, when equal facilities for education are afforded to both classes."

However, the United States Supreme Court did take a giant step in favor of black Americans in *Moore v. Dempsey*, 261 U.S. 86, in 1923. The step was really a judicial stomp in that the Court refused to assist the South by sanctioning a form of state assisted lynching.

Frank Moore and several other black men petitioned for a writ of habeas corpus (a legal document issued by a court or judicial officer that orders a prisoner to be brought before a judge) seeking to be freed from an Arkansas prison after being convicted of murder and sentenced to death. On the night of September 30, 1919, a number of black people had assembled in their church and were attacked and fired upon by a body of white men. In the disturbance that followed, a white man, Clinton Lee, was killed. It was for Lee's killing that the black men were convicted.

Shortly after the arrest of the black men, a white mob marched to the jail for the purpose of lynching them, but was prevented by the presence of United States troops. Phillips County, Arkansas, had a black majority of three to one,[145] yet blacks were systematically excluded from both the petit and grand juries in the county. An all-white grand jury handed down the indictment on October 27.

On November 3, the black defendants were placed on trial before a jury of white men. During the trial, the court and the neighborhood were thronged with an adverse crowd that threatened anyone who would interfere with the desired result. Counsel did not speak with the defendants before the trial, seek a change in venue, challenge members of the jury for bias, request separate trials, call witnesses for the defense, or call the defendants, themselves. All the black men were convicted and sentenced to death after a forty-five-minute trial.[146]

The Supreme Court's opinion mentions an affidavit that stated no juryman could have voted for an acquittal and continue to live in Phillips County, and if any prisoner by any chance had been acquitted by a jury, he could not have escaped the mob. The Court stated that if a state carries into execution a judgment of death or imprisonment based on a verdict produced by mob domination, the state deprives the accused of his life or liberty without due process of law. The case was sent to the federal trial court for further proceedings.

The *Moore* opinion represented an about-face from the high court, which refused to intervene in a similar case eight years earlier. In the Georgia pencil factory murder case, mentioned earlier, the evidence against Leo Frank, a transplanted northerner and a Jew, was suspect. When he was charged with the death of thirteen-year-old Mary Phagan, a torrent of anti-Semitism was unleased. Every day of the trial, a mob surrounding the courthouse could be heard screaming, "Hang the Jew" through the courthouse's open windows. The jury was present to hear the judge consult with the police chief about security measures. Neither Frank nor his lawyer were in court for the verdict, since the judge was concerned about a lynching in the unlikely event there should be an acquittal.

After his conviction and death sentence, Frank sought a writ of habeas corpus through the federal courts. When he reached the United States Supreme Court in

1915, in *Frank v. Magnum,* 237 U.S. 309, the Court rejected him, ruling the due process clause of the Fourteenth Amendment required only that the state afford him an opportunity to raise his claim of a mob dominated trial.[147] When the Supreme Court refused to intervene, Georgia Governor John Slaton courageously commuted Frank's sentence, remarking "feeling as I do, I would be a murderer if I allowed this man to hang." Slaton was hounded out of the state. A mob seized Frank from the state prison farm and lynched him. Perhaps the Court learned a lesson by the time *Moore* arrived at the Court in 1923.[148] [149]

The Court said the Fourteenth Amendment was passed with a special intent to protect blacks, and ruled that States may not classify by color when a private party acts on behalf of the state.

In the area of voting rights, the United States Supreme Court put more teeth into the Fourteenth Amendment during this decade. In the 1927 case of *Nixon v. Herndon,* 273 U.S. 536, election officials in Texas refused to allow blacks to vote in primary elections because a 1923 state statute made it illegal for a Negro to vote in the Democratic Party primary election. In this case, Dr. L.A. Nixon, a black physician in El Paso, sought to vote in the 1924 Democratic Party primary in El Paso, Texas. The defendants, who were magistrates in charge of elections, prevented him from doing so and they all ended up in court.

The *Nixon* case required another retrenchment by the Court. Until that case, the Court required state action before it would find the Reconstruction Amendments were implicated. Political parties are, nominally, private organizations, but the Court noted there are many situations where a state delegates public functions to private parties, and this was one of them. The Court said the Fourteenth Amendment was passed with a special intent to protect blacks, and ruled that States may not classify by color when a private party acts on behalf of the state.

In the property rights area, the Supreme Court applied the Fourteenth Amendment's due process rationale of the 1917 case of *Buchanan v. Warley,* where the Court said the white seller was denied his due process right when he was not permitted to sell his property to a black buyer, to rental property in *Harmon v. Tyler,* 273 U.S. 668, in 1927. Here, a Louisiana court, 160 La. 943; 107 So. 704, upheld a 1924 New Orleans ordinance that provided for the segregation of neighborhoods according to race. The state court restrained a landlord who owned property in a white neighborhood from renting to black renters and the Supreme Court reversed, citing *Buchanan.* While the Court was likely more concerned about the rights of white landlords than the rights of blacks, blacks benefited by these two decisions.

Another case sheds light on the motivation of the Supreme Court in *Buchanan* and in *Harmon,* which protected contract and property rights of white landowners, and not the civil rights of blacks. *Corrigan v. Buckley*, 271 U.S. 323, was issued in 1926. Corrigan and twenty-nine other white persons entered into an agreement which mutually covenanted that no part of the twenty-five parcels of land they owned "should ever be used or occupied by, or sold, leased or given to, any person of the negro race or blood; and that this covenant should run with the land and bind their respective heirs. . . ."

Curtis, a black woman, entered into a contract for the purchase of Corrigan's property. Buckley, one of the twenty-nine who had agreed to the covenant, argued the sale to Curtis would cause the other owners irreparable harm. Curtis argued the agreement of the white landowners ran afoul of the Fifth, Thirteenth and Fourteenth Amendments. The opinion, written by Justice Sanford, stated, "It is obvious that none of these amendments prohibited private individuals from entering into contracts respecting the control and disposition of their own property; and there is no color whatever for the contention that they rendered the indenture void." The Court dismissed Curtis's case, deciding there was no constitutional question at issue.

1921-1930
Hollywood

THE SOCIAL FORCES UNLEASHED BY World War I carried new ideas about the role of African Americans in the fabric of American life, but the 1920s Hollywood movie industry presented a white man's screen. Blacks had no choice but to tolerate it. African Americans who broke the old molds as soldiers, labor organizers and intellectuals were unseen on the silver screen. These were times of alcoholic prohibition and radical "reds." Race riots shocked America with news that racial problems were no longer purely a Southern question. And the need for working capital to make movies brought bankers into Hollywood.[150]

The bankers carried with them their conservative influence, and Hollywood film executives and politicians formed the Americanization Committee to encourage patriotism through films.[151] Artistic control shifted from directors to producers and studio supervisors. Even scripts of writers of the stature of F. Scott Fitzgerald were subjected to hierarchical approval. Studios then hired former U.S. Postmaster General Will Hays "to create a model of pious rectitude that included the American success myth, stratification along lines of wealth, secure segregation of the races . . ."

The Hays Office also prohibited miscegenation on the screen, which barred blacks from any role that called for serious relationships with whites. "Thus no studio depicted black despair, poverty, neglect, outrage, caste or discrimination."[152]

Other barriers to black issues on the screen were the absence of anyone at the studios who understood African Americans. "The most liberal Jews who managed the studios had no way of knowing how to render black life honestly." What this

The Hays Office prohibited miscegenation on the screen, which barred blacks from any role that called for serious relationships with whites.

meant was the exclusion of blacks from movies, except for a few traditional roles. For the black man, tradition often meant disrespect. Historian Thomas Cripps notes that even fine silent scripts included such text as, "The coon begins to apply the lather."[153]

A large wooden sign reading HOLLYWOOD was erected in 1923 by a real estate developer, and would remain as a symbol of the movie business. Studios became big during the 1920s. Columbia Pictures, owned by Harry and Jack Cohn, started on Sunset Boulevard. Metro-Goldwyn Pictures was formed with Louis B. Mayer as head. Paramount and Warner Bros. expanded. RKO was established. Fox Movietone News

was inaugurated. In 1927, the Academy of Motion Pictures Arts and Sciences was established "to improve the artistic quality of the film medium." That same year, Hollywood studios issued a list of "Don't and Be Carefuls" as part of a self-censorship move. Included in the list was a prohibition of showing *white* slavery and interracial marriage.[154]

Thomas Cripps describes most roles for blacks as "furniture and atmosphere." He says it was the invisibility of blacks on the screen that caused the most suffering. Because American racial lore found black women and prepubescent children benign, they found it a little easier to land acting jobs. A prudish veil was drawn over any kind of black masculinity. Meanwhile, white actors achieved fame by working in blackface.[155]

Insensitive and ignorant as Hollywood was to African Americans, it managed sensitivity and kindness to other groups. The solution to this inconsistency could be the fact that poverty and the rural Baptist tradition kept blacks out of moviehouses[156] while immigrants filled them.

A film that was kind to one immigrant group, the Irish, is *Juno and the Paycock* (1929), directed by Alfred Hitchcock. Based on a play written by Sean O'Casey, the story is set in Ireland. With much emotion, an Irish family is shown bearing many tragedies. Although it is very sad in parts, it is also amusing and colorful. Phrases such as "He that goes a borrowin', goes a sorrowin' " show the Irish as being whimsical and delightful.

Jews were the recipients of silver screen sympathy in *The Jazz Singer* (1927, AFI's #90). Here, Jewish immigrants are treated with great respect, while blacks are disrespected with blackface songs done by white people. Cantor Rabinowitz wants his young son, Jakie, to be the family's fifth generation cantor. Instead, Jakie runs away to show business. Seen ten years later as Jack Robin, the son works in a theater with ever-present black maids and paints his face black—leaving a lip area three times the size of his own lips—and dons a fuzzy-haired wig.

But when Jack Robin sings in black face, he does not poke fun. Rather, his presentation is sentimental and dignified. Historian Paul Johnson explains that Al Jolson was exceptionally nervous for a professional entertainer. He was told by an African American, "Yous'd be much funnier, boss, if you blacked your face like mine. People always laugh at the black man." [157] There is an overall bewildering ambivalence in this movie. On one hand, it is sentimental and culturally sensitive of immigrant Jews. On the other, it is highly disrespectful of, and wholly insensitive to, black people.

No doubt race was far more significant in 1920s movies than ethnic background. In *Murder* (1929), directed by Alfred Hitchcock, an innocent woman is prosecuted for murder. It turns out the woman who was murdered knew a terrible secret about the murderer, that he was a "half-cast." When discovered, the murderer kills himself. The implication is that he would rather die than have people know he was of mixed blood. And where did the half-cast murderer lay low to escape detection? The circus, of course. At one point, the leading man shakes his head and mumbles, "poor devil," as though understanding the man was in an abominable position because he was not born pure white and was in love with a white woman.

In several other of the decade's movies, blacks were also portrayed disrespectfully. *Champagne* (1928), directed by Alfred Hitchcock, has a scene where a message is delivered by a black messenger who cowers in fear as the man rants and raves. In *Manxman* (1929), also directed by Alfred Hitchcock, a man writes home to say he made his fortune in Africa. As he writes the letter, a parade of black men are seen behind him carrying heavy burdens. The obvious message is that white men can make money from the labor of black men.

When *Uncle Tom's Cabin* was released in 1927, blacks considered it high achievement. They expected white audiences to gain understanding of the black man, as seen through Mrs. Stowe's eyes. They hoped it "might finally eliminate the caricature he had acquired in years of gauche road shows."[158] The same sentimental "Swanee River" music that played at the South Carolina plantation of the Camerons in *The Birth of a Nation* is played at the opening of the story, but this time it is the Kentucky home of the Shelbys. The text on the screen reads, "Mr and Mrs. Shelby, whose gentle rule of the slaves was typical of the South."

Ignoring the fact that many main parts were played by fossils of the blackface era, *Variety* gave high praise to the film. But *Tom* was real, "barbed enough to earn censorship in Dixie." A strong black image was brought to the screen. While Southerners grumbled, blacks felt their cause received some representation.[159]

That African Americans perceived any sort of salvation from this film is affirmation of the dire straits they faced. Harriet Beecher Stowe's book does identify Eliza as "a young quadroon woman,"[160] but the only indication Eliza is in any way associated with other slaves in this movie is that the screen text says so. The other slaves are very dark, most constantly bear silly smiles or eat watermelon, and display a need for serious dental work. Whereas Eliza's and Harry's quarters look like a Ralph Lauren showroom, with flowered wallpaper, upholstered chairs, portraits hanging on the walls, and lovely curtains and carved wooden furniture,[161] Uncle Tom and his family really live in a cabin. While the other slaves are dressed in rags, Eliza and adorable little Harry are frocked in Laura Ashley-like frills. Eliza's hair and make-up are perfect, from eye shadow to lip liner. To be sure, Tom was portrayed as a man of character and physical strength. He was true and loyal to his family and his friends, and his facial expressions demonstrate kindness, sensitivity and intelligence.

Topsy was mischaracterized in the movie. The book does say her hair is "braided in sundry little tails" when she is purchased, but she is quickly "shorn of all the little braided tails." Yet the film gives her a comic appearance. She is wearing a steel wool wig that is made to stick out with about twenty tuffs of hair that look like question marks.[162]

But it is more than her appearance that filmmakers changed. In the book she is a sympathetic character who showed signs of neglect and abuse. "When she saw, on the back and shoulders of the child, great welts and calloused spots, ineffaceable marks of the system under which she had grown up thus far, her heart became pitiful within her."[163] Later, after Topsy was bathed, the novel says she confessed to stealing items she had not stolen because she was afraid she would be beaten. Yet the movie has a white woman beating Topsy for stealing. The scene is funny as Topsy jumps up and down, as though the flogging is harmless and humorous. The moviemakers reduced the humanity of the book, by making the child a jester. Another tired Hollywood joke at the expense of African Americans.

The Ring (1927), directed by Alfred Hitchcock, gives mixed messages. It is both impudent and enlightened regarding blacks. In an early scene at a carnival, with all white attendees, it is a black man with a simple grin who is dunked into water each time a ball hits the target. The crowd cheers with laughter and approval as the man is dumped into the drink. Later, a boxing promoter says in his discussion with a boxer, "You win this next fight with the nigger, you'll be in the running for the championship." But there is an interesting racial twist in this film. One of the actors who assists in the boxing ring, doing the same job as white men, is a black man. He appears in numerous scenes. He eats, drinks, talks, laughs, and jokes with his white co-workers as an equal. In one scene the champion boxer pours champagne for all of them, including the black man.

A movie with no race issues, but possible significance is another Hitchcock movie, *The Lodger* (1926). Here, an innocent man is arrested for murder. An incensed mob tries to kill him before he is saved by police who announce the real killer was just caught red-handed. This silent film demonstrates the savagery of a mob bent on revenge.

* Movies in the four categories not included in text appear in endnote.[164]

1921-1930
Decade Wrap-up

TREATMENT OF BLACKS BY THE Supreme Court was mostly positive during this decade, while it was mostly negative in Hollywood. The Court ruled in favor of African Americans in areas of criminal procedure, voting rights and housing. In a perverse sort of way, the Court's rejection of Takao Ozawa's request for naturalization recognized that black and white Americans were on the same level. The Court's analysis recognized that post-Civil War amendments and legislation provide that persons of the African race are eligible for citizenship, along with free white persons.

Movies, however, portrayed blacks being called "niggers," dunked into water with baseballs tossed by mocking whites, working as maids, being ridiculed by whites who painted themselves black, subjected to demeaning treatment, and bearing burden to make white men rich. There was only one black man who had a non-servile job. He played the boxing assistant in *The Ring*, and was portrayed with some dignity. While no dialogue was attributed to him in the text of the silent film, he was just as important, and just as unimportant, as the white boxing assistants with whom he interacted as an equal. The likes of this man would not be seen again in any of the popular movies studied for several decades. For the most part, blacks in film had menial jobs. There was no indication in films that black men such as Ossian Sweet, an educated professional, existed. Other than the black families living in slavery in *Uncle*

Tom's Cabin, there were no movies that portrayed black people in family settings, while most films portrayed white families at home.

Treatment of blacks by the two establishments had some similarities during the 1920s. Hollywood and the Court each did well by black men at least once. In *Uncle Tom's Cabin,* most blacks are shown as silly or simple, but Tom is portrayed as a real man. At the Supreme Court, in *Moore v. Dempsey,* a black man's plea was heard by the Court after his constitutional rights were violated in an Arkansas trial. *Moore* was freed because his conviction was a result of mob threat. The Court announced loud and clear that it would no longer condone trial by mob when it ruled that Frank Moore and his co-defendants deserved a new trial. Ironically, a few years later, in 1926, Hollywood portrayed an innocent man accused of a crime who also almost died as a result of mob violence. *The Lodger'*s most terrifying moment is when the real murderer is caught just as the mob is about to pounce on the innocent man.

While no dialogue was attributed to him in the text of the silent film, he was just as important, and just as unimportant, as the white boxing assistants with whom he interacted as an equal.

The rationale for the tender treatment of immigrants in movies, versus the often-vile handling of African Americans, was likely a result of a combination of circumstances. Most obvious is that our government was tainted from within with racism. The United States Supreme Court valued Caucasians. Also, African Americans were kept completely separate, so the races rarely had the benefits of exposure and contact, which might have bred sensitivity.

Besides the separateness, white America was given false information in advertising with the grinning Aunt Jemima and Uncle Ben. And, America was frightened. There had been race riots and the red scare. Meanwhile, the Hays Office's prohibition against miscegenation and the Americanization Committee's patriotism through films stood as firm reminders that Hollywood should not stray into experimental areas.

Of course, the reality was the absence of anyone at the studios who understood African Americans. So screenwriters, even if they were inclined toward sensitivity, probably had no idea how to present the true essence of the African American to the rest of America. Or, it could have come down to money. Immigrants bought more movie tickets than any other identifiable group.[165] African Americans on the other hand, both intellectuals and urban masses, shared an indifference to the cinema. Because of their deep puritan fundamentalist roots, black churches looked on film as needless frivolity.[166] Thus, the film industry could not look to black Americans to buy movie tickets; it did not pay to treat blacks decently.

The reality was the absence of anyone at the studios who understood African Americans.

But change was in the air. As Thomas Cripps astutely points out, while immigrants paid the price of integration from deteriorating ethnic cultures, African Americans sharpened their sense of urban group identity with a growing awareness that the melting pot excluded them.[167] As individuals and as a group, blacks pushed the envelope when they were able to do so without getting lynched.

While a college student in the late 1920s, Thurgood Marshall and a group of friends decided to integrate a movie theater in Oxford, Pennsylvania. Defying the "blacks in the balcony" rule, the young men sat in the whites-only orchestra section. An usher ordered them to move, and they ignored him. A harsh voice breathed down the back of Marshall's neck, "Nigger, why don't you just get out of here and sit where you belong?" The young men stayed where they were. And nothing happened.[168]

In the 1920s both African Americans and the United States Supreme Court were changing. It remained to be seen whether or not Hollywood would change along with them.

1931-1940
Racial Framework

THE GREAT DEPRESSION HIT HARDEST in areas of the economy where black workers were concentrated. For the average black person, the 1930s were economically bleak. By 1932, the Depression resulted in black unemployment in many cities as high as 40 or 50 percent.[169] African Americans fortunate enough to keep their jobs were generally paid lower wages than white workers doing the same work, and when in dire circumstances, African Americans relied on their families and the black community.

Most turned to the black churches, but newer forms of assistance were also at hand. Divine Kingdoms, religious cult installations led by a Father Divine, spread throughout the country. During the depression the kingdoms rented rooms for a dollar a week, served inexpensive meals, and helped the poor find jobs. Originally from Georgia, Father Divine's movement started in New York. His real name was George Baker, and his interracial following was in the tens of thousands. Authors James and Lois Horton say Father Divine's home on Long Island was thronged by cult supporters. But before too long, Father Divine was convicted of maintaining a public nuisance and sentenced to jail. When the judge died of a heart attack three days later, his followers said it was "Divine's retribution." His conviction was reversed on appeal, and his popularity soared.[170]

About this same time, W. D. Fard founded a charismatic religious movement in

Detroit that was later called the Nation of Islam. The movement built temples and schools, as well as an extensive network of economic self-sufficiency composed of farms, groceries, restaurants and apartment houses.[171]

Socialists also provided aid to poor blacks. The interracial Southern Tenant Farmers' Union drew ten thousand members. And it was the American Communist Party that provided legal aid to nine young black men who were falsely accused of raping two white women on a freight train in the famous Scottsboro Boys case in Alabama in 1931.

After being turned away by the law school at the University of Maryland, Thurgood Marshall graduated first in his class from Howard University in 1933.

In 1932, black Angelo Herndon was also helped by the socialists. He led a march protesting starvation after the city of Atlanta closed its relief offices. He was prosecuted under an old law that was passed to punish slave insurrection, and the prosecutor requested the death penalty. His eighteen to twenty-year sentence was tossed out after he spent three years in prison. [172]

Herndon was a coal miner and the son of a coal miner. He experienced discrimination, which forced black workers into the most difficult and dangerous jobs. He first met members of the Communist Party when he attended an unemployment council meeting in Birmingham in 1930.

The Hortons recount Herndon's reaction to Communism: "All my life I'd been sweated and stepped on and Jim-Crowed. I lay on my belly in the mines for a few dollars a week, and saw my pay stolen and slashed, and my buddies killed. I lived in the worst section of town, and rode behind the "Colored" signs on the streetcars, as though there was something disgusting about me . . . I had always detested it, but I had never known that anything could be done about it . . . [It] was like all of a sudden turning a corner on a dirty, old street and finding yourself facing a broad, shining highway."[173]

Several states to the east, a black man was emerging into the legal profession. After being turned away by the law school at the University of Maryland, Thurgood Marshall graduated first in his class from Howard University in 1933. At that time the ratio of black Americans to black lawyers was 200,000 to 1.

The local chapter of the NAACP hired Marshall in 1934. He soon arranged for a boycott of Baltimore stores that had a policy of not hiring black workers. Instead of hiring them when business plummeted, the stores sued the NAACP.[174]

Marshall and the NAACP later represented poor blacks and their causes all over the South. But there was a basic practical problem for African Americans that had to be solved before traveling to southern towns and cities, even for the sophisticated and educated likes of Thurgood Marshall. In the 1930s, public accommodations for blacks were either non-existent or so dismal the NAACP lawyers had to first arrange to spend nights with and obtain food from black families in the various communities.[175] One can only imagine how grateful and proud poor blacks were to have Marshall's tall, imposing, well-spoken figure in their community, acting as their crusader.

Migration of blacks northward continued so that the decade saw the black population of Chicago increase by 77 percent.[176] Soon, African Americans began to search for and gain political power in the North. After President Hoover did nothing to inspire black loyalty, countless African Americans voted democratic in the Presidential election, a change in political allegiance that was difficult for many. The *Pittsburgh Courier*, a black weekly advised, "My friends, go turn Lincoln's picture to the wall . . . that debt has been paid in full."[177]

The combination of changing racial dynamics in the 1930s and the presidency of Franklin Delano Roosevelt would make a difference in the lives of black Americans. Roosevelt's "New Deal" provided blacks with desperately needed economic relief,[178] and the Works Progress Administration gave poor blacks jobs doing manual labor for one dollar a day.[179]

Conservatives' negative reaction to Roosevelt's racial policy was obvious in 1938 when southern Democrats in the Senate defeated an anti-lynching bill. According to Senator Theodore Bilbo of Mississippi, the bill would open the floodgates of hell to the South.[180] That Roosevelt's treatment of minorities was resented can be assumed from a popular ditty of the time. According to the verse, Franklin supposedly told Eleanor:

> *"You kiss the niggers*
> *I'll kiss the Jews*
> *And we'll stay in the White House*
> *As long as we choose!"*[181]

The New Deal structured and reinforced racial inequality in significant ways. For example, the Wagner Act gave legal protection to labor unions, without doing anything to end racial discrimination in many of them. When it came to federal money used in housing programs, local authorities were allowed to segregate the races, and the Federal Housing Administration refused to provide loans to blacks moving into white areas.

While the language of the Social Security Act of 1935 was racially neutral, its numerous exceptions provided "a sieve with the holes just big enough for the majority of Negroes to fall through," according to NAACP's Charles H. Houston. Despite the prominent feature of Jim Crow dynamics in "New Deal" programs, in 1936 Roosevelt won 76 percent of the northern black vote. By the end of the decade, the only employment gains by blacks were in domestic service. When the New Deal ended, the color line remained.[182]

During the 1930s, Roosevelt attempted to explain the unequal treatment of the races to Walter White of the NAACP, who was trying to solicit Roosevelt's support for an anti-lynching measure. "I don't choose the tools with which I must work. Had I been permitted to choose them I would have selected quite different ones. But I've got to get legislation passed by Congress to save America. The Southerners, by reason of their seniority rule in Congress, are chairmen or occupy strategic places on most of the Senate and House committees. If I come out for that anti-lynching bill now, they will block every bill I ask Congress to pass to keep America from collapsing. I just can't take that risk."[183]

American opera singer Marian Anderson performed on the steps of the Lincoln Memorial accompanied by Finnish pianist Kosti Vehanen, in Washington D.C., on April 9, 1939. The African-American Anderson performed there after she was bared from two other D.C. venues due to her race. (Photo by Thomas D. McAvoy/Time & Life Pictures/Getty Images)

Though inequality in America was a way of life for blacks, great sympathy was shown to an African American contralto Marian Anderson who was prevented by the Daughters of the American Revolution from singing in Constitution Hall in Washington D.C. In response, the NAACP obtained permission to conduct an out-door concert featuring Anderson at the Lincoln Memorial on Easter Sunday, 1939. A large crowd of blacks and whites attended, while thousands of others listened on the radio. "Genius, like justice, is blind," remarked Interior Secretary Harold Ickes.[184]

But even outspoken advocates of racial liberalism in the 1930s who might have supported Marian Anderson, such as Eleanor Roosevelt and NAACP activist Ickes,[185] remained mum about Jim Crow. When Public Safety Commissioner Eugene "Bull" Connor, who years later turned fire hoses and dogs on black children during the Civil Rights Movement, seated the First Lady at a meeting of the Southern Conference on Human Welfare in 1938, she quietly complied with Birmingham's seg-regated seating policy.

In his diary, Ickes wrote, "As a matter of fact, I think it is up to the states to work out their social problems if possible, and while I have always been interested in see-ing that the Negro has a square deal, I have never dissipated my strength against the particular stone wall of segregation. I believe that wall will crumble when the Negro has brought himself to a high educational and economic status. After all, we can't force people on each other who do not like each other, even when no question of color is involved. Moreover, while there are no segregation laws in the North, there is seg-regation in fact and we might as well recognize this."[186]

America's repugnance at Nazi doctrines is obvious from its reaction to a Detroit heavyweight contender's defeat by a German boxer in 1936, compared with his vic-tory in 1938. When Max Schmeling defeated African American Joe Louis the first time, many white Americans acclaimed Schmeling as "The Great White Hope." Similarly, Nazi Germany viewed the match as a triumph for the white race over the black race.[187]

But when Louis clobbered Schmeling in a re-match, something had changed in white America's response. Historians Philip A. Klinkner and Rogers M. Smith say this turn of events tell us much about changing racial attitudes in the United States. "For in 1938, the specter of war with Germany loomed larger than the shadow of Jim Crow. Hence Max Schmeling was no longer first and foremost a white man fighting a black man. Schmeling was the symbolic representative of Nazism, and the soft-spoken Louis had become the standard bearer for the whole United States of America, and for the grand cause of democracy itself." [188]

1931-1940
The Supreme Court

PRESIDENT ROOSEVELT MIGHT HAVE LET African Americans down by allowing the color line to remain after his New Deal, but his appointments to the United States Supreme Court proved helpful to blacks. Five of his appointees would remain on the Court to hear *Brown v. Board of Education* in 1954.

The high court reviewed criminal procedure issues once again with the cases of the Scottsboro Boys. In 1932 in *Powell v. Alabama*, 287 U.S. 45, the Supreme Court reversed the convictions on grounds that Alabama failed to provide adequate assistance of counsel as required by the due process clause of the Fourteenth Amendment. In 1935, the Court, in *Norris v. Alabama,* 294 U.S. 587, overturned the convictions of defendants Norris and Patterson a second time because African Americans were excluded from sitting on the juries in their trials.

Once again the Court visited the question of a private political party preventing blacks from voting in a primary election in *Nixon v. Condon*, 286 U.S. 73, in 1932. The number of these white primary cases clearly reflected white opposition to true political democracy, since it would have meant a sizeable number of black voters—and sometimes a majority in counties in the South.[189]

The petitioner was a black man who was prevented from voting in a primary election. He came to the Supreme Court when his case was dismissed in Texas. Promptly after the Court rendered its 1927 decision in *Nixon v. Herndon* (discussed in the 1920s section), finding a Texas statute that prevented blacks from voting in the Democratic primary to be unconstitutional, the Texas Legislature passed a different statute. The new statute provided that all political parties in the state should set qualifications for its own members. Acting under the new law, the executive committee of the Democratic Party adopted a resolution that provided that only white Democrats would be allowed to vote in primary elections.

Writing for the Court, Justice Benjamin Cardozo noted the Fourteenth Amendment is a restraint upon the states, and not upon private persons unconnected with the state. Democrats said they represented a private voluntary association and, like any other voluntary organization, had the power to determine its own membership.

Reversing the lower court, Justice Cardozo noted, "The Fourteenth Amendment, adopted as it was with special solicitude for the equal protection of members of the Negro race, lays a duty upon the court to level by its judgment these barriers of color." Leaving open the possibility that the party could exclude blacks, as long as the state was not involved in the process, the Court found that the Democratic Party was an organ of the state of Texas, and was not acting in matters of private concern. In this instance, there was obvious discrimination between white and black citizens.

Three years later the same issue was back again, but this time the black man was kept from voting by a resolution of Texas's Democratic Party. In *Grovey v. Townsend*, 295 U.S. 45, the Harris County Clerk refused a ballot for the Democratic primary election to Grovey because he was black. The county clerk claimed to be following the law of Texas, which allowed the Democratic Party to decide who could vote in its primary. The Democrats had resolved that only whites were qualified to vote, so the county clerk would not give a ballot to a black man. Justice Owen Roberts wrote for the Court, and the Texas judgment against the black man was affirmed. The Supreme Court found the county clerk, in obeying the law of Texas, did not deny the black man any right guaranteed by the Fourteenth or Fifteenth Amendments. So even though the state regulated primaries in a variety of ways, the Court found no state action on the part of Texas.

The NAACP and Thurgood Marshall decided to attack the "equal" part of the "separate but equal" *Plessy* standard, first attacking policies in various graduate schools. The organization was able to extract admissions that facilities for blacks were woefully below the quality of those for whites.

One case involved a black college graduate who was denied admission to the University of Missouri Law School. Missouri actually offered to pay the student's tuition in another state. In court, the state university defended its refusal because it

A 1931 poster advertises a defense meeting for Haywood Patterson, one of the Scottsboro Boys, a group of African-American youths who were falsely accused of raping two white girls in Alabama. (Photo by MPI/Getty Images) was "contrary to the constitution, laws and public policy of the State to admit a Negro as a student in the University of Missouri." Missouri's Constitution provided that separate free public schools shall be established for the education of children of African descent; it had no provision regarding separating higher education students on the basis of race.

Missouri actually offered to pay the student's tuition in another state.

Chief Justice Charles Hughes noted in 1938 in *Missouri ex rel. Gaines v. Canada*, 305 U.S. 337, that it was not a question of the state's duty to supply legal training. Rather, it was a matter of equality of right. The white resident was afforded legal education; the Negro resident with the same qualifications, was refused it. The Court reversed the Missouri court, ruling the black man was entitled to admission to the law school of the state university in the absence of other and proper provision for legal training within the state.

A significant shift was made with the influx of Roosevelt appointees to the Supreme Court in the 1930s. The "Lochner Era" ended in 1937 with *West Coast Hotel v. Parrish*, 300 U.S. 379. In *West Coast,* the Court upheld a Washington State minimum wage law for women. After that case, the Court gave greater deference to the states regarding economic legislation. The Court would no longer interpret post-Civil War amendments to benefit business. A footnote in *United States v. Carolene Products Co.* 304 U.S. 144, heralded more attention given to civil rights by the Court. *Carolene Products* involved a statute that made it an offense to ship skimmed milk compounded with any fat other than milk fat across state lines. The company claimed its due process and equal protection rights were infringed upon by the legislation. In footnote 4, the Court stated: "There may be narrower scope for operation of the presumption of constitutionality when legislation appears on its face to be within a specific prohibition of the Constitution, such as those of the first ten Amendments, which are deemed equally specific when held to be embraced within the Fourteenth."

After 1937 the Court refused to seriously consider due process or equal protection challenges to economic regulation.[190]

1931-1940
Hollywood

THE DEPRESSION STRUCK AT EVERYONE, including Hollywood. Movie audiences decreased from a weekly attendance of ninety million to seventy million. When the number was eventually reduced to sixty million, theaters resorted to giveaway gimmicks such as "dish night" and double features. Still, the parent company of Paramount Pictures, Paramount Publix, filed for bankruptcy. Another studio, Grand National, which was launched in 1936, filed for bankruptcy in 1939. Fox Studio and Universal Films were sold at distressed prices.[191]

More controls over the content of movies were instituted, too. The Production Code was adopted to codify practices when filming scenes involving sex, violence, religion and other sensitive subjects. This self-censorship devised by the studios in 1930 was not strictly enforced until 1934, and continued to be until the mid-1960s. In 1936, Pope Pius XI issued an encyclical denouncing indecent films.[192]

Hollywood came to ignore all kinds of information about audiences and did not question anything but the amount of the box office receipts. In "The Myth of the Southern Box Office," historian Thomas Cripps wrote: "The Southern box office became a monolithic creature that predetermined the substance of racial images on the screens of the entire nation. After all, the reasoning ran, if it *would not* sell in the South, it *might not* sell in the North, and there go the proceeds. Besides, the profits

Hollywood came to ignore all kinds of information about audiences and did not question anything but the amount of the box office receipts.

made in the South, although smaller than those in other regions, would carry a movie out of the red."

Trade papers, such as *Variety*, routinely wrote that the Southern box office reflected the racial values and attitudes of America. Reviewers either predicted box office failure for black movies in the South, or justified success as an abnormality. About the successful movie *Imitation of Life* (1934), *Variety* timidly warned that "Its reception in the South, can of course, not be judged or guessed by a Northerner. Exhibs below the Mason-Dixon will have to make their own decisions."[193]

In fact, many local Southern factors served to place the South near the bottom of regional receipt totals. The hot climate limited the length of the movie season, and only a few large cities had comfortable theaters. Outdoor amusements such as picnics, baseball and county fairs distracted potential viewers. Six-day workweeks, Sunday theater closures, and high entertainment taxes further reduced Southern receipts. In Atlanta, theater managers were fined fifty dollars each for breaking Sunday blue laws, and Southern censors snipped away, ruining films with their scissors.[194]

Many potential black patrons refused to subject themselves to segregated movie houses. Studios found that moviegoers in the South were not predictable enough to influence national tastes. It was all a fiction, according to Cripps, since the movie sales of an entire Southern town were frequently less than those in a single New York theater.[195]

During the Depression years, Cripps says grosses decreased even more. By the end of 1932, only one theater in New Orleans was running at a profit. Even after air-conditioning made theaters bearable, Southerners did not go to the movies during the summer months. Before the decade was over, Warner Bros. announced it was dropping its Southern houses. "Yet, during the entire period there was no indication that the consistently low box office receipts could be traced to the appearance of black actors or racial themes."[196]

Cripps is of the opinion the myth of the Southern box office was "a rationalization for what Hollywood producers would have created anyway," since most whites saw blacks as social problems. Black actors were easily excluded from the normal Hollywood production. According to Cripps, even when black acts in nightclubs and live theatre were successful in the South, and evidence increased that Southern audiences would be receptive to black performers on the screen, "Hollywood clung to its myths of the happy darky maids and butlers."[197]

Criticism of the film industry when it did have black themes was not uncommon. When *Song of the South* premiered, Hollywood columnist Hedda Hopper wrote that several "Commie groups" were active in the movie capital. Cripps says a reviewer criticized the intermingling of the races when a movie had Martha Raye perform a dance routine with Louis Armstrong. In addition, racism was pervasive in Hollywood. Many marketing executives were Southerners and some directors retained racial prejudices. Racial attitudes soon hardened. The popular "how-to-write-for-the-movies" books warned writers to stay away from racial issues. Racial stereotypes gradually replaced any possibility of humane black characters. Industry advertisement for one movie read, "Your heart will beat with the tom-toms at this tragedy of a roaring buck from Harlem."[198]

The movie sales of an entire Southern town were frequently less than those in a single New York theater.

Hollywood sensitivity in movie themes dealing with ethnic, class and social issues, as compared with its treatment of blacks during this decade, is a contrast of opposites. Movies of the 1930s could demonstrate exquisite sympathy to many issues, while also demonstrating complete insensitivity—and sometimes cruelty—to African Americans. At times, this split personality was seen within the same movie.

The Grapes of Wrath (1940, AFI's #20), celebrates the underdog, the outcast and the oppressed. The film sympathetically demonstrates how poor tenant farmers can be displaced with machines. At a gas station stop, two attendants discuss the Joad family. "Human beings wouldn't live like that. A human being couldn't stand to be so miserable. Okies ain't got no sense." So moving was the film that after seeing it, a black friend of author James Baldwin swore that, by the way Henry Fonda walked down the road at the end of the film, he had "colored blood."[199]

Almost a testament to the film's compassionate treatment of the poor is the reaction of Adolf Hitler. He was deeply impressed with the social and economic devastation caused by the Great Depression, and argued the United States was incapable of mastering its problems because it was a mongrel society ruled by inferior elements. Having seen the movie several times, historian John Haag is of the opinion that Hitler regarded *The Grapes of Wrath*'s grim scenes as literal truth.[200]

Other sympathetic films of the time include *The Life of Emile Zola* (1937, Best Picture of the Year), which exposes anti-Semitism and abuse of power by bullies. It also emphasizes the suffering of a loyal man wrongfully accused. *All Quiet on the Western Front* (1930, Best Picture of the Year, AFI's #54), is a tragic story of the consequences of people from one country warring against those of another. In *You Can't Take it with You* (1938, Best Picture of the Year), a carefree family faces financial problems. The movie centers around class distinctions with a message that poor people are sometimes better than rich ones. The only actors treated disrespectfully in the film are the black maid and her simple-acting boyfriend. Out of the blue the boyfriend announces, "I'm on relief."

When blacks were not being degraded or ridiculed in movies, they were simply eliminated, much like a former relative-by-marriage who is airbrushed out of family photos.

Cimarron (1930-1931, Best Picture of the Year), managed to a show delicate and warm sympathy to Jews, Indians and women, while displaying excruciating cruelness to a black child. Before the story of the 1889 Oklahoma Land Rush begins, pictures of the main characters are displayed on the screen. As the characters are introduced, their first and last names are given as text. The last introduction is for a black child who is seven or eight years old. He is given only one name, Isaiah. He is shining shoes with a happy grin on his face as he pushes a brush back and forth. Then the story begins. In the opening scene Isaiah falls into a cream pie and is scolded by a very fat mammy who rushes in and swats him. The main male character remarks proudly that the boy has loyalty one can't buy. Later scenes show the boy happily doing chores for the white family. The film exposes biases against other groups by kindheartedly portraying characters that rise above the prejudices. Isaiah, however, stays constant: a contented servant for the white people. He has no family, and his only friend is a young man who is mocked due to his constant stuttering. No future or hope is considered for Isaiah.

Another film that deals with consideration to some, but is inconsiderate to African Americans is *Mr. Smith Goes to Washington* (1939, Best Picture of the Year, AFI's #29). A naïve young politician learns just how dirty politics can be, but eventually truth and justice prevail. The theme of the movie is that political change in the American system is available to the common man, if he is willing to stand up for what is right and true. Cherished actor Jimmy Stewart speaks from his heart, "Freedom is too important a thing to be buried in books." The most sentimental and moving music in the film is played as the camera slowly pans the Lincoln Memorial. Yet the only black actor in the movie, other than the black train conductors, was one little boy who appears for about three seconds among throngs of little white boys, and had no speaking part.

Many movies of the 1930s demeaned African Americans. When blacks were not being degraded or ridiculed in movies, they were simply eliminated, much like a former relative-by-marriage who is airbrushed out of family photos. *The Little Tramp* was kind to some but mocked a black man for no seeming purpose other than taking a cheap shot. In *City Lights* (AFI's #76), a big, brawny, dumb-looking black boxer is shown kissing a horseshoe and rubbing himself with a rabbit's foot before he is knocked out cold by a white man.

A Chaplin film, *Modern Times* (AFI's #81), is a satire of industrial life that shows the frustration of workers who are faced with such devices as an automatic feeding machine to avoid wasting time for lunch. There are numerous scenes of workers in factories, workers marching for rights, people crowded into streets and a restaurant, but there is not a black worker among them. The only two blacks in the movie are: a woman who is taken to jail in a paddy wagon and another who sits idly on a tiny back porch in the poor waterfront section of the city.

The little black boy in *Rich and Strange* (1932), directed by Alfred Hitchcock, is playing a banjo. In *Duck Soup* (1933, AFI's #85), someone tells the character Groucho, played by comedian Groucho Marx, that someone is headstrong. "Sure he's headstrong," says the Groucho character, "and his father was headstrong. But his mother was an Armstrong. So the Headstrongs married the Armstrongs, and that's why darkeys were born."

It Happened One Night (1934, Best Picture of the Year), has scenes on a bus trip from Florida to New York. There are no black characters on the bus, but there is a black actor at the bus stop. He is fat, wears a high chef's hat and bears a simple grin across his face, "Get yas red hot coffee." The film has white characters playing the part of food vendors and maintenance men, but only the black man is smiling and outwardly happy in his job.

The Great Ziegfeld (1936, Best Picture of the Year) has "If You Knew Suzie" sung in blackface, a blackfaced dancer, plus the unfortunately named maid "Flossie." Flossie says: "Ain't dat sumpin. Don't you like your flowers, Honey Lamb? And dare's a package, too. I done unwrapped it for you."

In *Young and Innocent* (1937), directed by Alfred Hitchcock, the murderer plays in a blackfaced band. A gentle twist was given to slavery when audiences of *Mutiny on the Bounty* (1935, Best Picture of the Year, AFI's #86) were informed that the ship, "Bounty," was dispatched to find fruit trees to feed slaves in the new world.

Jungle movies could be particularly insulting to blacks. Here, white men go to strange places and are immediately more adept with the terrain than the black natives.[201] *King Kong* (1933, AFI's #43) is a "beauty and the beast" story that values whites more than blacks. Most of the film takes place on an island. A character describes a wall on the island as being built by a "higher civilization" than the black natives who now inhabit it. The crew arrives on the island just as the natives are preparing a young black girl to sacrifice to the beast, Kong. As soon as the natives see the blond film actress among the crew, they realize the beast would much prefer the white girl to the black one, so they kidnap her and use her instead. Sure enough, the giant gorilla quickly fell in love with the white girl.

But at least one movie of this decade attempted to be sensitive toward African Americans. The 1934 film *Imitation of Life* portrayed a black woman with a light skinned daughter compassionately. It is a heartbreaking story of a white woman and a black woman who meet and develop a business together. The two lived in the white woman's home, so the audience never sees where black people live. When the black woman's pancake recipe develops into a thriving business, she asks the white woman to keep her share of the profits for her, sending the message that black people need whites to manage their affairs. Historian Daniel J. Leab says she ". . . responds like the mythical Southern slaves who renounced freedom in many a movie."[202] The beautiful young daughter eventually rejects her black mother so she can pass in the white world. Bogle describes the film as, "a conscious apotheosis of the tom spirit and an unconsciously bitter comment on race relations in America."[203]

> *Film historian Ed Guerrero noted that scenes depicting slaves contentedly picking cotton to orchestrated spirituals in the 1915 Griffith epic became a cliché that was used twenty-four years later in* **Gone With the Wind.**

For *Gone With the Wind* (1939, Best Picture of the Year, AFI's #4), David O. Selznick considered hiring D.W. Griffiths as director. Even Thomas Dixon tried to horn in. With the director and writer of *The Birth of a Nation* so close to the action, no wonder the two films seem similar. *Gone With the Wind* was based on a novel by Margaret Mitchell. The book was an immediate sensation around the country and a Book of the Month Club selection in 1936.[204] The movie, too, was sensational, and actress Hattie McDaniel won the Oscar for best supporting actress for her role as Mammy. She was the first African American to win an Academy Award.[205]

Film historian Ed Guerrero noted that scenes depicting slaves contentedly picking cotton to orchestrated spirituals in the 1915 Griffith epic became a cliché that was used twenty-four years later in *Gone With the Wind*. Both films featured loyal house servants who preferred slavery to freedom. Both also depict a strong mammy who is completely devoted to the master. But Guerrero says *Gone With the Wind* avoids the inflammatory propaganda of *The Birth of a Nation*, "revealing how much Hollywood had refined the art of suggestion."[206]

Surprisingly, the book version of *Gone With the Wind* was a best seller in the Third Reich. Within two days of its publication in Germany in 1937, it sold twelve thousand copies. In the autumn of 1937, German reviews were released, describing "a wonderful, strictly regulated life," and "patriarchal, well-defined relations between black and white." Scarlett's energy and tenacity were associated with her "Irish race." Another German reviewer raved, "Blood relationship transforms distant history into personal experience." Not surprisingly, Adolf Hitler, who believed the wrong side won the Civil War, loved the movie. Although it was banned to the public in Germany after 1941, it remained popular among the Nazi elite.[207]

The text of the opening scene sets up the story: "There was a land of Cavaliers and cotton fields. Here in this pretty world, gallantry took its last bow. Here was the last ever seen of Knights and their Ladies fair, of Master and of Slave . . . Look for it only in books for it is no more than a dream remembered . . . A civilization gone with the wind." Melanie remarks, "It is our world, wanting only to be graceful and beautiful."

There are three main parts played by black actors. Mammy is Miss Scarlett's personal maid. She is wise and tender, lectures Scarlett about the proper manners of a lady, and cares for all the white family members. Rhett Butler remarks about Mammy, "Mammy's a smart old soul, and one of the few people I know whose respect I'd like to have." Yet the character's comical grammar, frantic movements and red taffata slip

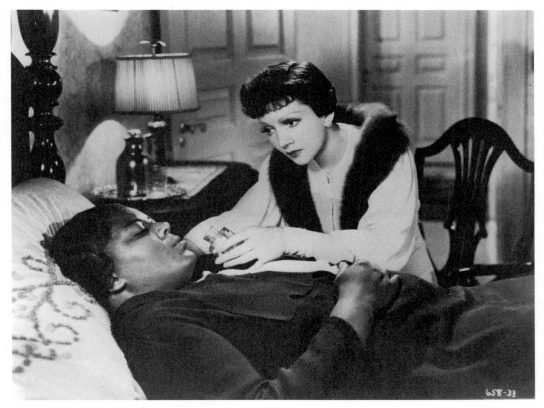

French-born American actress Claudette Colbert (1903-1996) (right) administers to actress Louise Beavers (1902-1962) in a scene from the film Imitation of Life, *directed by John M. Stahl, 1934. (Photo by Universal Pictures/Courtesy of Getty Images)*

render her too hysterical to take seriously, and her undying loyalty to Scarlett after the war is far-fetched. Author and historian Ed Guerrero attributes discussions of the mammy as a dominant representational figure of African American woman from *The Birth of a Nation* to *Guess Who's Coming to Dinner* to James Baldwin: "Baldwin's analysis, then is insightful when he comments that 'the inclusion of this figure is absolutely obligatory—compulsive—no matter what the film imagines itself to be saying by means of this inclusion.'" Guerrero says we still see her in contemporary films such as *Clara's Heart,* as she smiles at us in less caricatured versions. [208]

Prissy is another housemaid, referred to by Rhett as a "simple-minded darkey." She lacks Mammy's wisdom, and is absurd in her almost constant squealing. The third black character, Big Sam, is a field hand. He is seen in a troop of black men with spades and shovels over their shoulders singing while marching through Atlanta at the end of the war. He tells Scarlett, "So we'z goin to dig fo da Souf. Don worry. We'll stop dem Yankees." It is a far cry from W.E.B. DuBois's remarks about the desperate worship of freedom by the African American slave for two centuries.

An unnamed house slave at Tara looks like a buffoon, wielding a hatchet in one hand and an umbrella in the other, as he traipses through mud after a turkey. "Now you jus stan still so you can be a Christmas gif fo da white folks." This had nothing to do with surrounding scenes or the story as a whole, and appears to be added simply for the sport of making fun of black people.

Post-war black men are displayed as opportunistic scavengers. A man singing a song about marching through Georgia is heard over a scene of pitiful, defeated, wounded southern soldiers returning home. The camera then zooms to the fancy buggy carrying the singing man, who is foppishly dressed with a carpet bag at his side. He is black. Later, a white man from the north is shown telling a group of former slaves, "We're going to give every last one of you forty acres and a mule . . . cause we're your friends. And your gonna become voters and you're gonna vote like your friends do." Had the scene not been squeezed between displays of strolling black men looking fat and smoking cigars, as Scarlett, thin and hungry, searches for tax money to save Tara, it might have been sympathetic. Instead, it portrayed the freedmen as looking too dumb to know an obvious con when they saw one.

Not only was slavery not criticized in the movie, it was rationalized. When Ashley accused Scarlett of mistreating convicts who were hired to work in her post-war lumbar yard, Scarlett pointed out that he had not been so particular about owning slaves. Ashley replied, "That was different. We didn't treat them that way. Besides I'd have freed them all when father died if the war hadn't already freed them."

*Films in the four categories not discussed in the text are in endnote.[209]

1931-1940
Decade Wrap-up

THE UNITED STATES SUPREME COURT and Hollywood each had a message that they sent for more than a quarter of a century. The Supreme Court's message was that African Americans were equal. Hollywood's message was that African Americans were inferior and servile. Apparently Hollywood was not listening to the Court.

In 1914, the Supreme Court invalidated an Oklahoma statute that authorized railroads to exclude passengers in luxury compartments according to race, rather than provide separate but equal facilities (*McCabe v. Atchison, Topeka & Sante Fe Railroad Co*). The Court said the exclusion violated the Fourteenth Amendment's Equal Protection Clause.

In 1915, Hollywood said in *The Birth of a Nation* the white man was supreme and the black man was lesser. In 1938 in *Missouri ex rel. Gaines v. Canada*, the Court said the state of Missouri denied a black man equal protection of the laws when it refused to admit him to the law school of the state university because of his race.

In 1939, Hollywood portrayed African Americans happy and contented with slavery. *Gone with the Wind* had a black who man said he wanted the South to win the Civil War, a black woman was called a simple-minded darkey, showed little black girls happily fanning white women, and little black boys blissfully swinging and ringing the plantation bell.

White Southern newspaper editorials condemned Nazi racism but refused to acknowledge obvious similarities between Nazi Germany and the American South.

The *Gaines* opinion discusses the legality of allowing Missouri to send its black law students to four neighboring states, all of which accepted black students. There was not a black college graduate anywhere in a Hollywood movie. We know that Thurgood Marshall and his traveling troop of lawyers were trying cases across the South. Over four hundred thousand black Americans served in the military during World War I. Yet not one single popular movie from this decade portrayed a black person in any profession, trade, business or in the Armed Forces. Instead there were maids, grinning servants, savages, jail inmates and simpletons. Nor was there any future for a black child, as the films invariably showed little boys carrying shoe sign kits. In addition to no future, African Americans had no families or homes, at least none off the plantation. There was only one relationship

British-born actress Vivien Leigh (1913-1967) with Butterfly McQueen in a scene from the civil war epic Gone With the Wind *on June 26, 1939. (Photo by John Kobal Foundation/Getty Images)*

between blacks shown. It was the maid and her boyfriend in *You Can't Take it with You*. But it was tainted with the boyfriend's gratuitous announcement that he was on relief.

In *Imitation of Life*, while the black characters were treated with dignity, there was an underlying message that blacks should accept their lot with stoicism, and not complain. It is not that Hollywood did not know how to treat people with dignity or deal with serious subjects in a sensitive manner without attaching strings. There were scores of movies during this decade that sympathetically portrayed various groups and issues. It is as though the whole industry was in as state of denial. Denying racism, that is.

A similar phenomenon of wearing racial blinders occurred in the country during this decade. Most Americans were incapable of seeing the similarities in racial policies in America and Nazi Germany. The Nuremberg Laws prohibited sexual relations between Jews and Aryans while Southern laws banned interracial marriage. In both societies a minority was disenfranchised and dominated by a "master race."

Every Gallup poll during the 1930s and 1940s showed overwhelming support for segregation in the South. German-Americans in the South were hostile to the Nazis, and the Ku Klux Klan was hostile to the German Bund. Some American newspapers supported an American boycott of the 1936 Olympics and were outraged at the anti-Semitic outrages in Germany. At the same time, white Southern newspaper editorials condemned Nazi racism but refused to acknowledge obvious similarities between Nazi Germany and the American South. Newspaper editorials rejected comparisons between the persecution of Jews in Germany and the lynching of blacks in America, and the rare Southern editor who noted similarities was often viciously attacked. Even a 1936 *New York Times* article argued there was a difference between German racism and American treatment of blacks, since Germany's system was based on supposed laws of science and history, while Americans "do it in the good, old, thick-headed, prejudiced, irrational human fashion."

The African American press, on the other hand, saw the connection quite clearly. The Nazis also understood the similarities. Nazi publications frequently demonstrated an appreciation for the Southern way. Many of Hitler's speeches before 1933 were filled with vicious remarks about blacks. He clearly admired American Negrophobia. Some historans say the German ambassador to the United States reported to Berlin in 1936 that the overwhelming majority of Americans rejected any comparison between German racism and the discrimination against blacks in the South.[210]

1941-1950
Racial Framework

THE AMERICAN DEMOCRATIC SYSTEM, WHICH tolerated discriminatory laws in individual states, allowed for change when a person was smart enough to push the right buttons. African Americans pushed a lot of right buttons during this decade. The timing was right. "Hitler gave racism a bad name," one wit quipped according to historian Thomas Cripps who said the war came to stand against the Jim Crow order.[211]

In 1940, factories geared up and hired new workers, but black workers got little benefit from increased jobs and wages. A. Philip Randolph, head of the Brotherhood of Sleeping Car Porters, threatened to lead one hundred thousand African Americans in a march on Washington, D.C. unless industries working under federal government defense contracts provided equal employment opportunities.

On June 21, 1941 President Roosevelt issued Executive Order 8802, which prohibited employment discrimination based on race, creed, color or national origin by the defense industry working under federal contracts. Immediately, thousands of steady, well-paying jobs opened to black workers. These opportunities stimulated half a million African Americans to leave the South in search of jobs. [212]

Later that year, on December 7, 1941, the only position open to blacks by the United States Navy was that of a mess attendant. African American Dorie Miller was a mess attendant on the USS Arizona stationed in Pearl Harbor, Hawaii that Sunday morning. When the Japanese attacked the ship, Miller dropped the laundry he was gathering and hit the deck. He immediately pulled a wounded captain to safety and seized a machine gun, firing at the attacking planes. He shot down at least four Japanese planes before he was ordered to abandon the sinking ship. For his bravery, Miller received the Navy Cross and became America's first World War II war hero.[213]

On June 21, 1941 President Roosevelt issued Executive Order 8802, which prohibited employment discrimination based on race, creed, color or national origin by the defense industry working under federal contracts.

The NAACP asked African Americans to support the war effort. In the early 1940s, three million black men registered for service. Nearly one million black men and four thousand black women served in the military during the war, with close to half a million African Americans serving abroad.[214]

Despite valiant war contributions by black Americans, they continued to meet racial discrimination in the service. For example, the NAACP found racial bias in the grading of tests administered to potential draftees. White recruits were required to achieve a score of fifteen on the Army Intelligence Test; black recruits needed a thirty-nine.[215] Plus, blacks were kept in segregated all-black units. When stationed in the South, African Americans were forced to suffer all the humiliations, degradation and insults Jim Crow had to offer. According to the Hortons, one black chaplain recalled that, instead of allowing him to have quarters in a half-empty officer's barracks, the Army drew up plans to build a special "colored" officer's barracks in which he, alone, would be housed.[216]

The Army excluded from the military baseball team one black lieutenant from California who had been a star in football, basketball, track and baseball at UCLA. His name was Jackie Robinson. In 1944, while stationed at Fort Hood, Robinson refused to sit in the rear of a Texas bus, for which he was arrested, court-martialed and acquitted.[217] But what the military did not want, the major leagues did. After the war, in 1945, the Brooklyn Dodgers signed Robinson to their minor league farm team. On April 15, 1947, Robinson officially broke the color barrier in professional baseball by making his major league debut.[218]

On the night of July 17, 1944, Freddie Meeks, a sailor in the United States Navy, was on leave from his post as a munitions loader at the Fort Chicago naval base near Concord, California. Only black sailors with no training and fresh from boot camp were assigned the deadly duty of loading ammunition into ships bound for the Pacific theater. Their superiors told them the ammunition was not live. Meeks's constant nightmare came true when an explosion killed three hundred twenty men, including two hundred two black sailors, the deadliest stateside disaster of World War II. After the blast, injured whites who survived were sent home for extended leave. Black sailors, however, were sent back to the dock. Meeks refused to resume loading munitions until safety improvements were made, and was one of fifty who were convicted of mutiny and sentenced to prison. Meeks was pardoned by President Clinton on Christmas Eve, 1999.[219]

Black Americans at home also continued to suffer indignities. Those who wanted to give blood for the war effort had to do so at Jim Crow blood banks.[220] When returning on a bus with a few classmates from a high school oratorical contest in South Georgia, where Martin Luther King, Jr. had delivered a speech titled, "The Negro and the Constitution," the bus driver demanded the black youths, including high schooler King, give up their seats to whites. They had to stand the entire ninety miles to Atlanta. Later, in a summer job working for Railway Express, young King quit when a white superintendent kept calling him "nigger."[221]

White recruits were required to achieve a score of fifteen on the Army Intelligence Test; black recruits needed a thirty-nine.

Nonetheless, changes in civilian life were in the air, and one invention that would forever alter labor needs of the South was on the horizon. On October 2, 1944, a crowd gathered in Clarksdale, Mississippi for the first public demonstration of a new machine: a working, production-ready mechanical cotton-picker. Each unit picked as much as one thousand pounds of cotton in an hour compared to the twenty pounds a good field hand could pick in the same time. By machine, the cost of picking a bale of cotton was $5.26; by hand it was $39.41. This invention made the sharecropper system—a system that had satisfied the cotton planter's need for cheap labor since the Civil War—obsolete.[222]

In 1940, 77 percent of black Americans still lived in the South. For decades, cotton planters of the Mississippi Delta had been strongly opposed to migration of blacks to the North. But when word got around about the mechanical cotton picker, the attitude of whites regarding black migration changed. During the mechanization of cotton farming, five million blacks moved out of the rural South.[223]

Chicago was the first large northern city reached by migrating black Americans. The "Southside" of Chicago became the black capital of America. As the migrants crowded into the city, landlords converted more and more apartment buildings into kitchenettes to accommodate them. As a result, the neighborhoods became poorer and denser, and law enforcement was casual because, according to Nicholas Lemann, Chicago police didn't consider black on black crime to be a problem worth solving. Black people were regularly charged more rent and paid lower wages than white peo-

*In 1940,
77 percent
of black
Americans
still lived in
the South.*

*A new party,
known as the
Dixiecrats,
formed when
a group of
disgruntled
Democrats
stormed out of
the Democratic
convention after
the Democratic
Party adopted
a civil rights
plank.*

ple and were barred entirely from many good jobs. What made the overcrowded Southside look so good to the former sharecroppers was its comparison to the South.[224]

Middle class African Americans tried to get away from the slums by moving into white neighborhoods. It was a difficult process. Nearly all the white neighborhoods were segregated by fiercely maintained custom, and often by force of law with restrictive covenants that barred blacks from buying houses. Since the 1926 Supreme Court case of *Corrigan v. Buckley*, these covenants were perfectly legal. The Southside became, and still is, the largest contiguous settlement of African Americans in the country.[225]

In 1947, President Harry Truman appointed a prestigious bi-racial group of American citizens to study America's racial problems, "The President's Committee on Civil Rights." Truman saw the committee's report and asked Congress to make lynching a federal offense, outlaw the poll tax, eliminate segregated interstate transportation, and establish a fair employment practices commission to stop racial discrimination and hiring. In 1948, Truman ordered an end to discrimination in federal employment and to segregation in the nation's armed services.[226]

The civil rights bent proved too much for some southern Democrats. Remember Thomas Dixon, author of the play used as the basis for *The Birth of a Nation*? Well, his nephew, Frank Dixon, governor of Alabama from 1939 to 1943,[227] was the keynote speaker at the States Rights Party's 1948 convention in the city of brotherly love. He denounced civil rights as a diabolical plan. The new party, known as the Dixiecrats, formed when a group of disgruntled Democrats stormed out of the Democratic convention after the Democratic Party adopted a civil rights plank. The Dixiecrats nominated South Carolina Governor J. Strom Thurmond to be the next President of the United States. The new party professed to be motivated by states' rights rather than white supremacy. But historians Klinkner and Smith say this ploy was a reflection of the nation's declining tolerance for overt racism.[228]

1941-1950
The Supreme Court

EVEN THOUGH THE COURT DID not do well by all African Americans, tremendous advances for African Americans were made during this decade. In areas of criminal procedure, voting rights, interstate transportation, housing and school admissions, blacks were successful before the Supreme Court.

John W. Downer, a Colonel in the United States Army, was the commanding officer of Fort Upton, New York in 1942 when African American Winfred William Lynn sued him. Lynn complained, not about being inducted into the Army where he wanted to serve his country, but about being inducted as a member of a "Negro quota," in violation of the 1940 Selective Service Act, which provided, "no discrimination against any person on account of race or color."

Citing *Plessy v. Ferguson*, the Circuit Court of Appeals, 140 F.2d 397, affirmed the trial judge's rebuff of Lynn, stating, "If the Congress had intended to prohibit separate white and Negro quotas and calls, we believe it would have expressed such intention more definitely than by the general prohibition against discrimination. . . . In our opinion the statutory provisions which the appellant [Lynn] invokes mean no more than that Negroes must be accorded privileges substantially equal to those afforded whites in the matter of volunteering, induction, training and service under the Act; in other words, separate quotas in the requisitions based on relative racial proportions of the men subject to call do not constitute the prohibited 'discrimination.'"

Lynn did not give up and petitioned to the United States Supreme Court. Mr. Tom C. Clark, Assistant Attorney General, was one of the lawyers for the government. NAACP's Thurgood Marshall of Baltimore filed an amicus curiae or "friend of the court" brief. The Supreme Court, 322 U.S. 756, denied Lynn's petition.

In another case, the Court had to decide whether or not a peace officer's activity comprised state action in 1945 in *Screws v. United States*, 325 U.S. 91. Baker County, Georgia Sheriff M. Claude Screws arrested, handcuffed and beat to unconsciousness a black man named Robert Hall, who died shortly after. It was later found that Screws had a personal grudge against Hall. The arrest was made late at night at Hall's home on a warrant charging Hall with the theft of a tire. As the handcuffed Hall got out of the car onto the courthouse square, Screws and two deputies began beating him with their fists and a solid-bar blackjack, eight inches long and weighing about two pounds. They later claimed Hall had reached for a gun and used insulting language. But after Hall was on the ground, they continued beating him for fifteen to thirty minutes.

The Court ruled Screws acted under color of law under the civil rights statute. The opinion states: "Acts of officers who undertake to perform their official duties are included whether they hew to the line of their authority or overstep it, "

To the Southwest, Texas continued its pastime of depriving blacks of their voting rights by excluding them from participation in primary elections. African American Lonnie Smith brought suit against election judge S.E. Allwright because Allwright would not permit him to cast a ballot in a Democratic primary election on July 27, 1940 for nomination of Democratic candidates for the United States Senate, House of Representatives, Governor and other state offices. In 1932, the Democratic party had adopted a resolution at its convention that stated: "Be it resolved that all white citizens of the State of Texas who are qualified to vote under the Constitution and laws of the State shall be eligible to membership in the Democratic party and, as such, entitled to participate in its deliberations." It was by virtue of that regulation that the Democratic party refused to permit Smith to vote in the primary election.

In Smith's case, the Supreme Court made note of its earlier ruling in 1927 in *Nixon v. Herndon* where it held the action of Texas in denying the ballot to Negroes by statute was in violation of the Equal Protection Clause of the Fourteenth Amendment. It also noted its 1935 opinion in *Grovey v. Townsend* where a Texas county clerk refused to furnish an absentee ballot to an African American solely on the ground of race. In that case, the Court did not find any Constitutional violation

The "separate but equal" coach for black passengers was not air-conditioned and was divided by partitions into three parts, "one for colored smokers, one for white smokers and one in the center for colored men and women." The toilet did not flush, and there were no wash basins, soap, towels or running water.

because the election was a primary held by the Democratic party, and not a general election held by the government.

In Lonnie Smith's case, the Supreme Court issued its 1944 opinion, *Smith v. Allwright*, 321 U.S. 649. The Court overruled its earlier holding in *Grovey v. Townsend*, reasoning that because the candidate for the general election was selected in the primary election, Smith's rights under the Fifteenth Amendment had been violated.

Two significant events occurred in the interim between *Grovey* and *Smith*. First, the make-up of the Court had changed with seven appointments by President Roosevelt. Second, a few years earlier, the Court issued an opinion in the matter of *United States v. Classic*, 313 U.S. 299, holding that Section 4 of Article I of the Constitution authorized Congress to regulate primary as well as general elections.

After *Smith v. Allwright*, reducing African American participation in the voting process was practiced on an individual, rather than a group, level. Registrars of voters became more aggressive in enforcing literacy tests and levying poll taxes against prospective black voters.[229]

Being sophisticated, educated and well connected did not insulate a black American from Jim Crow. United States Congressman Arthur W. Mitchell, an African American, purchased a first class ticket and traveled by railroad from Chicago to Hot Springs, Arkansas. Shortly after leaving Memphis and crossing the Mississippi River into Arkansas, the train conductor forced Congressman Mitchell, under threat of arrest, to move into the car provided for "colored passengers." Arkansas law, referred to as the "Arkansas Separate Coach Law," provided for separate but equal facilities for the races. The conductor advised the Congressman to seek a refund for the portion of his payment for the upgraded Pullman accommodations which were air-conditioned, had hot and cold running water, and separate flushable toilets for men and women.

The "separate but equal" coach for black passengers was not air-conditioned and was divided by partitions into three parts, "one for colored smokers, one for white smokers and one in the center for colored men and women." The toilet available to Mitchell did not flush, and there were no wash basins, soap, towels or running water.

Congressman Mitchell charged unjust discrimination, and filed a complaint with the Interstate Commerce Commission. The Commission dismissed his complaint, finding there was "comparatively little colored traffic." Mitchell filed a suit in federal court, which ruled it lacked jurisdiction and also dismissed his complaint. Mitchell then appealed to the United States Supreme Court.

In *Mitchell v. United States*, 313 U.S. 80, the Court concluded the Congressman had been denied a fundamental right of equal treatment. It ordered the case back to the Interstate Commerce Commission with directions to set aside its previous order, and conduct further proceedings.

Racial prejudice existing in the United States is shown in Supreme Court opinions involving Japanese Americans, too. Bigotry was unleashed by all branches of the national government after the Japanese attack on Pearl Harbor. Gordon Hirabayashi, an American citizen, was convicted of a misdemeanor for a May 9, 1942 violation of a curfew for persons of Japanese ancestry. Hirabayashi, who grew up in Seattle, had been educated in Washington public schools, was a senior at the University of Washington and had never been to Japan. He admitted being out of his home at eight P.M. He also failed to report to the Civil Control Station, the first step toward an anticipated exclusion evacuation of persons of Japanese ancestry, stating it was his belief he would be waiving his rights as an American citizen by doing so. The curfew was set in force by Executive Order 9066, and made punishable as a crime by an act of Congress. Hirabayashi contended the act violated the Fifth Amendment, which he said prohibited discrimination between citizens of Japanese Ancestry and those of other ancestry.

In *Hirabayashi v. United States*, 320 U.S. 81, the Supreme Court upheld the constitutionality of the law, rationalizing the war power of the Executive and Congress extends to every matter and activity related to war, and is not restricted to the winning of victories in the field and the repulse of enemy forces. The justices said it is not for any court to sit in review of the wisdom of their action or substitute its judgment for theirs.

Another Supreme Court case that illustrates the Court's attitude toward race during this time involved Fred Korematsu. Like Hirabayashi, Korematsu argued he was denied due process under the Fifth Amendment after he was convicted of violating a war powers act. He grew up in the San Francisco area. Civilian Exclusion Order No. 34 directed that all persons of Japanese ancestry were excluded from prescribed West Coast military areas as a protection against espionage and sabotage. Korematsu's attempt to avoid concentration camps by altering his features with plastic surgery were compared by the Court of Appeals, 140 F.2d 289, to actions of some persons of African American heritage. "This attempt is as pathetic as that of another of our minority groups—of those of one-sixteenth negro blood hoping to conceal the fact that they have not 'passed over' into general Caucasian social intercourse."

In *Korematsu v. United States,* 323 U.S. 214, the Supreme Court stated that all legal restrictions that curtail the civil rights of a single racial group are immediately suspect: "That is not to say that all such restrictions are unconstitutional. It is to say that courts must subject them to the most rigid scrutiny."

The Tenth Amendment of the United States Constitution reserves to the individual states the right to exercise police power; that is, to pass laws for the health, safety and welfare of its citizens.

The Court went on to discuss investigations that revealed loyalties to Japan and that exclusion of those of Japanese origin was deemed necessary, and concluded there was no constitutional violation: "He was excluded because we are at war with the Japanese Empire, because the properly constituted military authorities feared an invasion of our West Coast and felt constrained to take proper security measures, because they decided the military urgency of the situation demanded that all citizens of Japanese ancestry be segregated from the West Coast temporarily, and finally, because Congress, reposing its confidence in this time of war in our military leaders—as inevitably it must—determined that they should have the power to do just this."

Justices Owen Roberts, Robert Jackson and Frank Murphy dissented. Murphy wrote, "Racial discrimination in any form and in any degree has no justifiable part whatever in our democratic way of life. It is unattractive in any setting but it is utterly revolting among a free people who have embraced the principles set forth in the Constitution of the United States. All residents of this nation are kin in some way by blood or culture to a foreign land. Yet they are primarily and necessarily a part of the new and distinct civilization of the United States. They must accordingly be treated at all times as the heirs of the American experiment and as entitled to all the rights and freedoms guaranteed by the Constitution."

With regard to racial discrimination against African Americans, still to come was a direct constitutional attack of state laws that interfere with travel. In a country as vast as the United States, travel often involves journeying through several states, and sometimes a state statute comes into conflict with the federal Constitution. The Tenth Amendment of the United States Constitution reserves to the individual states the right to exercise police power; that is, to pass laws for the health, safety and welfare of its citizens. But the Commerce Clause assigns Congress the power of regulating interstate commerce.

Virginia had a statute that required segregation of bus passengers according to race, and made it a misdemeanor for a person to refuse to change a seat on a bus when directed to do so by the bus driver. Greyhound Lines, Inc.'s company regulation reserved full control of seating to the discretion of the bus driver. On July 16, 1944, Irene Morgan, an African American, purchased a bus ticket at Hayes Store in Gloucester County, Virginia for travel to Baltimore, Maryland. When the bus left the town of Saluda in Middlesex County, Virginia, six white passengers were standing. The driver directed Morgan and her seatmate to move to two vacant seats in the rear of the bus. Morgan refused. The seatmate attempted to move, but Smith pulled her back. A sheriff and a deputy boarded the bus and again told her to move. The other black woman moved, but Morgan again refused. She was arrested, tried and found guilty.

The Supreme Court of Appeals of Virginia reasoned that if Congress wanted to nullify State segregation statutes that were applicable to interstate passengers, it had power to do so under the Commerce Clause. "However, until Congress pre-empts this legislative field by proper enactment, the States continue to have the right to segregate the white and colored races on public carriers. That Congress probably will not enter this field is evidenced by the fact that since January 5, 1938, for more than seven years it has refused to act, though at each session since then it has had the subject before it and has been urged to abolish segregation."[230]

The next step was to the United States Supreme Court. Thurgood Marshall argued to the Court, "Today we are emerging from a war in which all of the people of the United States were joined in a death struggle against the apostles of racism. How much clearer, therefore, must it be today that the national business of interstate commerce is not to be disfigured by racial notions alien to our national ideals."[231] Marshall was successful in *Morgan v. Virginia*, 328 U.S. 373. The Court held that Virginia's statute interfered with the need for national uniformity in commerce.

Restrictive covenants between white home buyers and sellers agreeing not to sell homes to people of other races were preventing the nation's black veterans from obtaining decent housing.

In addition to travel hindrances, blacks faced barriers in housing. Restrictive covenants between white home buyers and sellers agreeing not to sell homes to people of other races were preventing the nation's black veterans from obtaining decent housing.[232] In 1948, what have come to be known as the "Restrictive Covenant Cases,"[233] were decided by the Supreme Court. The Court held that, in granting judicial enforcement of racial covenants (which amounted to official approval of private agreements) States denied black home buyers equal protection of the laws. By invalidating enforcement of the covenants, the Court destroyed one of the most formidable instruments ever developed to enforce racial discrimination.[234]

Higher education was again before the Supreme Court in *Sweatt v. Painter*, 330 U.S. 620. Heman Marion Sweatt, wanted to become a lawyer. The University of Texas denied him admission because he was black. With Thurgood Marshall and the NAACP on the case, Texas scrambled to assemble a law school for African Americans. It didn't work. The Supreme Court found lacking the elements that made a law school distinguished, such as faculty, reputation, alumni prestige, tradition and history. Under the Equal Protection Clause of the Fourteenth Amendment, the Court ordered Texas to admit Sweatt to the University of Texas.

1941-1950
Hollywood

TO JUDGE FROM 1940s MOVIES, the film industry was blind both to the achievements of blacks in American society and opinions issued by the United States Supreme Court. It is too bad Hollywood didn't get to Oz first to receive that Triple Cross Legion of Courage medal from the Wizard. It needed it a lot more than the cowardly lion. The industry's true stripes were shown in its movies during this decade. Prior to this time, the film trade might be excused for various reasons. With its popular movies, it first portrayed what it saw in American society at large. Later, with most African Americans still in the South, there wasn't that much exposure to the race. But by the 1940s there were millions of blacks in the North. There were black doctors and lawyers and war heroes. Blacks were in industry. There were thriving African American universities. Difficult though it was, blacks managed to move into some neighborhoods besides the ghettos. Surely Hollywood could see what was all around it. Yet it did not accurately portray African Americans in movies.

In spring of 1942, a group from the NAACP met with the heads of several Hollywood studios. The studios agreed to abandon derogatory roles, place blacks as extras in roles they could reasonably be expected to occupy in society and begin to incorporate blacks as studio technicians. A 1942 article in the film industry's newspaper, *Variety*, had a front page headline, "BETTER BREAK FOR NEGROES IN H-WOOD." [235]

Did Hollywood keep its promise to the NAACP? Let's look at *Sunset Boulevard*

(1950, AFI's #12). Several scenes take place at Paramount Studios. Flocks of actors, extras, executives, technicians, and other behind-the-scenes personnel are shown busily about their work. Not one of them is black. In fact, the only black actor in the film appears in a non-speaking part for about one second. He is called Rudy and he operates a shoe-shine shack. The main character parks his car behind Rudy's business, instead of near his apartment, to throw car repossessors off the scent. Apparently, the film suggests, no one would think of looking near a black man's business for a white man's car.

Likely, on the Paramount lot somewhere are huge storage rooms containing items such as medieval suits of armor, tiki torches and covered wagons, props to be brought out when necessary to set a scene. That is how blacks are used in popular movies during this decade. As props. None of the black actors used as props add anything to the movies except to give signals about wealth or status. A few say a line or two in a movie, but most have no speaking part.

Witness, for example, *The Lost Weekend* (1950, Best Picture of the Year). A would-be writer who has not been successful since school days, drowns himself in alcohol. It is painful to watch his useless life. At one point, he finds himself with no money to pay for his drinks, and steals from a woman sitting next to him, whose purse is within his reach. Afterward he goes to the restroom where a smiling black man obsequiously brushes jackets, wipes shoes and hands out towels.

The comparison of the two men is stunning. One works hard for a living, appreciating his tips, and the other, a drunken thief, contributes absolutely nothing. The black bathroom attendant apparently was used as a prop to show how much more difficult it is to find happiness in work when a person is white, and far more discerning.

Later, the drunk wakes up in the alcoholic ward of a hospital. His degradation is demonstrated with another black "prop." To show just how low the drunk had sunk, the camera flashed to the bed next to him: a black man in delirium tremens.

Citizen Kane (1941, AFI's #1) is a story about a poor boy who is raised by a rich man. The movie challenges the old order by pointing out the inherent failure of capitalistic success. "If I hadn't been very rich, I might have been a really great man," the Orson Wells character states. To demonstrate how well-kept Kane's mistress is, a giggling, smiling black maid in a frilly apron is used as a prop.

In *Mr. and Mrs. Smith* (1941), a comedy set in New York directed by Alfred Hitchcock, a little black boy is the only one of a group of children who carries a shoe shine box to demonstrate just how shabby the neighborhood has gotten. And jokes at the expense of blacks were used instead of props to underscore the wealth of white people. Hilariously funny, *The Philadelphia Story* (1950, AFI's #51) has two magazine reporters pretend they are friends of the family so they can secretly cover a socialite's wedding. When the two are shown into the parlor, they are aghast at the display of wealth. One of them cracks that she half expected to see pickaninnies and banjos.

For some reason, even after promising the NAACP it would show black actors in a more positive light, Hollywood insisted upon having virtually every show business dressing room scene contain a black maid.

How about the promise not to use black actors in derogatory roles? At first, the movie *Lifeboat* (1943), also directed by Alfred Hitchcock, appeared to show Hollywood kept its word. The story takes place on the Atlantic Ocean. After a ship is sunk by Germans during World War II, several survivors manage their way to a lifeboat. One is a black sailor named Joe. He brings with him to the lifeboat a woman and her baby he just saved from drowning. Joe is the one who knows enough verses of the bible to recite them during a burial at sea. He plays beautiful tunes on the flute, and is a genuinely good person, saintly at times, well liked and respected by the others. But instead of permitting a black man to be portrayed in purely positive terms, the plot later reveals Joe to be an able pick-pocket.

Or, how about the very patriotic *Yankee Doodle Dandy* (1942, AFI's #100)? James Cagney plays George M. Cohan who grows up in a family of entertainers, and stays in show business throughout his life. The characters playing the four singing, dancing members of the Cohan family perform a number in blackface. Real black actors play the part of a chef, valets, butlers, and a maid; as well as a group of slaves singing "Glory" beseechingly to a statue of Abraham Lincoln. But during the scene that shows volunteers lining up to enlist to fight in World War I, only whites are shown, even though hundreds of thousands of African Americans served in that war.

For some reason, even after promising the NAACP it would show black actors in a more positive light, Hollywood insisted upon having virtually every show business dressing room scene contain a black maid. *Going My Way* (1944, Best Picture of the Year) is a prime example. The ever-popular *Double Indemnity* (1944, AFI's #38) is also degrading to blacks. In *Double Indemnity*, only whites appear in the Los Angeles street, supermarket, train and office scenes—except a black night janitor and a black man who washes cars. In one scene, the female lead admires the apartment of the male lead, and asks who takes care of it. He tells her that a colored woman comes in once a week to clean.

Beloved Jimmy Stewart made *It's A Wonderful Life* (1947, AFI's # 11) memorable for all of us. Its unnamed ideal little American town has lots of public scenes. But the only two blacks are an inexplicably smiling train porter, who presumably will soon leave town, and a maid/cook at the boarding house.

In the 1940s, Hollywood continued to display sensitivity to other groups, while ignoring African Americans. *Gentleman's Agreement* (1947, Best Picture of the Year) was about anti-Semitism. A magazine writer is assigned to write a series of articles on the topic. There are numerous scenes where there is preaching about how unfair Americans are in their treatment of Jews. When it turns out that the magazine, itself, has no Jews on staff, the editor remarks, "I'm ashamed of myself and this magazine, too. The sloppy, slovenly notion that everybody's busy doing bigger things. Well there isn't anything bigger than beating down the complacence of essentially decent people about prejudice. Yes, I'm ashamed of myself."

At a few places in the movie time is given to prejudice against others besides Jews. There is a mention of anti-Catholicism, and twice words such as "coon" and "nigger" are scorned. But the movie does not practice what it preaches. There are countless New York street scenes including inside taxis and elevators, Central Park, La Guardia Airport, crowded restaurants, bars, hotels, office buildings, and department stores. Undoubtedly, there must have been at least one black person in New York City in 1948. Yet none were in this movie.

A still from the film Casablanca, *with the star Humphrey Bogart, and Sam, the piano player, who was played by Dooley Wilson. Photo circa 1942. (Photo by Bob Thomas/Popperfoto/Getty Images)*

It is implausible that Southern lawyers, judges and doctors of the time would have sided with a black person who had something white people wanted.

To give Hollywood its due, there were a few movies that portrayed blacks positively, albeit quickly. *The Best Years of Our Lives* (1946, Best Picture of the Year, AFI's #37), about the travails of returning soldiers, finally portrays the first signs of racial integration. In a supermarket scene, there is a quick shot of a black soldier and a few other well-dressed black people, probably the soldier's family, shopping and intermingling with whites. They served no apparent purpose as a prop; rather they are representative of typical shoppers.

In *The Maltese Falcon* (1941, AFI's #23), there are several scenes around San Francisco with crowds in the streets, hotel lobbies, office buildings and a theater entrance. Yet there is not one black actor to be found at any of those places. There is, however, one nicely dressed black couple, standing apart from others and talking to each other, at the bus terminal where Sam Spade hides the falcon in a locker.

And, of course, there is the other Sam. Who could forget Sam, Rick and Ilsa in *Casablanca* (1943, Best Picture of the Year)? The piano player at Rick's café is an African American, Sam, who has a share in the café's profits and is fiercely loyal to Rick. Sam is in charge of the fez-wearing band, but Rick is clearly in charge of Sam. Sam calls Rick "Mr. Richard" and "boss," and takes orders from him. When Rick decides to leave Casablanca, he sells his establishment. In the sale, Rick negotiates for Sam, who stays in Casablanca, giving the impression that Rick is smarter than Sam, and can strike a better deal. Hierarchical though the relationship between Rick and Sam is, there is mutual loyalty and respect. Their bond is the first indication of personal feelings and collegiality between black and white men.

Pinky (1949) is about the daughter of a black washerwoman who passes for white. When she returns to her hometown in the South to stay with her grandmother, after graduating from nursing school in the North where she enjoyed the privileges of the white world, she is subjected to the cruel treatment reserved for blacks. When Pinky has contact with law enforcement, the double standard for the races is revealed and police attitudes turn from respect to hostility when they find out she is black. The rest of the movie was quite unbelievable. Pinky ends up a defendant in a will contest after a white woman dies and leaves her estate to her. The white relatives are furious and bring a legal action. It is implausible that Southern lawyers, judges and doctors of the time would have sided with a black person. Elia Kazan won the best director award. His obituary says "the film seems timid and stagy today."[236]

* Movies not discussed in above text appear in endnote. [237]

1941-1950
Decade Wrap-up

ARMED WITH THE BENEFIT OF favorable Supreme Court decisions, millions more African Americans made it to the North during this decade. Shabby though their living conditions often were, they were finally able to exercise their right to vote under the Fifteenth Amendment, and they used their new power to their advantage. Incredible advances were made by African Americans in the 1940s, as they thrust themselves into areas previously closed to them. Jobs such as those involving federal defense contracts were now open to blacks, and the United States military would begin desegregation before the end of the decade. White owners and buyers of homes would no longer have their racial covenants enforced by the courts. But, during times when the topic of Adolf Hitler's racial discrimination was being discussed worldwide, it is astonishing how persistent racism still was in America.

While the 1940s Supreme Court would not pass muster under a twenty-first century microscope, it did not do too badly for the times. During this decade, the Court reversed some earlier cases, and clarified others, many benefiting African Americans. Judicial enforcement of restrictive covenants would no longer be allowed. In voting primaries and criminal procedure cases, the Court found state action where it did not find it earlier. The Commerce Clause was brought to the forefront to crush discriminatory state statutes. In higher education cases, no longer would the Court go along with winking at the equal part of the separate but equal standard under *Plessy v. Fergeson.* Much like knowing the need for a schoolyard monitor, the United States Supreme Court came to the realization that democracy sometimes has some of the same tendencies as recess bullies. The Court's rulings implied the states, left to their own devices, could not be trusted to respect the rights of persons. The total effect was more control over people's lives by the federal government, and less by individual states.

But while both African Americans and the Supreme Court made tremendous strides against racism during this decade, Hollywood remained in a time warp with many of its popular movies. The film industry knew the powerful effect movies had on the public psyche, and here Hollywood was at the height of the message movies. Even the military knew the clout of a lesson learned in a movie. The Army's manual warned "When the Negro is portrayed in the movies, or elsewhere, as a lazy, shiftless, no-good, slew-footed, happy-go-lucky, razor-toting, tap-dancing vagrant, a step has been taken in the direction of fixing this mental picture in the minds of whites."[238]

> *The Court's rulings implied the states, left to their own devices, could not be trusted to respect the rights of persons.*

One area underscores Hollywood's lack of sensitivity to blacks during this period: it is obvious from looking at films from this era that Hollywood still did not care about American blacks. Neal Gabler says Jews from the East looked yearningly at Hollywood for its ability to influence public opinion. RKO decided to use a Jew as the victim of anti-Semitism in a proposed movie loosely based on a contemporary novel, *The Brick Foxhole.* The novel used the murder of a homosexual as a ploy for a sermon on tolerance. There was concern by American Jewish Committee representative Dick Rothschild that it was dangerous to kill a Jew on the screen, simply because he was a Jew. "With astounding insensitivity," Gabler says, a suggestion was made by Rothschild to studio executive Dore Schary that, because the movie might prove hazardous to Jews, the book be adapted to be about blacks instead.[239]

Pinky was sympathetic to blacks to a point, but the overall message of the film was more negative than positive. First, Pinky was played by a white woman, instead of a black woman, probably to try for audience identification, a technique similar to that used in *The Birth of a Nation*, where whites in blackface were used in speaking parts. In the movie, local authority figures—doctor, lawyer and judge—all sided with Pinky when she was the defendant in a lawsuit. Such an unrealistic plot sent the false message that blacks had the same legal protections afforded to whites. In the real world at the time, had authority figures turned their backs on local folk, there would have been problems.

Hollywood, in effect, eliminated black Americans from normal, everyday life in many of the movies shown to white America.

In fact, in the novel, written by Cid Ricketts Sumner, Pinky won her lawsuit just as she did in the movie, but the Ku Klux Klan burned down the mansion Pinky inherited from the white woman—a more honest and believable ending than that dished out by Hollywood.[240] The film also sent the same stoic message as 1934's *Imitation of Life* in that Pinky's black grandmother, who was portrayed as happy and content with her lot, was better off than Pinky, who was confused and befuddled when she tried to "pass." In the end, when Pinky accepted her race, along with the restrictions imposed by whites, she, too, was happy.

Hollywood misrepresented actual conditions of blacks within the American system in other films, too, even though there were many opportunities for Hollywood to show life the way it really was. Factories during the war could have easily shown black workers. *Saboteur* came out a year after the President's executive order prohibiting racial discrimination by holders of federal contracts, yet not one black worker is among the thousands of white workers seen at the aircraft plant.

Hollywood, in effect, eliminated black Americans from normal, everyday life in many of the movies shown to white America. In all those crowded scenes, with throngs of people rushing around America's cities doing their everyday business, how effective it would have been to have African Americans among them, as they often were in real life. Then white America could have gotten used to how normal it was to have black and white people going about their business side by side. Instead, Hollywood misrepresented that there were no blacks in many of the cities shown in its films. Many popular movies stuck to the format of using blacks to send a signal about wealth or status, but to otherwise keep the story white. And when Hollywood did allow for the portrayal of a nice black person, he was either far off on the Atlantic Ocean picking pockets, as in *Lifeboat*, or in Africa having his affairs negotiated by a shady white man, as in *Casablanca*. A few movies portrayed travel, such as *Shadow of a Doubt* and *Spellbound*. During the 1940s, black people such as Irene Morgan in *Morgan v. Virginia* suffered constant indignities while traveling in the South. Hollywood could have sent an effective message by having a single black passenger. Or how about just one black politician in *Citizen Kane*? That movie was released the same year black Congressman Arthur W. Mitchell's case made its way to the Supreme Court.

When it came to African Americans during the 1940s, Hollywood's message in many of its popular movies was that the good old U.S. of A. could get along just fine,

Each message from Hollywood piled up to dam a stream of changing public opinion, thus shaping, rather than reflecting, what was occurring in America.

thank you, without them. This communication flies in the face of respect that Americans have always had for people who pull themselves up by their own bootstraps, as many African Americans had done by that time. Each message from Hollywood piled up to dam a stream of changing public opinion, thus shaping, rather than reflecting, what was occurring in America. To paraphrase the Army manual, each time Hollywood treated African Americans in an insensitive manner, a step was taken to fix this mental picture in the minds of whites.

There are a few possible explanations for Hollywood's treatment of blacks. The first is the continuing "Myth of the Southern Box Office." Based on mythical data regarding what sold in the South and how Southern tastes mirrored all Americans, the film industry persisted in marketing its movies as though white Americans would not tolerate any kindness, sensitivity or realistic portrayal of blacks.

Zooming in . . .

Did HUAC Prevent Hollywood from Being More Sensitive to Blacks

THE HOUSE COMMITTEE ON UN-AMERICAN Activities (HUAC) was an investigative committee of the House of Representatives. It functioned from 1934 until 1975 and was made up of nine representatives that investigated suspected threats of subversion or propaganda that attacked "the form of government guaranteed by our Constitution." The committee and its series of hearings frightened Hollywood from racially advancing after World War II. As a result, while some films initially portrayed blacks realistically and with sensitivity after the war, such depictions did not last long. It is my opinion that had it not been for the HUAC hearings, films would have been far more realistic, sympathetic and empathetic in their portrayals of blacks and racial issues at a much earlier time in American history. Films took a big step backward in the late 1940s and early to mid-1950s. Coincidentally, the first hearings conducted by HUAC were in 1947. The second round was in 1951.

Logically, Hollywood should have been in line with many in this country and the rest of the world regarding attitudes about and treatment of blacks. But it wasn't. The landmark *Brown v. Board of Education* (1954) stated "separate educational facilities are inherently unequal." As a result, racial segregation was ruled a violation of the Equal

Protection Clause of the Fourteenth Amendment and the victory paved the way for integration and the Civil Rights Movement. A statement written by Chief Justice Earl Warren in his unanimous decision draws one to this issue:[241] "Today, in contrast, many Negroes have achieved outstanding success in the arts and sciences as well as in the business and professional world."

. . . had it not been for the HUAC hearings, films would have been far more realistic, sympathetic and empathetic in their portrayals of blacks and racial issues at a much earlier time in American history.

When that statement is compared with the jobs Hollywood films showed black characters performing in popular movies of the time, one has to wonder how nine conservative white men living in an ivory tower knew more about the successes of blacks than Hollywood liberals. Hollywood did not portray blacks achieving outstanding success in the arts, science, business or professions.

During World War II, many Americans believed that racism was fundamentally at odds with the principles of democracy and inconsistent with all that the United States stood for.[242] In the years following World War II, racial discrimination against blacks in the United States received increasing attention around the world. Non-white visiting dignitaries from other countries were subjected to humiliating discrimination. At a time when America was trying to reshape the world in its own image, the international attention given to racial segregation was troublesome and embarrassing.[243]

In its Friend of the Court brief filed in the *Brown* case, the Justice Department's desperation with America's racial policy is obvious.[244] Justice spelled out some of the conditions in Washington, D.C. and stated: "This city is the window through which the world looks into our house. The embassies, legations, and representatives of all nations are here, at the seat of the Federal Government. Foreign officials and visitors naturally judge this country and our people by their experiences and observations in the nation's capital; and the treatment of colored persons here is taken as the measure of our attitude toward minorities generally."

In its brief, the Justice Department included quotes taken from letters written by the State Department: "The United States is under constant attack in the foreign press, over the foreign radio, and in such international bodies as the United Nations because of various practices of discrimination against minority groups in this country. As might be expected, Soviet spokesmen regularly exploit this situation in propaganda against the United States, both within the United Nations and through radio broadcasts and the press, which reaches all corners of the world. Some of these attacks against us are based on falsehood or distortion; but the undeniable existence of racial discrimination gives unfriendly governments the most effective kind of ammunition for their propaganda warfare. The hostile reaction among normally friendly peoples, many of whom are particularly sensitive in regard to the status of non-European races, is growing in alarming proportions. In such countries the view is expressed more and more vocally that the United States is hypocritical in claiming to be the champion of democracy while permitting practices of racial discrimination here in this country."

One has to wonder how nine conservative white men living in an ivory tower knew more about the successes of blacks than Hollywood liberals.

In fact, after World War II, it did at first appear the film industry was reflecting an awakened democratic spirit. Initially there was some movement toward showing empathy toward blacks by portraying them more accurately in films. The film *The Best Days of Our Lives* (1946) cast a black veteran in uniform shopping with his family in an otherwise all-white grocery store, which may not seem like much, but it was something. It was the first Hollywood film I saw that showed black people mingling as ordinary Americans. *Gentleman's Agreement* (1948) has statements condemning bigotry against African Americans. *A Streetcar Named Desire* (1951) shows several outdoor scenes where blacks and whites freely mingle, chat and interact.

To set the stage for the impact of the HUAC hearings and appreciate the flavor of the times, one should understand the then-existing level of censorship of the movies. Public criticism of Hollywood climaxed in the 1920s as scandals and crimes were publicized. The motion picture industry began to regulate itself when it formed the Motion Picture Association of America in 1924 and hired Will H. Hays to write a code that would govern motion pictures. What became known as the Hays Code went into effect in 1930 and was, at first, weakly enforced. But nudity in films such as *Tarzan and His Mate* (1932) and aggressive responses by groups watching the film industry resulted in more enforcement of the Hays Code. The Code forbade films involving miscegenation and stated, "No picture shall be produced which will lower the moral standards of those who see it." The Code was in effect until 1968.[245]

In addition, in 1934, the Roman Catholic Church formed the Legion of Decency to review and rate films. It rated films in 'approved,' 'morally objectionable,' and 'condemned' categories.[246] From that time until the 1960s, a 'condemned' rating by the Legion doomed a movie to financial failure because no Catholic would attend.[247]

Various states also set up boards and groups to oversee content of films. In 1915, state censorship was given approval by the United States Supreme Court when it said that the states watching over movies in the interest of public morals and welfare was reasonable. The Court quickly discarded an argument that movies were forms of speech and expression. The Court acknowledged that movies were a powerful means of communication, but said they are "a business pure and simple, originated and conducted for profit," and were only incidentally a form of expression.[248] Later constitutional challenges to censorship were also unsuccessful.[249]

What became known as the Hays Code went into effect in 1930 and was, at first, weakly enforced.

In Connecticut, for example, the commissioner for censorship had power over permits and licenses to exhibit motion pictures in Connecticut. It would not permit exhibition of films that might "offend the racial or religious sensibilities of any element of society."[250] Ohio's Division of Film Censorship rejected one film because it, "contributes to racial misunderstanding, presenting situations undesirable to the mutual interests of both races."[251]

The standards used by all the censors were subjective and broad. Before World War II, Hollywood moguls, almost all of whom were Jewish, were alert to the anti-Semitism that was widespread throughout much of the country. Sensitive to the potential for movies to indoctrinate, they were watchful for charges they were trying to change existing American values. It was in such a highly stifling atmosphere that HUAC emerged.

Ironically, HUAC began with the exact opposite mandate of what it eventually did. In 1934, New York Representative Samuel Dickstein, an Eastern European Jew, introduced a resolution to create a committee to investigate Nazi activities in the United States. This was how the House Committee on Un-American Activities was born.[252]

The committee's undertaking broadened, and some suspected that conservative Texas Democratic Representative Martin Dies was motivated by anti-Semitism when he was chosen to take over HUAC in 1937. Dies's mission was to investigate subversion of all sorts, including attempts to upset the racial status quo.[253] In 1939, Dies turned his attention to the Jews in Hollywood. After meeting with Hollywood leaders, Dies remarked, "I told the producers we had reliable information that a number of film actors and screen writers and a few producers either were members of the Communist Party, followed the Communist line, or were used as dupes, and that there was evidence that the Hollywood Anti-Nazi League was under the control of Communists." That investigation ended almost as quickly as it began. Then the war came.[254]

New Jersey's Edward Hart took over the reigns of HUAC after Dies, but it was Mississippi's John Rankin, with the committee since its inception, who set HUAC's agenda and tone. When Hart fell ill, John Rankin was appointed acting head. The day after he took charge in 1945, he announced he was about to unearth "one of the most dangerous plots ever instigated for the overthrow of the government" and he explained how he would go about the task, "We are not trying to hound legitimate writers, but we are out to expose those elements that are insidiously trying to spread subversive propaganda, poison the minds of your children, distort the history of our country, and discredit Christianity . . . Communism is older than Christianity. It is the curse of the ages. It hounded and persecuted the Savior during his earthly ministry, inspired his crucifixion, derided him in his dying agony, and then gambled for his garments at the foot of the cross; and has spent more than 1,900 years trying to destroy Christianity and everything based on Christian principles . . . They are trying to take over radio. Listen to their lying broadcasts in broken English and you can almost smell them . . . They are now trying to take over the motion-picture industry and howl to high heaven when our Committee on Un-American activities propose to investigate them. They want to spread their un-American propaganda, as well as their loathsome, lying, immortal, anti-Christian filth before the eyes of your children in every community in America."[255]

There was suspicion the Civil Rights Movement was a Trojan horse filled with Communists and other radicals who wanted to make wholesale changes in American society.

HUAC's chief counsel, Robert Stripling, was a Southern white supremacist.[256] One of the committee's investigators warned a suspect in 1946, "You should tell your Jewish friends that the Jews in Germany stuck their necks out too far and Hitler took care of them and that the same thing will happen here unless they watch their step."[257]

There was suspicion the Civil Rights Movement was a Trojan horse filled with Communists and other radicals who wanted to make wholesale changes in American society.[258] Scholar and civil rights activist W.E.B. Du Bois was charged with Communist activities, taken to trial and acquitted by a jury in 1952.[259] Baseball player Jackie Robinson was called as a witness during the HUAC hearings in 1949 because of concerns of Communist infiltration of minority groups.[260]

HUAC concluded the movie industry harbored a Jewish conspiracy to undermine American values. Between 1951 and 1954, HUAC named 324 Hollywood personalities, all of whom were blacklisted. Eventually ten of the screenwriters who refused to testify about their political affiliations were held in contempt of Congress and sent to prison. Hollywood's tragic experience with HUAC provides some explanation why

Hollywood's tragic experience with HUAC provides some explanation why the film industry under the studio system was not more progressive in its depictions of African Americans.

the film industry under the studio system was not more progressive in its depictions of African Americans in movies at a time when the world's recent experience with Nazism had spawned worldwide discussion of democratic ideals. Eventually, the appeals of the screenwriters who refused to testify about their political affiliations slowly wound their way to the United States Supreme Court.

Hollywood steered away from showing sympathy to the Civil Rights Movement after World War II because it feared accusations of having Communist sympathies. The combination of HUAC's suspicion of Communist infusion in minority groups, the censors' concerns about racial depictions interfering with American values, and the anti-Semitism of some heads of HUAC proved to be fatal to films displaying the beginnings of postwar broad-mindedness.

1951-1960
Racial Framework

ON DECEMBER 1, 1955, ROSA Parks, a seamstress and member of the local NAACP chapter in Montgomery, Alabama, tired after a day's work, boarded a bus home. She chose a seat in the first row behind the rail of the rear section of the bus reserved by law for black people. The seats quickly filled. When a white man was left standing, the bus driver came back to the row where Mrs. Parks was seated, and said, "All right, you folks, I want those seats." The other three black passengers in the row compliantly stood and walked to stand in the back of the bus. Mrs. Parks quietly said, "No," and was arrested.[261]

The black community rallied to Mrs. Parks' defense, and made modest demands for change. There was not a request for segregation to end, blacks merely wanted the system reformed so they would begin sitting from the back of the bus forward, and whites from the front of the bus backward. They also requested that bus drivers give equal courtesy to both races. Once the seats were filled, everyone would stay where they were when the bus got crowded. Montgomery leaders refused. Blacks boycotted Montgomery's segregated bus system, and so began the Civil Rights Movement in earnest.[262]

A young preacher had recently moved from Atlanta to Montgomery to head a congregation. Possibly because he had not yet been incorporated into black politics in the city, he was chosen to lead the black community in its efforts.[263] A gifted orator, he addressed over four thousand Montgomery blacks, and stirred them with commitment by amplifying their sentiments; he was the man of the hour.

During the bus boycott, over 90 percent of Montgomery's blacks carpooled and walked for three hundred eighty-one days, despite threats and attacks by whites.

Something needed to be done about discrimination. Since World War II, America had done little to address the denial of basic rights to its black citizens, while speaking ever more forcefully about being dedicated to equality and democracy.[264] It was then, December 5, 1955, four days after Rosa Parks was arrested, that the world met the young preacher, Martin Luther King, Jr.

King's career was launched as leader of the nonviolent fight for African American rights. Many compared his tactics with Ghandi's, but King said he went to Ghandi through Jesus. King explained his strategy to his congregations, "In every human being, black or white, there exists, however dimly, a certain natural identification with every other human being, so that we tend to feel that what happens to a fellow human being also, in some way happens to us. Therefore, no man can very long continue to abuse another human being, without beginning to feel in himself at least some dull answering stir of discomfort. And in the catharsis of a live confrontation with wrong, when an oppressor's violence is met with a forgiving love, he can be vitally touched and even, however partially or momentarily, reborn as a human being. You are shaming them into decency."[265]

During the bus boycott, over 90 percent of Montgomery's blacks carpooled and walked for three hundred eighty-one days, despite threats and attacks by whites. The tactics prompted spirited complaints from different sectors. Whites in the city were suspicious that northern agitators were to blame. As one white citizen of Alabama put it, "In Montgomery, the niggers are not that smart." Even the NAACP was wary of any popular protest out of the carefully controlled and calibrated program of court actions.[266]

For years, tensions had been building in the South. The summer before, a fourteen-year-old black youth from Chicago was visiting his relatives near Money, Mississippi. One version of what happened in a sundries store is that the boy whistled at a white woman; another account is that he spoke disrespectfully to her. Young Emmett Till's body was found so severely beaten, some said his face looked like a monster mask. It took an all-white jury only sixty-seven minutes to acquit the woman's husband and his half-brother of the murder. The boy's mother sent a telegram to President Dwight D. Eisenhower, and allowed the world to see her son's mangled body. As many as ten thousand mourners came to the viewing. When the president did not respond, Roy Wilkins, head of the NAACP, remarked, "Eisenhower was a fine general and a good, decent man; but if he had fought World War II the way he fought for civil rights, we would all be speaking German today."[267]

The rest of the country was not oblivious to the need for racial change. By 1952, six states passed fair employment practices legislation (Massachusetts, Connecticut, New Mexico, Oregon, Rhode Island and Washington) and six states passed public accommodations legislation (Connecticut, New Jersey, New York, Rhode Island, Massachusetts and Oregon). Similar measures were passed by local governments and some states began enforcing Reconstruction-era laws.[268]

The Chicago Housing Authority's and the Daley machine's response to the black migration was to keep as many of the migrants as possible from white Chicago by building housing projects.

Meanwhile, the great migration north continued. During the 1950s the black population of Chicago increased by another 65 percent, to 813,000. At one point twenty-two hundred black people were moving into Chicago every week, as the sharecropper system had been phased out on most plantations.

Chicago whites were upset with the movement of blacks into their city. In 1950, Joseph Beauharnais, president of the "White Circle League," passed out lithographs and other literature to volunteers for distribution on downtown Chicago street corners. One leaflet was titled, "PRESERVE AND PROTECT WHITE NEIGHBORHOODS! FROM THE CONSTANT AND CONTINUOUS INVASION, HARASSMENT AND ENROACHMENT BY THE NEGROES (WE WANT TWO MILLION SIGNATURES OF WHITE MEN AND WOMEN)."[269]

Richard Daley was mayor of Chicago, and his Chicago democratic machine was dependent on the neighborhood system. Neighborhood racial transition was the only powerful force at work in the city that posed a real threat to the machine. Ward bosses were essential actors in the system and delivered the votes. If a ward went from white to black it created havoc, since good machine voters were lost to the suburbs.

The Chicago Housing Authority's and the Daley machine's response to the black migration was to keep as many of the migrants as possible from white Chicago by building housing projects. When African Americans did make it into Chicago neighborhoods, all races were victimized by sleazy Realtors known as "panic peddlers" who would move a black family into a neighborhood, often subjecting it to a terrifying round of fire bombings and snarling crowds. Then they would tell the white families they'd better move out before it was too late, thereby obtaining their houses at rock bottom prices.[270]

But African Americans continued to move forward in sports. Althea Gibson, daughter of a South Carolina sharecropper, became the first black player, man or woman, to win the U.S. Open tennis tournament, Wimbledon and the French Open. She integrated Wimbledon in 1951 and won the French Open in 1956. In 1957, she won Wimbledon and the U.S. Open at Forest Hills, New York. In all, Gibson won eleven Grand Slam titles in her career.[271]

In the South, the Civil Rights Movement continued to spread. On February 1, 1960 four college students sat down at a Woolworth's lunch counter in Greensboro, North Carolina and ordered coffee. They were refused service. The next day fifteen went to the lunch counter. They were not served. The third day one hundred fifty went to the counter, and eventually one thousand went. Whites hurled insults, and at times attacked the students. Within days there were sit-ins in at least fifteen places across the South.[272]

Television in American society during this decade grew in popularity. Powerful media coverage was given to the Montgomery boycott as well as the rest of the growing movement. The South was no longer able to inflict its cruelty in private. Viewers all over the world witnessed the outrages, and were inspired by the courage of the civil rights activists. Lynchings, beatings of African Americans, and discrimination drew world concern. The United States was cast as the champion of the free world as the Cold War with Russia heated up, but American racial discrimination had become an international embarrassment.[273]

1951-1960
The Supreme Court

THE UNITED STATES SUPREME COURT was reacting to America's embarrassment before the world when it ruled on class actions that challenged segregated schools brought by African American children in Kansas, South Carolina, Virginia, Delaware and the District of Columbia.[274] Scholars believe these school desegregation cases to be the beginning of many Supreme Court decisions. The federal district court in Kansas denied relief on the ground that public education was substantially equal for both races. In South Carolina and Virginia, the courts found education for African Americans to be inferior and ordered equalization of the facilities. The Supreme Court of Delaware, on the other hand, adhered to the *Plessy* principle, but ordered the plaintiffs to be admitted into white schools because of their superiority to black schools. The federal district court in the District of Columbia dismissed the complaint.

Brown v. Board of Education, 347 U.S. 483, as heard by the Supreme Court, was a combination of five cases. The court posed the issue before it as: "Does segregation of children in public schools solely on the basis of race, even though the physical facilities and other 'tangible' factors may be equal, deprive the children of the minority group of equal educational opportunities?"

Thurgood Marshall argued to the Court, "I got the feeling on hearing the discussion yesterday that when you put a white child in a school with a whole lot of colored children, the child would fall apart or something. Everybody knows that is not true. These same kids in Virginia and South Carolina, and I've seen them do it. They play in the streets together. They play on their farms together. They go down the road together. They separate to go to school. They come out of school and play ball together. They have to be separated in school."275

Speaking with one voice in a unanimous decision, the Court announced that segregation in public education is a denial of equal protection of the laws.

The Court concluded that segregation does deprive minority children of equal educational opportunities, saying separation by race "generates a feeling of inferiority as to their status in the community that may affect their hearts and minds in a way unlikely to be undone." The Court explained that a sense of inferiority affects the motivation of a child to learn, especially when segregation has the sanction of law. As a result, according to the Court, the educational and mental development of black children can be hindered.

The opinion compares the status and importance of education at the time of the *Plessy* decision: "Education of white children was largely in the hands of private groups. Education of Negroes was almost nonexistent, and practically all of the race was illiterate," versus 1954: "Today, in contrast, many Negoes have achieved outstanding success in the arts and sciences as well as in the business and professional world;" "Today, education is perhaps the most important function of state and local governments;" and "In these days, it is doubtful that any child may reasonably be expected to succeed in life if he is denied the opportunity of an education."

Speaking with one voice in a unanimous decision, the Court announced that segregation in public education is a denial of equal protection of the laws. The parties to the action were invited to submit further argument in support of what relief each thought the Court should order. What the Supreme Court actually did in *Brown* was different than in preceding decisions. The Court not only strayed from its own precedent, it gave great weight to changing times and social studies. To support its analysis and conclusions, the Court did not cite to the usual case and statutory authorities. Instead, the sources were psychological and sociological studies by Witmer, Kotinsky, Deutscher, Chein, Brameld, Frazier and Myrdal.

Bolling v. Sharpe, 347 U.S. 497, the school desegregation case from the District of Columbia was heard by the Court the same time as *Brown.* It was the first time the Court explicitly questioned the existence of differences between obligations of the federal government and the states to avoid racial classifications. *Bolling* noted that equal protection of the laws in the Fourteenth Amendment is a more explicit safe-guard of prohibited unfairness than due process of law in the Fifth Amendment, and then concluded it would be unthinkable that the same Constitution would impose a lesser duty on the federal government.

Whether or not the Supreme Court's 1954 decision in *Brown* made much differ-ence with regard to segregation is open to debate. But some say *Brown* sent a wind of exhilaration through the black community. No doubt it made a tremendous difference in the minds of African Americans. And perhaps that was the intended result. Chief Justice Earl Warren revealed in his memoirs that he wrote the opinion in a short, non-accusatory, non-technical style so it could be easily understood and even reprinted in the public press.[276] If he intended to motivate, he succeeded.

When Martin Luther King, Jr. addressed Montgomery's black residents for the first time after Rosa Parks said, "No," just one year after the Court's decision, Dr. King was able to speak to the gathering in shorthand. He must have assumed that each of the four thousand African Americans crowded into and around the church knew exactly what he was talking about when he said, "We are here this evening for seri-

Lawyer for the NAACP (and later jurist) Thurgood Marshall (1908-1993) (center) speaks to reporters on the steps of the United States Supreme Court about the landmark legal case, Brown v. Board of Education, in August of 1958. (Photo by Ed Clark/Time Life Pictures/Getty Images)

ous business. . . . And, if we are wrong, the Supreme Court of this nation is wrong."[277]

For King to make that assumption, and for the huge assembly to have responded with thundering applause and stomping feet, indicates *Brown* was a common topic among America's black population, and provided a credible sense of confidence, support and energy to their cause.

The May 17, 1954 decision was courageous, and calls to mind one of Martin Luther King's remarks that, while a court can declare rights, it cannot deliver them.[278] In 1954, the Court made a declaration, and then sent everyone home to think about how integration should be implemented. Thurgood Marshall and his staff were unsuccessful in persuading the Court, at arguments about implementation in April, 1955, to either issue firm instructions or set a fixed date for compliance.[279] On May 31, 1955, an order was issued from the Court in what is often called *Brown II*, 349 U.S. 294. It was to be left to the federal trial courts to administer integration and to ensure that public schools were operated on a "racially non-discriminatory basis with all deliberate speed."

And so the games began. Three years earlier, when school segregation cases first arrived at the Supreme Court, Justice Felix Frankfurter stated: "Nothing could be worse from my point of view than for this Court to make an abstract declaration that segregation is bad and then to have it evaded by tricks."[280] A prophet if there ever was one.

That it would not be an easy task for federal judges to desegregate Southern schools was confirmed by a remark made by a well-dressed woman, a leader of segregationist Mothers League of Central High School, standing in a corridor outside a Little Rock federal district courtroom: "I don't give a damn what that stupid little judge in there says; my children are never going to school with monkeys."[281]

Communities used a variety of tactics to prevent desegregation of public schools. Their best chance was a segregationist judge, and the Little Rock School Board, pleading chaos and disorder, requested and received federal Judge Harry J. Lemley's permission to resegregate, after desegregation efforts were prevented by Arkansas's governor, Orval Faubus. As school authorities went forward with desegregation by arranging for nine black children to attend Central High, the governor ordered the state's National Guard to place Central High School off-limits to black students. Until that time, no crowds had gathered around the school and there were no acts of violence.

The School Board's petition to the court requesting postponement of desegregation said, "The effect of that action [of the Governor] was to harden the core of opposition to the Plan and cause many persons who theretofore had reluctantly accepted the Plan to believe there was some power in the State of Arkansas which, when exerted, could nullify the Federal law and permit disobedience of the decree of the [District] Court, and from that date hostility to the Plan was increased and criticism of the officials of the [School] District has become more bitter and unrestrained."

In *Cooper v. Aaron*, 358 U.S. 1, the Court stated interpretation of the Fourteenth Amendment voiced by the Supreme Court in *Brown* is the supreme law of the land. "No state legislator or executive or judicial officer can war against the Constitution without violating his undertaking to support it," the Court castigated Arkansas officials, concluding there was no legal excuse for delay in desegregation.

Various other strategies to circumvent *Brown* were instituted. Pupil placement was simple. A school board would announce that students would no longer be assigned to

African American elementary school children get off a bus in Kansas in 1953. The photo depicted segregation of elementary grade schools, an issue that prompted the famed legal suit Brown vs. Board of Education. (Photo by Carl Iwasaki/Time & Life Pictures/Getty Images)

schools according to race, and then proceed to assign black students to segregated schools, but for reasons such as residence, health and educational achievement. When school boards were unable to have a black complainant's action dismissed from court, it would often avoid an injunction with a contention it had acted in good faith, and was doing the best it could under the circumstances.

Another approach was to request permission to remain segregated until the aptitude of black students could be raised. A spin on the same approach was instituted by the Houston board, which insisted it was moving with deliberate speed because it had established a summer training program for black teachers. Other school boards attempted escape from desegregation by explaining the schools were voluntarily segregated due to residential location. The Louisiana legislature encouraged resistance to desegregation citing the doctrine of "interposition," a view that the legislature had inserted its authority between the federal courts and the people, and by doing so, had relieved any person from any obligation to obey federal injunctions.[282]

Despite the fact that many Americans favored desegregation, segregationists were willing to fight harder for what they wanted than the desegregationists. Besides fear of bombs, beatings and economic harassment, most blacks simply did not have the sophistication, money or wherewithal to mount an attack. After all, school boards were able to hire the highest paid legal talent in town, with the public coffers and the state attorney general's office always open for assistance. Blacks, on the other hand, usually had no help (except from the NAACP), and much to lose. As one parent explained to her minister why she did not want to enroll her child in Nashville's newly desegregated school: "I have an older child in the Negro school, and my first-grader needs his protection." Another said, "I don't want my child a guinea pig."[283]

Without the moral, financial and legal help of the NAACP, few blacks had the money, knowledge or courage to seek legal redress. Attacks on the NAACP were commonplace. During the fall of 1955, a black civil rights leader was killed each month in Mississippi, one at midday in front of the Pike County Courthouse. After that there were no attempts for several years by Mississippi blacks to bring lawsuits. Additionally, various tools of the government were used to intimidate the NAACP.

In Texas, Attorney General John Ben Sheppard asked and received from a state judge, without notice to the NAACP, a restraining order that required all one hundred twenty-two branches of the organization to immediately cease operations. Texas' basis was the NAACP incited racial prejudice. Another strategy was to charge the organization with one irregularity or another, and then use the charge as an excuse to demand its membership list. Members knew that if their NAACP membership were publicly known, employers would fire them, and they would be denied credit and suffer other forms of retaliation.[284]

Matters involving NAACP membership lists reached the Supreme Court a few times. Alabama had a statute that required a foreign corporation, except as exempted, to qualify before doing business in the state. The NAACP had never applied for qualification since it considered itself exempt as a non-profit corporation.

The Attorney General of Alabama brought an action against the NAACP in 1956, claiming it had given financial support and furnished legal assistance to black students who sought admission to the state university, and supported a boycott of Montgomery bus lines to force the seating of passengers without regard to race. The bill recited the NAACP was causing irreparable harm to the citizens of the State of Alabama. On the day the complaint was filed the state court issued an order that restrained the NAACP from doing further business in the state and forbidding it to take steps to qualify itself to do business in Alabama. The state moved for production of large numbers of documents and records, including the names and addresses of all Alabama members. The organization produced everything but the membership list, was fined $10,000 and informed that the fine would be increased to $100,000 within five days, unless there was compliance.

In Dallas, Houston and New Orleans, judges construed "all deliberate speed" to mean a school district could take six years or longer.

In *National Association For the Advancement of Colored People v. State of Alabama*, 357 U.S. 449, the Supreme Court held that the order requiring the records production and membership lists was a denial of due process and caused the likelihood of a substantial restraint upon members' exercise of their right to freedom of association.

Arkansas tried a similar tactic. In 1957 two cities, Little Rock and North Little Rock, added identical amendments to their occupation license tax ordinances. They required that, upon request of the city clerk, any organization that operated within the cities must supply extensive information, including "a statement as to the dues, assessments, and contributions paid, by whom and when paid, together with a statement that reflected the disposition of the funds and the total net income." In *Bates v. City of Little Rock*, 361 U.S. 516, the Supreme Court ruled that municipalities could not constitutionally require that organizations such as the NAACP submit membership lists.

In Dallas, Houston and New Orleans, judges construed "all deliberate speed" to mean a school district could take six years or longer. In Atlanta, six years after the Supreme Court's order, the judge gave the board two more years to *start* to desegregate. Harry Briggs, Jr., one of the original *Brown* plaintiffs, was nine years old when his parents first brought suit against South Carolina's Clarendon County School

Board. In 1960, he graduated from an all-black high school. In Washington, President Eisenhower commented: "We are going to whip this thing in the long run by Americans being true to themselves and not merely by law."[285]

Maybe the second phase of the Civil War took place in the 1950's as a result of *Brown*. Again, the battle was between the South and the North, as well as the states and the federal government, and primarily concerned African Americans. Casualties like Little Rock Mayor Woodrow Wilson Mann were left wounded and unattended. When Arkansas's governor interfered with orderly school desegregation, Mayor Mann asked for federal assistance. President Eisenhower sent eleven hundred members of the Army's 101st Airborne Division to Little Rock to safely escort nine black youths into Central High.

For his attempt to follow the law of the land, Mann received hate mail and threats to his life. In 1958 he lost his job and was vilified by the people of his home state for taking a stand. His son was quoted as saying, "When he was elected mayor he had the largest independent insurance agency in the state. When his term was over, he was basically out of business because he had lost his clientele."[286]

As a footnote to history, it was not until September, 2002 that federal Judge William Wilson ended more than forty years of court-supervised desegregation in Little Rock's schools. This finally closed a chapter in the battle over desegregation that began with the *Brown* ruling.[287]

1951-1960
Hollywood

FROM THE CONTENT OF MOVIES during the 1950s, the film industry was oblivious to the *Brown* decisions and the nationwide struggle with the physical implementation and moral implications of desegregation. Various dynamics were at play in Hollywood at the time. With few notable exceptions, in the majority of popular movies studied, African Americans were either ignored or placed in the same old, tired stereotypical roles.

Neal Gabler describes postwar Hollywood as like the South after the Civil War: plantations were wasted and the slaves emancipated. A way of life was gone forever.[288] After World War II there were conservatives who expected a return to Hollywood's antebellum ways, deleting all but the most benign references to race or ethnicity. Prewar filmmakers were sensitive to Southern racism, always in search of a monochromic movie that muted political debate. The object was to reach across cultures to produce profits.[289] Postwar, the formerly stable film industry was faced with soaring labor costs, the threat of strikes deferred by the war, migration to the suburbs and inflation. Changes included a liberal bent, since everyone, including Hollywood, was aware that Nazi crimes had been committed in the name of racial superiority.

Many filmmakers had learned through the use of wartime documentaries that film was an effective means of advocacy. Documentaries, as a voice of liberalism, may have taught Hollywood some tolerance. Unlike its practice before the war, the industry began to be receptive to message movies that contained politically sensitive material. Interestingly, many of the most provocative ideas for documentaries and feature films grew out of Myrdal's *An American Dilemma*,[290] the same text cited by the Supreme Court in *Brown*.

As previously mentioned, Hollywood's reflection of racial mores and attitudes was distorted between World Wars I and II based on a, mythic Southern box office that supposedly corresponded to American racial values. Hinging decisions on incorrect information, Hollywood created a generation of servile blacks who rarely stepped out of stereotyped roles. The movie industry depended on box office receipts as an index of American taste. Essential to production decisions was a belief that certain regional markets would refuse to patronize movies with racial themes.

There was wide-spread racism in Hollywood, and the presumed existence of a regional market in the South permitted filmmakers to disguise their own racial attitudes. In film, black Americans were banished to groveling, bumbling roles, unless it was more convenient to make them invisible. In fact, as shown by historian Thomas Cripps, there was no Southern box office as the South was unpredictable and not profitable. Fairs, carnivals, radio, roller derbies and vaudeville acts combined with hot movie houses, a six-day work week, Sunday blue laws, regional amusement taxes and ardent censors to keep Southerners away from the movies. But once the myth was in place, Hollywood could rationalize that if a film did not sell in the South, it might not sell in the North, excusing itself from having to be accurate.[291]

Many filmmakers had learned through the use of wartime documentaries that film was an effective means of advocacy.

Still, considering the awakening of worldwide racial consciousness and real life racial dramas that occured on the stage of American life, one might expect intense racial presentations on the 1950s silver screen. On the contrary, newly energized liberals took lukewarm, perfunctory steps to present blacks as integrated into American life. Hollywood's prewar failure to accurately reflect blacks in films may have had an adverse impact on postwar films.

Another less subtle influence was probably the main reason civil rights advancements were not reflected by the film industry during the 1950s. Before the war, Hollywood moguls, almost all of whom were Jewish, were alert to existing anti-Semitism that was widespread throughout much of the country. Sensitive to the potential for movies to influence, they were watchful for charges they were trying to change existing American values. Sam Goldwyn is reputed to have said, "if you want messages, go to Western Union."[292]

Following the war, Hollywood did produce some movies that involved social issues, such as *Gentleman's Agreement* and *It's a Wonderful Life.* Some say it was Hollywood's experimentation with challenging American values that brought about additional Congressional investigation to uncover the influence of Communism in the film industry.[293] Investigations in Hollywood took place in 1947 and again in 1951. HUAC focused on nineteen Hollywood screenwriters, fifteen of whom were Jewish. One of them, Ring Lardner, Jr. lamented of the times, "Under this kind of censorship this inquisition threatens, a leading man wouldn't even be able to blurt out the words, 'I love you' unless he had first secured a notarized affidavit proving she was a pure, white Protestant gentile of old Confederate stock."[294]

Eventually ten screenwriters who refused to testify about their political affiliations were held in contempt of Congress, and their appeals slowly wound their way to the Supreme Court. In 1950 the Court denied a writ and the "Hollywood Ten" were all sent to prison. HUAC concluded the movie industry harbored a Jewish conspiracy to undermine American values,[295] and in 1951 the hearings were renewed.[296] Producers promised HUAC they would not knowingly employ a Communist, and Harry Warner fired one writer whose name appeared on a blacklist. The writer said it was a mistake, since he was actually an *anti*-Communist. Warner fired back, "I don't give a shit what kind of Communist your are, get out of here."[297]

Meanwhile, Communists were suspected to be elsewhere in America, too. Junior Senator from Wisconsin, Joseph R. McCarthy, made a sensation by charging that the State Department was filled with Communists and spies. At that point, a witch-hunt was organized by conservative elements. "McCarthyism," as the times came to be known, resulted in hysterical pressure for Americans to conform.[298]

Indeed, there were some Communists, as well as "Old Lefties," "New Lefties," labor unionists and black nationalists.[299] Communists had been promoting racial equality since the 1930s, and they used racial incidents, such as the case of the Scottsboro boys as propaganda to bash democracy in America.[300, 301]

Hollywood probably steered away from showing sympathy to the Civil Rights Movement during this decade because it feared additional accusations of having Communist sympathies. However, there were changes in some 1950's films. Tepid though racial advances in movies were, there is a discernible distinction between films displaying the beginnings of postwar broad-mindedness and the old-time conservative course. In one kind of film, all but subservient blacks were invisible, and in the other, race issues were either frankly discussed or African Americans were starting to be part of the crowd of ordinary people.

Rebel Without a Cause (1955, AFI's #59) best exemplifies the older view. There is only one black actor in the film, an unnamed woman whose status is unidentified.

She is a combination housekeeper/ baby-sitter for a lonely rich white teenage boy, whose father lives in parts unknown, and whose mother travels a lot. The African American woman is clearly not up to the task. She talks incessantly, but the boy never once pays her the courtesy of a response. During a scene at a police station, the police officer also ignores her. She sobs and definitely cares, but the message is that the troubled youth was left with an inept black woman who meant well, but could not function without supervision.

Reactionary as the racial treatment in the movie is, the war touched the film nonetheless. The Nuremberg defense, which might have had an effect on the Supreme Court's *Brown* decision, must have been on everyone's mind, since the film did not have to explain one vignette. In the scene, after the teenagers discuss a drag race called "chicken," a security guard intervenes. A boy places his finger above his lip to simulate a mustache, puts on the guard's hat, gives a Nazi salute and says, "Achtung! Achtung! Ve vere just clucking out." Scenes at a high school underscore continuing segregation a year after *Brown* came down. Not one black student is among the throngs of students in *Rebel*.

Tepid though racial advances in movies were, there is a discernible distinction between films displaying the beginnings of postwar broad-mindedness and the old-time conservative course.

One film, however, did have a black student, *Blackboard Jungle*. This 1955 film, one year after *Brown* and the same year as the December, 1955 Alabama bus strike triggered by Rosa Park's refusing to give up her seat, shows virile young Sidney Poitier as the only black student in this expose of American high schools. The story has the lone black student at times leading the student rebellion against the teacher. It is difficult to believe a black youth of the time, without the protection of other black students, could have such power. While the black student eventually behaved decently, the film sends the message the problems in American schools stems from allowing blacks to attend formerly white schools.

From Here To Eternity (1953, Best Picture of the Year, AFI's #52) completely ignores African American presence in the military. Set in Hawaii in 1941 just before, during and after the Japanese attacked Pearl Harbor, there are no blacks among the hundreds of military personnel who are shown in the movie, even though we know the first American military hero of the war was a black man at Pearl Harbor.

And how could there be no African Americans in New York City in 1955? *Marty* (1955, Best Picture of the Year) is a sympathetic and sentimental story of two lonely, plain-looking white people who meet at the Star Dust Ballroom. Numerous street,

restaurant and bus scenes show no black people, but there is a black bathroom attendant at the Star Dust.

Blossoming liberalism can be seen in other films, and race was the subject of a few
films. Two convicts, one white and one black, escape a chain gang while chained to
each other in *The Defiant Ones* (1958). As he chains them together, a prison official
says, "If they escape, we don't worry about catching them. They'll kill each other
before they can get fifty miles." At first the official's wisecrack seems like a prophecy,
as the two bicker and quarrel. But a friendship is formed and before it is over, each
risks his welfare to save the other, although the Sidney Poitier character is portrayed
as morally and physically stronger than the Tony Curtis character.

Ultimately it is the black man who gives up his freedom to save the white man's
life. Donald Bogle said, "When he saved his honky brother, he was jeered at in ghetto theaters. Black audiences were consciously aware for the first time of the great
'tom-ism' inherent in the Poitier character, indeed in the Poitier image."[302]

Arguably more eloquent than the ghetto theater group, James Baldwin adds his
criticism of the symbolism in the film, "A black man knows that two men chained
together have to learn to forage, eat, fart, shit, piss and tremble, and sleep together:
they are indispensable to each other, and anything can happen between them, and
anyone who has been there knows this. No black man, in such a situation, and especially knowing what Poitier conveys so vividly Noah Cullen knows, would rise to the
bait proffered by this dimwitted poor white child, whose only real complaint is that
he is a bona-fide mediocrity who failed to make it in the American rat-race."[303]

In *No Way Out* (1950), Poitier plays Dr. Luther Brooks whose felon patient, Johnny
Biddle, dies while the doctor tries to save his life, only to face a charge from the dead
man's brother that the "nigger doctor" murdered him. Hospital administration is
supportive of the black doctor, and the doctor's home scenes show a quiet, dignified
lifestyle. Eventually a riot breaks out in a slum area, the crowd protesting that a black
doctor was working on one of theirs. "Once again," author Daniel Leab commented,
"racism is relegated to the lower classes, to the Biddles and the other slum inhabitants, one of whom spits at Brooks when he tries to treat a white injured in the race
riot."[304]

A few of the black characters are as anti-white as the white characters are anti-
black. Censorship in Chicago and other areas resulted in deletion of portions of the
film showing black rioters attacking white slum dwellers. Daniel Leab says the Poiter
character in *No Way Out* was a precursor of the "ebony saint," the black man who
remains nonviolent and cool, no matter the provocation.[305]

On the Waterfront (1954, Best Picture of the Year, AFI's #8) was ahead of its time.
White and black workers in the movie are stevedores, and members of a local long-

shoremen's union. While the story could have been based on a real integrated union, much of the industry had racially separate local unions throughout the country until after the 1964 Civil Rights Act. In 1959, black labor leaders formed the Negro American Labor Council to pressure AFL-CIO president George Meany toward a position of complete integration. By the end of 1961, Meany verbally agreed to the elimination of segregation in labor unions.[306] After 1964, Attorney General Ramsey Clark began filing suits against the International Longshoremen's Union under Title VII, alleging a pattern or practice of discrimination on the grounds of race, color and national origin, and requesting mergers of the segregated locals.[307]

On the Waterfront deals with mob corruption, which prevents longshoremen from working. The major racial difference between this movie and previous ones involving labor issues is that black men appear among the masses of white workers. One black character, while speaking very few lines, is in six or seven scenes. The black workers are not used as props, but exist among the ordinary masses.

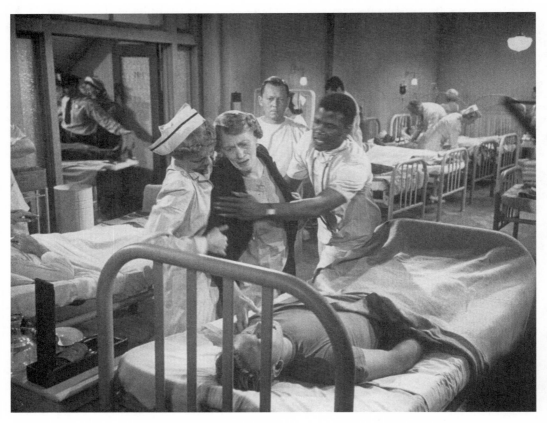

Circa 1950: Actor Sidney Poitier (center) in hospital scene from the movie No Way Out. *(Photo by Peter Stackpole/Time & Life Pictures/Getty Images)*

Set in a seedy neighborhood in New Orleans, *A Streetcar Named Desire* (1951, AFI's #45) cannot quite be characterized as courageous, yet it showed both integration and segregation. There are several outdoor scenes where blacks and whites freely mingle and interact. And, there is one quick shot of passengers aboard the streetcar. The white people are sitting in the front, and a lone black man is in the rear, although seeing this required modern technology in the form of rewind/forward options to make certain what was in the scene, quick as it was.

The Greatest Show on Earth (1952, Best Picture of the Year) shows muscular, hardworking black men every time the circus tents are raised or lowered. However, blacks are never seen mingling among the carneys or when the circus is operating. White characters who are part of the set-ups and tear-downs, however, are also circus entertainers, and seen throughout the movie. At one point, the film reverts to the old Hollywood technique of telling a joke at the expense of African Americans. A white actress makes a wisecrack when the circus manager says the circus will continue so long as it is in the black. She responds, "You mean we all gotta play in blackface?"

Although the filmmakers did not depict the black and white roustabouts mixing together, they did show that the circus audience was integrated as there are a few black patrons among the entering crowds. But while there are numerous camera shots focused on popcorn-eating, ice cream-licking whites, the camera never once rests on, or even shows, black patrons under the big top.

As it did during earlier decades, Hollywood continued to wear racial blinders even when it was supposedly being liberal and brave. This is so similar to the white South's denouncing Nazi tactics during the war, while remaining unconscious to many similarities between its own racial system and that of the Third Reich.[308] Like the South, Hollywood could not connect the intolerance dots, and remained insensitive to African Americans while showing the evils of prejudice to other groups.

Giant (1956, AFI's #82) is an example. A Texan visits a horse ranch in Maryland and returns to Texas with both the horse and a wife. When the liberal young bride treats the Mexican servants with dignity by chatting with them while they serve her, she is reprimanded for treating servants as equals. One of the Texans says, "I know how to handle Mexicans . . . doin' it all my life. They'd sit on their honkers all day if I didn't keep after them."

The young woman is disgusted and alarmed at the biased attitudes she sees in the Southwest. Yet, in the Maryland scenes, she never said a word to the black servants who served her. Even when the woman returns to Maryland years later, she apparently finds her black servants just as invisible as they were before she learned so much about prejudice. In fact, at one point, an African American asks her a question, and she is too absorbed with her own thoughts to even respond.

While not on any of the lists of films being studied, the 1960 version of *Cimarron*, a remake of a 1931 film, was included to see how Hollywood treated Isaiah, the young black boy. In the earlier version, while fanning the dining family, Isaiah fell from a board across the chandelier onto a cream pie, and was subjected to other buffoonery throughout the movie. At the same time, sensitivity was shown to Indians, women and Jews. By 1960, Hollywood was able to connect a few dots. Apparently someone either noticed the disparity or did not have the stomach to demean a little boy in such a cruel manner.

But the later version of *Cimarron* deserves no accolades for its racial approach to African Americans. The beginning scenes of the earlier film had black servants looking simple. The later version substituted white servants who conducted themselves in a dignified manner. Instead of seizing the opportunity to display Isaiah in a respectful and kindly manner, Hollywood left him on the cutting room floor while keeping a delicate and compassionate storyline about Indians, women and Jews, showing how "liberal" it was.

A scene in both versions has a darling little Indian girl, whose father was killed by racist white men, show up for her first day of school. She waves goodbye at the schoolhouse door, and a moment later comes running back. "They don't want me," she cries. The next scene shows the school board making its decision to deny admittance to her because she is Indian. Certainly a 1960 audience would have questioned why a little boy was not in school, so Hollywood's excluding Isaiah from the film allowed it to avoid the issue of school segregation of African Americans.

*Movies not discussed in text appear in endnote.[309]

1951-1960
Decade Wrap-up

THE ACHIEVEMENTS OF AFRICAN AMERICANS in society were so great by 1954 the United States Supreme Court said in *Brown*, "Today, in contrast, many Negroes have achieved outstanding success in the arts and sciences as well as in the business and professional world." Yet the popular movies of the decade that were studied had but one educated black. There was the ubiquitous bathroom attendant in *Marty*, the ineffectual housekeeper/baby-sitter in *Rebel Without a Cause*, and the house servants in *Giant*. And of course, the uneducated black voice in *Rear Window*. The closest Hollywood came to the Supreme Court's characterization was the doctor accused of malpractice in *No Way Out.* In that way, nine isolated old white men noticed much more about what was going on in society than Hollywood, that bastion of liberalism, which eliminated much of it from the screen.

Exclusion of Isaiah from *Cimarron* discloses the depth of Hollywood's insensitivity. It is an ironic illustration as to why the Court did what it did in *Brown*. The whole country was avoiding the problem. The novel and the earlier version of *Cimarron* included a black child. Everyone loves kids. Children need guidance and love and schooling. What an opportunity to portray a young black actor with decency. The movie was all about dignity. Dignity to Indians. Dignity to women. Dignity to Jews. One reason for Hollywood's elimination of the child's role likely was to avoid having

At the time of the Cimarron *sequel, education was on everyone's mind.*

to face *Brown*'s issue of school desegregation. At the time of the *Cimarron* sequel, education was on everyone's mind. As stated by the Supreme Court in *Brown*, "In these days, it is doubtful that any child may reasonably be expected to succeed in life if he is denied the opportunity of an education."

Audiences at the time could not have avoided sympathizing with the bitter sting of rejection on the basis of color when a Mexican family was refused service in *Giant*, and when the Indian child was turned away from school in *Cimarron*. Sit-ins were occurring at lunch counters across the South. Public accommodations bills were being passed by many states, and in the early 1960s, President John F. Kennedy would introduce a federal bill to make it illegal to refuse service on the basis of race. School integration issues had been front-page stories in American newspapers since *Brown*. But the clear message given by *Giant* and *Cimarron* was that African Americans are different from

Members of the House Committee on Un-American Activities (HUAC) sit for an executive meeting in Washington, D.C. on August 8, 1948. From left, future American President Richard Nixon (1913-1994), chief investigator Robert Stripling, and U.S. Representatives John McDowell (1902-1957), committee chairman J. Parnell Thomas (1895-1970), and F. Edward Hebert (1901-1979). (Photo by New York Times Co./Getty Images)

others. Indians and Mexican Americans deserve respect and equality, but African Americans deserve to be ignored.

Also witness what was done in *The Greatest Show on Earth*. By showing black laborers and a few blacks entering the circus, filmmakers could pound themselves on their chests, boasting how liberal their movie was. But, by not having black laborers intermingle with white ones, the film side-stepped the integration issue, and by not showing any black patrons under the big top, the movie carefully avoided dealing with the sticky problem of integrated seating.

With real life black protagonists like Rosa Parks and genuine black leaders and heroes such as Thurgood Marshall and Martin Luther King, Jr., how could Hollywood limit its popular movie portrayals to babysitters, bathroom attendants and a few dock-workers?

Whether *On the Waterfront's* presentation was courageous, accidentally forward or wishful thinking, it demonstrated how black and white workers share similar concerns and bonds, and, banded together, could fight union corruption. Hollywood deserves kudos for this film. It said to Americans that both races want to work; and share the same fears, concerns and hopes. Acclaimed director Elia Kazan's films ushered in an era of socially conscious drama and emotional realism. These scenes are good examples of what the Supreme Court was protecting in the NAACP cases of *Cooper v. Aaron* and *Bates v. City of Little Rock*: freedom of association for the purpose of advancing ideas and airing grievances as protected by the Constitution.

Alas, other films did not contain similar messages. While the 1950's Supreme Court shaped and reflected current American values, Hollywood, by and large, remained in the dark ages by reflecting times long gone, likely misshaping some American minds along the way.

A scene in the 1952 film, *Singin' in the Rain* (AFI's #10), portrayed the inability of some silent screen actors to make the transition to talking pictures. During filming, the curtain was raised behind the set to show it was the melodious Debbie Reynolds, and not the leading lady with the scratchy, high-pitched voice, doing the singing. It was during the 1950's, too, that Hollywood's curtain was raised to reveal its true self. The industry did not accurately reflect African Americans. Early immigrant filmmakers had a different excuse: they did accurately reflect what they saw. In the post World War I 1920s, America was changing. In the 1930s and 1940s the industry hid safely behind the myth of the Southern box office. By the 1950s, the curtain was up, and Hollywood's stereotypical roles for African Americans were exposed for all to see.

With real life black protagonists like Rosa Parks and genuine black leaders and heroes such as Thurgood Marshall and Martin Luther King, Jr., how could Hollywood limit its popular movie portrayals to babysitters, bathroom attendants and a few dockworkers? Why did it not notice it was ignoring a black servant, while preaching sensitivity to a Mexican servant in *Giant*?

There are a number of reasons. Many of the old time conservatives from the pre-war days were still in Hollywood, along with the remains of the myth of the Southern Box Office. In those frightening days of the 1950s, the film industry was fighting for its own survival by avoiding charges it was a hotbed of Communism, bent toward changing American values. HUAC was largely controlled by Southern Congressmen and white supremacists. And the Civil Rights Movement was suspected of having Communist origins and ties. Jewish executives, mostly anti-Communist themselves, were acutely aware of HUAC's anti-Semitic views, and knew it was a short step from having permitted propaganda in their movies to being seen as condoning it.[310]

There was no way for Hollywood to win in those days. For many reasons, mainly to stay under the red scare radar, Hollywood played it safe. Director Elia Kazan testified before HUAC on April 10, 1952, and informed on eight of his old friends. Many in Hollywood never forgave Kazan, and his adamant refusal to apologize afterward provoked a whirlwind of protest that reverberated for the rest of his life. Parallels have been drawn between Kazan's real life part as an informer and the Brando character in *On the Waterfront* who yelled at the end of the film, "I'm glad what I done—you hear me?—glad what I done!"[311]

Little wonder more of the decade's films did not demonstrate a social conscience.

This photo of members of the Supreme Court who delivered the school-desegregation opinion was taken on November 13, 1953: Seated, from L to R: Felix Frankfurter, Hugo L. Black, Earl Warren, Stanley F. Reed, William O. Douglas. Standing, from L to R: Tom C. Clark, Robert H. Jackson, Harold H. Burton and Sherman Minton. (Photo by George Tames/New York Times Co./Getty Images)

Zooming in . . .

Was Alfred Hitchcock a Racist?

HITCHCOCK MOVIES HAVE ALWAYS HINTED that Alfred Hitchcock had an issue with race and ethnicity. His films boosted racial stereotypes and at times seemed malicious and abusive with regard to race. By the end of his career, Hitchcock's films were sometimes blatant in ridiculing African Americans. But since one of his earliest films, *The Ring* (1928), was advanced for its day in that a black man mixed it up with whites as just one of the guys, it is not clear what Hitchcock's racial notions really were.

Murder (1929) had a villain who committed murders because he was trying to hide his racial impurity. When his secret is uncovered at the end of the movie, the murderer is referred to as a half-cast. In Hitchcock's other earlier films, such as *The Man Who Knew Too Much* (1934), *Sabotage* (1936), and *The Lady Vanishes* (1938), he cast the villain as a dark-skinned, swarthy character. In *The Lady Vanishes*, Hitchcock used an ethnic joke. When the male lead has a scuffle with an Italian, he feigns dizziness, waives his hand before his nose and explains, "garlic!" Hitchcock also pokes fun at dark-skinned people in *Foreign Correspondent* (1940). *The Young and Strange* (1932) heavy plays in a blackfaced band. In *The 39 Steps* (1935), the main character makes a crack about someone being the "white man's burden." Among a group of children, the only one who carries a shoe shine kit in *Mr. and Mrs. Smith* (1941) is black.

Lifeboat (1943) is based on a story written by John Steinbeck that was later turned into a screenplay. In Steinbeck's story, the lone black character is larger than life. He is pure and innocent, and represents goodness. But Hitchcock changed the black character in his film. Instead of the saintly person in Steinbeck's work, Hitchcock's "Joe" is a reformed pickpocket who is asked to demonstrate his skill by taking a compass from the pocket of a sleeping character.

One cruel treatment of blacks in Hitchcock films was their complete eradication across the country. In many Hitchcock movies, there are throngs of people in public places, but no blacks to be found. *Shadow of a Doubt* (1943) begins in Philadelphia and then continues across the country in Santa Rosa, California. Not one black person. *Spellbound* (1945) has scenes in several locations, many in crowded public places such as hotel lobbies, train stations and along the streets of New York City. No blacks. There are numerous indoor and outdoor public scenes in both Florida and Rio de Janeiro in *Notorious* (1946), but none of the actors or extras are black.

Saboteur (1942) begins at a defense plant in Los Angeles during World War II. Thousands of white workers are seen, but no blacks. Other scenes take place around Los Angeles, and other parts of California, then across the country in Manhattan, the Brooklyn Navy Yard and Liberty Island. There are no blacks in any of those scenes either. It is particularly surprising there are no black workers at any of the defense sites because, as previously noted, in 1941 Roosevelt issued Executive Order 8802 prohibiting employment discrimination based on race, creed, color or national origin by the defense industry working under federal contracts.

There is a conspicuous absence of black people in several other films directed by Hitchcock. *The Wrong Man* (1957) takes place in New York City. There are no black people in the subways, a nightclub, an all-night diner, a bus, various street scenes, an office building, liquor stores, police headquarters, a grocery store, the jail, a paddy wagon or in a courthouse. The setting for *Vertigo* (1958) is northern California, primarily San Francisco. Restaurants, office buildings, street scenes and tourist locations showed no black people. In *North By Northwest* (1959), there are a few black actors in the New York City street scenes, but none in the Chicago street scenes or the Chicago airport, even though that city had the highest population of African Americans in the country.

Other films in the 1950s, especially *Rear Window* (1954), clearly indicate Hitchcock boosted racial stereotypes and was, at times, malicious and abusive regarding blacks. The scenes in *Rear Window* were shot from inside an apartment into the courtyard of the complex. It is crowded with residents, and has a view of a bustling New York City street and a crowded restaurant. Deliverymen are coming and going. Visitors are in and out, and children are running and playing. But not a single black person is shown. Nonetheless, when the suspense is at its height and the cavalry is needed, Jimmy Stewart dials the number of his buddy, the detective. A cheerful, slow-speaking woman answers the phone. "Dis da babysitter . . . Ahm hired til one . . . Do he have yo number, Mr. Jeffries?"

Why did Hitchcock have a babysitter, who sounded black and uneducated, but not one black on the screen? When the Jimmy Stewart character made the phone call, it was at a point when he was most frustrated and anxious that the killer would harm Grace Kelly's character. To have a slow speaking, grammatically incorrect, black voice was likely Hitchcock's way of heightening the character's frustration and conveying to the audience that the person on the other end of the line would be of no help at all.

Film credits showed the movie was based on a novelette by Cornell Woolrich. Woolrich's story has the same scene, but the part about the phone call is much different.[312] The immobile man in the full-leg cast, played by Jimmy Stewart in the movie, called the police station searching for the detective. The watch commander said the detective went home, but before he could give out the home number, the telephone line was cut. So, the black voice in the phone call was added by Hitchcock.

Segregation was obviously a volatile concern in the 1950s, but that did not prevent Hitchcock from taking a cheap shot in *Strangers on a Train* (1951). A drunken professor is on a train with the lead actor and makes a crack about "integration." The lead looks perplexed, so the professor pauses for effect so the joke can sink in, then gives the punch line and explains he is talking about differential calculus.

The setting in *To Catch a Thief* (1955) is the south of France. There are no blacks in the film. But the Cary Grant character goes to a masquerade ball where all the costumes are of royalty. Grant goes as an African prince, and wears a black mask.

In *Topaz* (1969), Hitchcock used race as a gimmick to get a negative reaction from the audience. Leon Uris's book, on which the movie is based, is sympathetic to blacks.[313] In the book, members of the Cuban delegation to the United Nations in New York City are mistreated at their hotel because the group includes blacks, so they move to another hotel in Harlem. Adhering to the book plot in the movie could have sensitively demonstrated the unfair treatment to which blacks were subjected when they needed public accommodations. But the movie manages to twist the story just enough to eliminate sensitivity for blacks. The delegation is only seen in Harlem, and Hitchcock created a scene where a spy, a black operative, poses as a reporter for *Ebony* magazine. In the book, the spy never meets with the Cuban official. But the movie has the black spy meet a high Cuban official in order to use the race card. When the official refuses an interview, the black actor asks, "What's the matter, are you anti-Negro?" The embarrassed official grants the interview, responding, "There are no color bars in Cuba. We are a free and democratic nation. All men are comrades." Thus,

Racism can be a ritual assertion of supremacy, like animals sneering and posturing to maintain their places in their hierarchy.

Hitchcock managed to cleverly switch Leon Uris's sympathy for the plight of blacks, who were denied equal accommodations, to sympathy for the Cuban official who is manipulated by the black man.

Hitchcock's last film was *Family Plot* (1976). In it, the main characters interview several people in their quest to track down an heir named Arthur Adamson. One of the persons being interviewed is standing on a ladder and has his head in an attic while he answers some questions. When he pulls his head out of the ceiling he is revealed to be black, and that is the joke.

Racism can be a ritual assertion of supremacy, like animals sneering and posturing to maintain their places in their hierarchy.[314] That was not what Hitchcock did. Rather he did a lot of racial and ethnic sneering and posturing in his films, especially in the 1950s. If he was merely being clever, it was mean-spirited at best. In many ways, his use of blacks in his films was similar to the old black face clown in Jim Crow roadshows. Hitchcock used blacks as props and to get laughs, but he was probably no more or less racist than most of America. Perhaps his technique could be called opportunistic racism.

1961-1970
Racial Framework

By the 1960s, Americans were embarrassed that their racial policies were an international scandal. The country was ready for change in racial relations. When Gunnar Myrdal's book, *An American Dilemma*, was re-published in 1962, it contained a preface stating that racial changes in the previous twenty years were at a far more rapid rate than was anticipated when Myrdal initially published his study. "Prejudice as an attitude was still common, but racism as a comprehensive ideology was maintained by only a few." Additionally, a 1961 Gallup Poll found that 76 percent of white Southerners expected there would soon be complete integration of the races in public places.[315]

Before President Eisenhower left the White House, he urged the country to move toward the goal of greater autonomy for all so "we shall be better prepared to work for the cause of freedom under law throughout the world."[316]

Not all Americans were prepared to follow Ike's counsel, however. A widely publicized 1961 incident in a restaurant along a highway just outside Washington, D.C. caused worldwide embarrassment for the United States. Malik Sow, the newly arrived Ambassador for Chad was refused service while on his way to present his credentials to President Kennedy. The waitress later explained, "He looked like just an ordinary run of the mill nigger to me. I couldn't tell he was an ambassador."[317]

Vice President Lyndon Johnson feared another international incident and worked to prevent a similar diplomatic disgrace in Texas when the Dallas Hilton at first refused a room to Ghana's ambassador to the United States.[318]

Soviet Premier Nikita Khrushchev called for the United Nations to move its headquarters to another country, citing other incidents of African and Asian members being subjected to racial discrimination. Khrushchev claimed the Soviet Union could guarantee complete freedom and security for all U.N. representatives regardless of the color of their skin. During another session of the United Nations, a dark-skinned delegate denounced Soviet intervention in Hungary, to which the gentleman from Bulgaria quipped, "Something worse could happen to you in Little Rock."[319]

In 1967, President Johnson nominated Marshall to fill a vacancy on the United States Supreme Court, and diehard Southern Senators did their best to humiliate him during the Senate hearings.

This decade wrought greater international scrutiny of America's commitment to freedom and democracy.[320] A humiliated U.S.A. listened to the rebukes and worked to remedy some of its less than democratic racial policies.

Thurgood Marshall's advancement is a prime example of the country's changing racial practices. He proved to be a quintessential American success story. In 1962, after a solid year before the Senate Judiciary Committee, Marshall took his seat on the Federal Second Circuit Court of Appeals. In 1965, he was confirmed as Solicitor General, holding the third highest legal position (after Attorney General and Assistant Attorney General) in the land. While Solicitor General, Marshall was able to argue some of the same civil rights issues he formerly did while championing NAACP causes. Then, in 1967, President Johnson nominated Marshall to fill a vacancy on the United States Supreme Court, and diehard Southern Senators did their best to humiliate him during the Senate hearings. Senator Strom Thurmond was the roughest, supposedly administering "a simple history test" by asking Marshall to name the congressional research committee members who had worked on the Fourteenth Amendment in 1868. Despite Southern harassment, Marshall won Senate approval by a vote of 69 to 11. He took the oath of office on October 2, 1967, and was the first member of the Court from Maryland since Roger Taney, the justice who authored the Dred Scott case.[321]

The spring and summer of 1963 were busy for the Civil Rights Movement. On April 21, mailman Bill Moore started two weeks vacation by stepping off a bus in Chattanooga. He intended to walk through the South to deliver a letter to the Governor of Mississippi, asking for an end to racial segregation. He carried a sand-

wich board that read, "BLACK AND WHITE EAT AT JOE'S." "Nigger lover," people taunted from passing cars. Bill Moore never made it to Mississippi. His body was found
just outside of Birmingham two days after he began his trek.

That same month, Martin Luther King, Jr. wrote his "Letter From A Birmingham
Jail." In June, National Guard troops were required to protect two black students who
were enrolling at the University of Alabama despite outspoken objection of Governor
George Wallace. The next day, NAACP's field secretary, Medgar Evers, was murdered
in the driveway of his Jackson, Mississippi home.[322] That summer, civil rights
marchers struggled with Birmingham Police Chief Bull Connor, and his dogs and fire
hoses. In August, there was a march of hundreds of thousands of protestors to the
steps of the Lincoln Memorial in Washington, D.C. where King delivered his "I Have
a Dream" speech.[323] Four little girls died from a Ku Klux Klan bomb in the basement
of a Baptist church.[324] And, of course, in November of 1963, President Kennedy was
assassinated.

During this time,
school desegregation was
progressing at a snail's
pace in the South. There,
just over 0.15 percent of
black schoolchildren in
1960 and 1.2 percent in
1964 attended school with
whites. Not one black
child attended an integrated public grade school in
South Carolina, Alabama
or Mississippi during the
1962-1963 school year.[325]

*Rev. Martin Luther King Jr.
sat on a chair against a wall
in a police station after his
arrest for directing a city-
wide boycott of segregated
buses. (Photo by Don
Cravens//Time Life
Pictures/Getty Images)*

Boxer Cassius Clay, who later changed his name to Muhammad Ali, won a medal in the 1960 Olympics in Rome, only to return to his hometown in Louisville, Kentucky and be refused service at a lunch counter.

Black migration continued North. As blacks moved into cities, whites moved to the suburbs in droves, leaving blacks behind in slums with persistent social disorganization, official neglect and abuse.[326] In 1962 the largest public housing project in history, the Robert Taylor Homes, was built in Chicago. The project consisted of twenty-eight identical sixteen-story buildings. Crime ran unchecked and the housing quickly deteriorated.

Black projects in other cities, such as St. Louis, also were complete failures. Presidents Kennedy and Johnson set up numerous agencies and programs such as The Urban Renewal Program, the Community Action Program, Head Start, Office of Economic Opportunity, Mobilization For Youth, Community Development and the Model Cities Program, to respond to the migration. Twenty years later, President Ronald Reagan quipped, "In the 1960s we declared a war on poverty, and poverty won."[327]

In 1965, a police officer in Los Angeles made a routine traffic stop in a section of the city known as Watts. By the time the riot stopped, thirty-four people were dead and over one thousand injured.[328] The 1960s saw race riots throughout the country, including Harlem, Philadelphia, Detroit, Cleveland and Chicago. After Martin Luther King, Jr. was assassinated on April 4, 1968, riots broke out in one hundred twenty five cities. More than seventy-five thousand National Guardsmen and federal troops were required to quell the disturbances. Over twenty thousand people were arrested, and there was over 40 million in property damage.[329]

Racial overtones in the Vietnam War resulted in the war's being connected with civil rights. Comments about the "white man's burden" and "yellow peril," and comparisons of reported atrocities in Vietnam with Nazi extermination camps, gave the anti-war movement a racial hook. Many of the groups that were most vocal in support of civil rights were the same ones outspoken against United States involvement in Vietnam. Boxer Cassius Clay, who later changed his name to Muhammad Ali, won a medal in the 1960 Olympics in Rome, only to return to his hometown in Louisville, Kentucky and be refused service at a lunch counter. Later, he refused to be drafted into the military because of religious beliefs, which resulted in the World Boxing Association's stripping him of his world heavyweight title.[330] The Vietnam War, and a vague notion of community that crossed national lines, resulted in blacks broadening their racial awareness and sharing racial consciousness with others.

By the 1960s, American blacks had achieved adequate sophistication, self-involvement, organization and leadership to accomplish mass collective action. Race scholar Louis E. Burnham remarked: "One hundred years would seem time enough and more for so rich and strong a nation as ours to redeem the promise of freedom made to an unoffending people it once held as slaves."[331]

1961-1970
The Supreme Court

DURING THIS DECADE, THE UNITED States Supreme Court served as the hub of the anti-discrimination wheel, intent upon taking the internationally embarrassing issue of white supremacy off the nation's table. The Court infused energy into the Civil Rights Movement. Soon after Congress passed legislation banning racial discrimination in public accommodations, voting rights or housing, the Court set the Acts into motion by affixing its mighty stamp of approval. As Court rulings were issued, civil rights workers, using the decisions as a compass, spread throughout the South and challenged local practices.

The preface to a reprint of an article in *Freedomways*, an African American intellectual periodical of the times states: "The Supreme Court had ruled in 1961 that bus terminal restaurants could not discriminate against interstate travelers. The Freedom Riders set out to test the enforcement of federal law in the terminals in the South. A member of the Congress of Racial Equality (CORE), Jimmy McDonald, was in the first group of seven black and six white Freedom Riders. Segregationists bombed and burned their bus when it reached Anniston, Alabama."[332]

Indeed, the Supreme Court ruled in 1961 that the arrest of seven African Americans who sat down at a lunch counter in a bus terminal violated their Fourteenth Amendment rights in *Briscoe v. Louisiana*, 368 U.S. 157. The Court also dealt with the public accommodations issue in other cases during this decade. In the 1964 case of *Heart of Atlanta Motel v. United States*, 379 U.S. 241, a motel owner in Atlanta, patronized primarily by transient interstate travelers, refused to serve blacks as required by the Civil Rights Act of 1964. In a companion case, *Katzenbach v. McClung*, 379 U.S. 294, a barbeque restaurant that served mostly in-state customers, but purchased much of its food and supplies through interstate commerce, also refused service to blacks. The 1883 *Civil Rights Cases*, 109 U.S. 3, had interpreted the Fourteenth Amendment as inapplicable to privately owned restaurants and hotels, so Congress employed the Commerce Clause as primary authority for the Civil Rights Act. The Court held that racial discrimination has a disruptive and adverse effect on the free movement of people and goods.

As Court rulings were issued, civil rights workers, using the decisions as a compass, spread throughout the South and challenged local practices.

New twists on existing laws were also brought before the Court. Maryland's trespass law was used to charge black sit-in protesters who were refused service at a Baltimore restaurant on the basis of their race. Almost immediately, a public accommodations local ordinance and state statute were passed, making it unlawful to deny service on account of race in both the city of Baltimore and the state of Maryland.

Nonetheless, the protesters' trespass convictions were upheld by the Maryland Supreme Court, and protesters placed their plight before the United States Supreme Court, claiming their Fourteenth Amendment rights had been violated. Providing the state with another chance to right its wrong, the Court sent the matter back to state court in *Bell v. Maryland*, 378 U.S. 226, in 1964, with directions for the court to specifically determine whether or not the convictions survived the new public accommodations laws.

But just a few years later, in 1966, the Court was far more vigorous when Georgia protestors were arrested and charged with criminal trespass after being refused service at privately owned restaurants. In *State of Georgia v. Rachel*, 384 U.S. 780, the Court held that prosecutions for trespass based on refusal to leave after being denied service solely for racial reasons was sufficient basis to predict denial of federal civil rights.

On the voting front, various states tried creative schemes to keep blacks from being politically represented. In 1960, the Louisiana Legislature passed a statute that required the Secretary of State to print the race of each candidate opposite his name on the ballots. Louisiana was slapped on the wrist by the United States Supreme Court in 1963 in *Anderson v. Martin*, 375 U.S. 399, "We have concluded that the compulsory designation by Louisiana of the race of a candidate on the ballot operates as a discrimination against appellants and is therefore violative of the Fourteenth Amendment's Equal Protection Clause. . . . Race is the factor upon which the statute operates and its involvement promotes the ultimate discrimination which is sufficient to make it invalid."

In 1964 the Twenty-fourth Amendment to the United States Constitution banned poll taxes as a condition for voting in national elections.

Baker v. Carr, 369 U.S. 186, opened the federal courts to urban interests that had previously been unable to force state legislators to reapportion their legislatures. Some say this case represented a revolution in redistributing political power.[333] Populations had been moving to the cities and suburbs, but legislatures, dominated by small-towners and farm districts, dragged their heels at changing the boundaries for electoral districts, refusing to legislate themselves out of jobs. In *Baker*, the Court sent word to all the states that their citizens might be deprived equal protection under the United States Constitution unless their state electoral districts were equitably drawn. City dwellers received the message, and within a year, there were lawsuits in more than thirty states.

In *Westberry v. Sanders*, 376 U.S. 1, the Court held that state districts must be as nearly equal as practicable to electoral districts for seats in the House of Representatives. Historian Lawrence M. Friedman commented: "In the end, if anybody gained, it was not the urban masses but the middle class in suburban bulges ringed around the midriff of metropolitan areas."[334]

In 1964 the Twenty-fourth Amendment to the United States Constitution banned poll taxes as a condition for voting in national elections. By 1966, when the Court issued its opinion in *Harper v. Virginia State Board of Elections*, 383 U.S. 663, only a few states still had a poll tax.[335] The 1937 case of *Breedlove v. Suttles*, 302 U.S. 277, had unanimously upheld Georgia's poll tax, finding the Equal Protection Clause did not require absolute equality. Partially overruling *Breedlove*, the *Harper* Court held state requirements for fees as a condition to voting were unconstitutional since the political franchise is a fundamental right, and cannot be denied because of a lack of wealth.

In 1966, *South Carolina v. Katzenbach*, 383 U.S. 301, and *Katzenbach v. Morgan*, 384 U.S. 641, were milestones in the development of Congressional power to enforce post-Civil War amendments, after Congress passed a Voting Rights Act in 1965 that prohibited racial discrimination in voting. The Court held Congress had the power to proscribe a class of suspect practices by, for example, selecting areas where racial discrimination was likely to be prevalent. The Court declared Congress needed only to have a rational basis for its laws.

The 1960s saw further attempts at thwarting the NAACP, requiring yet another intervention by the United States Supreme Court. For example, solicitation of legal business, such as lawyers advertising for clients, had been illegal in Virginia since 1849. It was not until 1956 that Virginia changed its definition. The Court held the activities of the NAACP and its affiliates and legal staff are modes of expression and association protected by the First and Fourteenth Amendments. "We cannot close our eyes to the fact that the militant Negro Civil Rights Movement has engendered the intense resentment and opposition of the politically dominant white community of Virginia," the Court noted in *National Association For the Advancement of Colored People v. Robert Y. Button, Attorney General of Virginia*, 371 U.S. 415. Virginia was thus prohibited, under its power to regulate the legal profession from finding the NAACP improperly solicited legal business.

A more emotional issue was presented later the same year in *McLaughlin v. State of Florida*, 379 U.S. 184, and three years later,

Married couple Mildred and Richard Loving (1933-1975) embrace at a press conference the day after the Supreme Court ruled in their favor in Loving v. Virginia, on June 13, 1967. The court, in a unanimous verdict, overturned Virginia's anti-miscegenation statute, which had resulted in the Loving's arrest shortly after their 1958 marriage. (Photo by Francis Miller/Time & Life Pictures/Getty Images)

From school desegregation cases that were before the Court during the 1960s, it is obvious that some Virginians did not like the **Brown** *decision.*

in 1967, in *Loving v. Commonwealth of Virginia*, 388 U.S. 1. In both cases, the Supreme Court discussed an 1883 case, *Pace v. State of Alabama*, 106 U.S. 583. In *Pace*, the Court upheld a conviction under an Alabama statute forbidding adultery or fornication between a white person and a black person that imposed a greater penalty than that of a statute prohibiting similar conduct by persons of the same race. The *Pace* Court reasoned the statute could not be said to discriminate against blacks since the punishment was the same for both the white and black participant.

The *McLaughlin* matter involved criminal convictions under a Florida statute. It provided that any black man and white woman (or any white man and black woman) who were not married and who lived in the same room be punished. The Court rejected the proposition that the requirement of equal protection is satisfied by laws that define offenses based on racial classifications—as long as white and black participants are equally punished.

But the issue of interracial marriage was squarely before the Justices in *Loving v. Virginia*. Mildred Jeter, a black woman, and Richard Loving, a white man, married in the District of Columbia in 1958. When they returned to their native Virginia, they were prosecuted. Their jail terms were suspended for twenty-five years on the condition they leave the State of Virginia and not return for twenty-five years. The trial judge stated, 206 Va. 924, "Almighty God created the races white, black, yellow, Malay and red, and he placed them on separate continents. And but for the interference with his arrangement there would be no cause for such marriages. The fact that he separated the races shows that he did not intend for the races to mix."

The Lovings moved to Washington D.C. and in late 1963 filed a motion to vacate the Virginia judgment. When Virginia did not hear the motion, they filed a class action in the United States District Court in Virginia. When the matter reached the United States Supreme Court, the Court unanimously struck down Virginia's statute, noting "The Fourteenth Amendment requires that the freedom of choice to marry not be restricted by invidious racial discrimination."

Although not a black man, Clarence Earl Gideon's case in *Gideon v. Wainwright*, 372 U.S.335, paved the way for many poor blacks to have counsel appointed when they are charged with a crime punishable by imprisonment and do not have the money to hire a lawyer. This ruling extended the 1932 holding in *Powell v. Alabama* that due process for an indigent charged with a capital crime required a state to appoint counsel for him.

From school desegregation cases that were before the Court during the 1960s, it is obvious that some Virginians did not like the *Brown* decision. The Supervisors of Prince Edward County closed the public schools, explaining they were "confronted with a court decree which requires the admission of white and colored children to all the schools of the county without regard to race or color."

The Supreme Court was not sympathetic. "The time for mere 'deliberate speed' has run out, and that phrase can no longer justify denying these Prince Edward County school children their constitutional rights to an education equal to that afforded by the public schools in the other parts of Virginia."

Green v. County School Bd. of New Kent County, Va., 389 U.S. 1003, involved a school district in a rural county in Eastern Virginia where the School Board continued the segregated operation of the system after the *Brown* decisions, presumably on the authority of several statutes enacted by Virginia in resistance to those decisions. One statute, the Pupil Placement Act, rid local boards of authority to assign children to particular schools and placed that authority in a State Pupil Placement Board. Under that Act, children were each year automatically reassigned to the school previously attended unless, upon their application, the State Board assigned them to another school. Disallowing the system, the Supreme Court ruled the pattern of separate 'white' and 'Negro' schools in the New Kent County school system established under force of state laws is precisely the pattern of segregation to which *Brown I* and *Brown II* were particularly addressed, and which *Brown I* declared unconstitutionally denied black school children equal protection of the laws.

Finally, the Court closed another door to housing discrimination in *Jones v. Alfred H. Mayer Co.,* 392 U.S. 409. The Thirteenth Amendment, which has been interpreted to prohibit badges of slavery as well as slavery, was utilized by Congress to legislate against private discrimination in house sales. On September 2, 1965, Joseph Lee Jones filed a complaint in the Eastern District of Missouri, claiming he was unable to purchase a home in the Paddock Woods community of St. Louis County for the sole reason that he was a Negro. The Court held that all racial discrimination, private as well as public, in the sale or rental of property is barred.

1961-1970
Hollywood

BESIDES WINNING COURT BATTLES, AFRICAN Americans were also more favorably treated in films during the 1960s. While not presenting issues in depth, Hollywood was willing to reflect some societal changes.

For numerous reasons, filmmakers began to reappraise and revise their product during this decade.[336] The old studios were severely weakened, becoming places where movies were made, rather than monarchies. The industry was faced with rising labor strife and costs, along with decreasing revenues.[337, 338] Conglomerates, industrialists, lawyers, businessmen, talent agents and stars took over where the old moguls left off. Television presented major competition to Hollywood, portraying more realistic racial situations than movies. The number and composition of movie audiences altered just as American racial attitudes were rapidly changing.

Throughout the 1960s, the NAACP kept continuous pressure on the movie industry to upgrade the film image of blacks and to employ them in all capacities within the industry.[339] As a result, central casting began giving blacks equal access to available assignments, and other additional employment opportunities were forthcoming.[340] Actually getting black actors on the screen was another matter. When persuasion did not work, and legal action was threatened by both the NAACP and the Equal Employment Opportunities Commission, blacks began to play policemen, civil servants, students, and workers in films.[341, 342] African Americans became more militant as the 1960s progressed, and the new motion picture makers wanted their products to take a stand on current social, political and economic issues.[343]

Television changed America's movie tastes, and familiarized people with incredible scenes of blood and brutality.[344] Movies could now be seen for free in the comfort of living rooms. On race issues, television had a direct impact on African Americans. This industry did not hold back the truth about American racial conditions from its audiences, as Hollywood had done for decades. Viewers saw the violence used by whites in resisting racial change, and the quiet dignity of black leadership in documentary footage of bus boycotts, sit-ins and the March on Washington. Television was referred to as "the chosen instrument of the Civil Rights Movement."[345]

Television changed America's movie tastes, and familiarized people with incredible scenes of blood and brutality.

After World War II, whites had been increasingly drawn away from noisy cities into the open spaces of the suburbs, far away from urban movie houses where they formerly went twice a week. Movie audiences declined and thousands of theaters closed.[346] African Americans filled in some of the gap. Periodically, *Variety* and other trade journals noted the "growing Negro audience" in movie houses, which by the 1960s represented a sizable segment of film patronage. According to a 1967 estimate, although blacks represented only 15 percent of the population, they accounted for 30 percent of movie audiences.[347]

The film industry bid farewell to its myth of the American Dream in the 1960s. *West Side Story* (1961, Best Picture of the Year, AFI's #41) is about alienated Puerto Rican and Anglo gangs in New York, and illustrates how Hollywood reflected America's attitude about the country sometimes falling short in its ideal of democracy. *Dr. Strangelove* (1964, AFI's #26) pokes fun at America's commitment to democracy when an Air Force officer delivers a pep talk to his crew, which includes one black man. After telling them citations may be in order on completion of the mission, he adds, "That goes for every last one of you, regardless of your race, color and your creed." Later, the mad doctor's paralyzed arm keeps inadvertently shooting up in a "heil Hitler" salute, and he repeatedly calls the President of the United States "Mein Fuhrer."

The Manchurian Candidate (1962, AFI's #67) is an example of the use of black actors in parts that were not race specific, and could easily have been played by whites. An Army officer and his beautiful young wife, as well as an intelligence officer, are portrayed as dignified, competent and respected African Americans.

To Kill a Mockingbird (1962, AFI's #34) is about the prosecution and conviction of an innocent black man for rape of a white woman in a small Southern town in 1932. The powerfully built man with a crippled hand and head hung low is pitiful and emasculated in a town where he has no or credibility and where white supremacy reigns. While the film portrays Tom Robinson on trial, it actually exposes the crippled apartheid system. It might have been modeled after the well-publicized Scottsboro boys trials from the 1930s. In fact, the holding in one of the Scottsboro boys cases, *Powell v Alabama*, which required effective assistance of counsel in capital cases, was illustrated at the beginning of the film when the judge visited Atticus Finch to ask him to represent Robinson. The film accurately portrays rural Southern courtrooms where whites sat downstairs and blacks upstairs, and that some states ignored the 1880 holding in *Strauder v. West Virginia*, which said that blacks could not be barred from juries.[348] The message was that African Americans had no opportunity for justice in the Jim Crow South. This movie portrayed blacks with kindness and dignity.

According to a 1967 estimate, although blacks represented only 15 percent of the population, they accounted for 30 percent of movie audiences.

The public accommodations issue was also addressed in film during this decade. *Lawrence of Arabia* (1962, Best Picture of the Year, AFI's #5) has a scene where Lawrence accompanies a young Bedouin boy into the Officer's Club and orders a lemonade from a bartender who does not want to serve the dark boy. Lawrence insists and prevails. In *M*A*S*H* (1970, AFI's #56) the question of quarters for an African American neurosurgeon is discussed. "We'll stick him in here with us," Hawkeye says. When the doctor from the South asks, perplexed, "You're serious, ain't ya?" Hawkeye ridicules him for his prejudice. The black doctor, indeed, bunks in the same tent with the white doctors.

*M*A*S*H* demonstrates the moral linkage of the anti-war and Civil Rights Movements. The film must have jolted viewers with its irreverent humor and shocking realism, and challenged traditional notions about morality, racial prejudice, sexuality and the United States involvement in the Vietnam War. In fact, both the United States Army and Air Force banned showing the film on their bases because of its cynical attitude toward the military.[349] In addition to openly dealing with accommodations for the black doctor, the film has numerous other racial nuances. Black characters mixed with white in many of the scenes but, except for the one hero neurosurgeon, were not distinguished in any way.

During the 1960s many articles criticized the country's fascination with Sidney Poitier. Black dramatist Clifford Mason called him a "showcase nigger."[350]

In the Heat of the Night (1967, Best Picture of the Year, 1968) displays Poitier in a white world without a woman and assisting a white sheriff solve a crime. But black author James Baldwin points out that while *In the Heat of the Night* (1967) unrealistically has a black man voluntarily change trains in a backwater Southern town in the middle of the night, it turns on a plot designed to camouflage bitter questions.

Both the United States Army and Air Force banned showing [M*A*S*H] on their bases because of its cynical attitude toward the military.

In the film, Virgil Tibbs, played by Poitier, comes face to face with racism at every turn. His sophisticated big city manners sharply contrast with those of cowed local black folk and crude whites. He stays in the small town at the insistence of the rich widow of a murdered man, to help the local sheriff solve the murder. The Mississippi town has no hotel for him to stay, no restaurant where he can eat and no white people who are prepared to treat him as an equal. Baldwin refused to dismiss the film as helplessly conveying, without confronting, the anguish of people trapped in a legend. "The film gave me the impression, according to my notes the day I saw it, of 'something strangling, alive, struggling to get out.'" Not convinced things had changed all that much, Baldwin concluded, "In *The Birth of a Nation*, the sheriff would have been an officer of the Klan. The widow would, secretly, have been sewing Klan insignia. The murdered man (whether or not he was her husband) would have been a carpetbagger. Sam would have been a Klan deputy. The troublesome poor whites would have been mulattoes. And Virgil Tibbs would have been the hunted, not the hunter. It is impossible to pretend that this state of affairs has really altered: a black man, in any case, had certainly best not believe everything he sees in the movies."[351]

The emotional topic of integrated neighborhoods was also the subject of a Sidney Poitier movie. James Baldwin wrote of *A Raisin in the Sun* (1961) that with the Younger family there are no conclusions, only commitment to new levels of personal and public struggle.[352] Perhaps he was right regarding the family's moving into a white Chicago neighborhood over the protests of their new neighbors. But there is a conclusion in the male/female relationships in the film when Sidney Poitier's character makes the decision to reject the white neighborhood representative's offer of a bribe to change the family's mind about the move, explaining, "Negro families are happier when they live in their own communities." In the end, Poitier's character gains self-respect and becomes head of the household before the viewer's eyes.

Poitier was the first black man to win an Academy Award. He won for his performance in *Lilies of the Field* (1963), where he played a chaste black man with no love interest.

*Since World War II, and especially since the **Brown** decision in 1954, many Americans were relieved to see the United States finally living up to the ideals of racial equality.*

Guess Who's Coming to Dinner (1967, AFI's #99) deals with the taboo subject of interracial marriage, and the confounded reaction both races had to integration. A twenty-three-year-old white woman and a thirty-seven-year-old "perfect" black man tell their parents they are in love and are soon to be married. Sidney Poitier is playful and fun, albeit sexless, in his role. The white family's black maid probably spoke for all of them when she cracked, "Civil rights is one thing. This here is sumpin' else." She also says, "Well, I got a right to my own opinion. I don't care to see a man of my own race gettin' above hisself." When the bride-to-be tells her father about her plans, she says, "If you had objections, I wouldn't let him go, even if you were the governor of Alabama." Her father tells her, "There'll be one hundred million people in this country who will be shocked, offended and appalled with the two of you."

The groom's father tells his son, "In sixteen or seventeen states, you'd be

1967: From left to right: Actor Sidney Poitier with actors Spencer Tracy (1900-1967) and Katharine Hepburn (1907-2003) in a still from director Stanley Kramer's film Guess Who's Coming to Dinner. *(Photo by Columbia Tristar/Getty Images)*

breaking the law. You'd be a criminal." Poitier's character responds, "You think of yourself as a colored man. I think of myself as a man."

Since World War II, and especially since the *Brown* decision in 1954, many Americans were relieved to see the United States finally living up to the ideals of racial equality.[353] Just as soon as one victory was had, more was demanded. The mid to late 1960s saw rapidly changing outlooks, opinions and attitudes.[354] From 1965 on, there was a growing and dramatic rise in black militant political activism and cultural consciousness.[355] Yet the movie industry was cautious in taking steps to keep up with these changing attitudes. Hollywood was coasting along on Martin Luther King nonviolent attitudes, even after Malcolm X had been assassinated and Stokley Carmichael had arrived.[356]

Reaction to *Guess Who's Coming to Dinner* is an example of the rapidly changing and racially diverse attitudes of the 1960s. For over a decade, Sidney Poitier had been held up as a milestone for American blacks, but this film was a hit among whites, the second biggest moneymaker of 1968, and one of the top ten moneymaking films of the 1960s. At the Academy Awards it won two Oscars and five other nominations. But blacks ridiculed the film for its shallowness.[357] They no longer considered Sidney Poitier roles to be pertinent to the black revolution. One angry black writer, Maxine Hall Elliston, called it "warmed-over white shit."[358] James Baldwin wrote, "A black person can make nothing of this film—except, perhaps, *Superfly*—and, when one tries to guess what white people make of it, a certain chill goes down the spine."[359]

*Movies not discussed in text appear in endnote.[360]

1961-1970
Decade Wrap-up

DURING THIS DECADE, THE UNITED States Supreme Court reshaped much of the civil rights landscape. While criticized for not keeping up with the rapid pace of change, Hollywood often accurately reflected American society. The 1960s was a very good time for African American in both institutions.

By the sixties, Hollywood had outgrown its basic way of doing business. The original immigrant founders of the motion picture industry created an image of America out of their own idealism. Their vision proved to be so powerful that it ultimately came to shape the myths, values, traditions and archetypes of America.[361] From what immigrants saw in this country at the time they started the movie business, there was no room in traditional American values for anyone but whites. But movies in the 1960s drove a Mac truck through the American Dream. A song in *West Side Story* went:

> *I like to be in America*
> *Okay by me in America*
> *Everything's freer in America*
> *For a small fee in America . . .*
> *Life is all right in America*

By the sixties, Hollywood had outgrown its basic way of doing business.

If you're all white in America . . .
Here you're all free and you have pride
Long as you stay on your own side . . .
Free to be anything you chose
If you wait tables and shine shoes

Synchronization between the Court and Hollywood, insofar as they each accurately reflected true conditions of blacks in American society, was almost reached. The Supreme Court's opinion in *Heart of Atlanta Motel v. United States* involved a segregated motel in Atlanta, and held it was unconstitutional to refuse service to blacks. At virtually the same time, Hollywood presented *In the Heat of the Night*, involving a black man from the North who has no motels available to him while visiting Sparta, Mississippi. Then there was Hawkeye's ridicule of another doctor's questioning that a black neurosurgeon bunk in the same tent with whites in *M*A*S*H*. Compare also

In 1967 actor Sidney Poitier was surrounded by an angry mob of armed men in a still from the film In the Heat of the Night, *directed by Norman Jewison. (Photo by United Artists/Getty Images)*

Katzenbach v. McClung, the barbeque restaurant that discriminated against blacks, with the lemonade scene in *Lawrence of Arabia* and Sidney Poitier being refused service in the diner in *In the Heat of the Night.*

Hollywood's 1961 film, *A Raisin in the Sun,* demonstrated the impact of the Supreme Court's 1948 decision, *Shelley v. Kraemer,* which made restrictive covenants illegal. Without that decision, the movie's black Younger family could never have moved into the white neighborhood. And the 1962 release of *To Kill a Mockingbird* must have helped shape the country's mind to accept the Supreme Court's 1963 holding in *Gideon v. Wainwright.* The movie portrayed the need for a poor black man to have effective counsel. This had to help Americans understand how bleak an unrepresented defendant's chances were, and the importance of *Gideon*'s requirement of effective counsel in felony cases.

A common denominator between 1960s Hollywood and the Supreme Court was the NAACP.

Not only was the issue of interracial marriage tackled by both the Court and Hollywood in the same year, 1967, Chief Justice Earl Warren and Sidney Poitier's father in the movie, played by Cecil Kellaway, shared an almost identical line. Warren wrote in the *Loving v. Virginia* opinion "Virginia is now one of sixteen States which prohibit and punish marriages on the basis of racial classifications." The movie character advises his son, "In sixteen or seventeen states, you'd be breaking the law."

However, the film keeps some racial stereotypes clearly in place. Author James Baldwin points out the maid in *Guess Who's Coming to Dinner* is the same one seen before in numerous movies including *Gone With the Wind* and *Imitation of Life.* "How many times have we seen her?" Baldwin points out she has a real family somewhere, and she does not love the white family nearly as much as the viewer is compelled to suppose.[362]

A common denominator between 1960s Hollywood and the Supreme Court was the NAACP. The organization, relentless, but not militant, kept constant pressure on both the Supreme Court and Hollywood throughout the 1960s, and both responded by opening doors of opportunity to African Americans.

1971-1980
Racial Framework

In the 1970s, African Americans made major progress toward integrating themselves into mainstream American society, politics and business. As blacks progressed, political divisions developed among African Americans. Whites reacted, sometimes positively and sometimes negatively.

African Americans also achieved significant political power in this decade. In 1970 there were twelve African Americans in the House of Representatives and one in the Senate. Blacks were mayors of Gary, Indiana; Cleveland, Ohio; Newark, New Jersey; and Washington, D.C. After the 1972 election, the number of blacks in Congress increased to sixteen.

In Congress, blacks formed the Congressional Black Caucus to set a national agenda for the progress of African Americans. When President Nixon delivered his annual State of the Union address in 1971, caucus members refused to attend as a protest to the president's refusal to discuss racial issues with them.

In 1972, eight thousand African Americans gathered for the first National Black Political Convention, and passed two controversial resolutions. The first called for black control of black schools, and opposed busing as a remedy for school segregation. The second called for self-determination for all people of color, which was assumed by some to be a condemnation of Israel and an endorsement of the Palestine Liberation Organization. The Congressional Black Caucus, not wanting to alienate

While the Democratic Party's structure was on the left, its electorate was moving to the right.

longtime Jewish supporters, distanced itself from the National Black Political Convention.[363]

As the 1972 election approached, white conservatism became more vocal. Code words such as "law and order," "silent majority" and "busing" were used to signify racial issues during the 1972 presidential elections.[364] On the other side were the civil rights and antiwar forces. While the Democratic Party's structure was on the left, its electorate was moving to the right. Even George Wallace, an outspoken segregationist, received more popular votes in some Democratic primaries than either Hubert Humphrey or George McGovern. Historians Philip A. Klinkner and Rogers M. Smith say this signified national opposition to the advancement of racial equality.[365] Nixon won by one of the largest margins in American history, carrying forty-nine states and more than 60 percent of the popular vote. Blacks were the only traditionally democratic group that consistently voted for his opponent, George McGovern.[366]

Later, Richard Nixon was accused of emphasizing the decline of law and order in an effort to appeal to white fears of black riots, and to white stereotypes of black criminality.[367] Radical conservatism increased, and national membership in the Ku Klux Klan nearly tripled between 1971 and 1980. Black churches, schools and residences were firebombed.[368]

In 1976, African American Barbara Jordan, a U.S. representative from Texas and a member of the House Judiciary Committee, delivered the keynote address before the Democratic National Convention. Blacks overwhelmingly supported candidate Jimmy Carter. Once in office, President Carter appointed a significant number of blacks to important positions in his administration. Corporate lawyer Patricia Harris was appointed secretary of Housing and Urban Development. Andrew Young became ambassador to the United Nations. Judge Wade McCree was named Solicitor General, and John Reinhardt headed the International Communications Agency. Several other African Americans were appointed as Ambassadors.[369]

By the time the great black migration was over (around 1970) the country had acquired a good measure of the tragic sense that had previously been confined to the South. During the 1970s, roughly half of America's nonwhite children lived in the twenty largest school districts, which were 60 percent nonwhite. The middle class, both blacks and whites, fled the cities for the suburbs.[370] Over time, the tenuous nature of the War on Poverty began to fade. It seemed to many Americans that the government had tried everything. Nothing had worked, including the numerous

1960s federal programs. "Model cities . . . flush it," President Richard Nixon is supposed to have said shortly after the 1972 election.[371]

The whole country was injected with a black history lesson when African American author Alex Haley's book, *Roots*, the story of his family's suppression into and then emergence from slavery, was presented on television. The mini-series drew 130 million viewers. Black travel agencies initiated "Roots" tours. Public funds were allocated for "Roots" projects. ABC immediately went to work on a sequel. Public Broadcasting's *Black Journal* interviewed Haley, and community colleges presented black history courses.[372]

Once in office, President Carter appointed a significant number of blacks to important positions in his administration.

Other black personages became high profile figures in American society during this decade. Angela Davis was a black activist who drew much attention. She was affiliated with the Communist Party, the Black Panther Party and the Student Nonviolent Coordinating Committee. By the early 1970s, Panther members had been arrested on charges ranging from conspiracy to commit murder to bombing police stations and assaulting police officers. Under pressure from California Governor Ronald Reagan, she was fired from her job teaching philosophy at UCLA. Davis was arrested and jailed for sixteen months on charges she supplied the weapons used in an escape attempt that resulted in the death of a judge and three others. Her trial before an all-white jury resulted in an acquittal.[373]

African Americans perceived law enforcement to be just as racist in 1976 as it was in 1876. In the 1970s, blacks saw their chances of being arrested, convicted, sentenced, imprisoned and executed as disproportionately high. In Pennsylvania, most white persons convicted of felony murder had their sentences commuted to life imprisonment; blacks did not.[374] In New York, 65 percent of those brought before the court on delinquency charges were black. A panel of judges reported the most frequently leveled charge against white children in stolen car cases was "unauthorized use of a vehicle," but virtually all black children were charged with grand larceny auto.

"Our young Blacks learn more in prison than they do at many of our urban schools," Judge Bruce McM. Wright, an African American judge in New York, remarked in 1975. He added: "A shockingly large proportion of the Black young men were unable either to read or write, although close questioning revealed that they had gone as far as the eleventh grade and sometimes had even been graduated."[375]

1971-1980
The Supreme Court

EVEN WHILE OUTSPOKEN SEGREGATIONIST GEORGE Wallace was receiving a record number of votes in the real world, the Supreme Court was ordering school busing and affirmative action. But as the 1970s wore on, African Americans could no longer count on victories as they often could in the 1950s and 1960s. Chief Justice Earl Warren, author of *Brown*, left the Court. Nixon critics noted that after observing Chief Justice Burger in action, President Nixon's administration sought the appointment of more conservative Supreme Court Justices.[376] On October 22, 1971 Justices Lewis F. Powell, Jr. and William H. Rehnquist were nominated to the Court. But there were many significant changes in addition to different judges that could account for the seemingly dissimilar results.

In the area of school desegregation, for example, the *Brown* opinion noted that the impact of segregation was greater when it has the sanction of law. By the end of the 1970s, while there was considerable segregation in American schools and industry, legally sanctioned segregation was all but gone. Pre-1970s Supreme Court cases involved small rural southern districts. In the 1970s, cases often concerned large urban or suburban areas all over the country, not just in the South. Historians Klinkner and Smith noted, "[T]he North now had to confront its own dark and dirty secrets."[377]

In numerous decisions, the Supreme Court allowed lower courts to use various means to accomplish school desegregation, but drew the line at school district boundaries, thus leaving open the option of white flight to the suburbs. In *Swann v. Charlotte-Mecklenburg Board of Education*, 402 U.S. 1, decided in 1971, seventeen years after *Brown*, the Court approved busing to implement desegregation. The district's 29 percent black population was concentrated in one quadrant of the sprawling school district, and more than half of the black pupils had no white students or teachers in their schools. In affirming the trial court's order, the Supreme Court, chiding, said, "Deliberate resistance of some to the Court's mandates has impeded the good-faith efforts of others to bring school systems into compliance." The Court further noted that, once a constitutional violation is shown, the district court has broad and flexible powers to remedy inequities.

President Richard Nixon tried to slow school desegregation to satisfy conservative whites.

Swann was a unanimous decision delivered on April 20, 1971, by the Court's new Chief Justice, Warren Burger. According to Klinkner and Smith, busing as a means to remedy segregation in public schools aggravated a growing disenchantment with civil rights. Reacting to public sentiment, President Richard Nixon tried to slow school desegregation to satisfy conservative whites.[378] Nixon said busing was "a symbol of helplessness, frustration and outrage—of a wrenching of children away from their families, and from the schools their families may have moved to be near, and sending them arbitrarily to others far distant."[379]

A few years later, the justices declined to permit a lower court to order a desegregation plan, severely limiting the ability of federal courts to achieve racial balance in schools. The plan called for crossing school district boundaries into districts not part of illegal segregation. In the case of *Milliken v. Bradley*, 418 U.S. 717, in 1974 the Court reversed the lower federal courts' plan encompassing fifty-three schools in three counties, which were not parties to the action and against which there was no claim of violations. The Court commented that such a plan might be in order where racially discriminatory acts of a school district caused racial segregation in an adjacent district, or where district lines were deliberately drawn on the basis of race. "Conversely, without an interdistrict violation and interdistrict effect, there is no constitutional wrong calling for an interdistrict remedy."

Justice Thurgood Marshall, who had argued *Brown I* and *Brown II* for the NAACP, now had to watch a bitter defeat of his former colleagues at the hands of his new colleagues. A dissent authored by Justice White and joined by Marshall observed, "The result is that the State of Michigan, the entity at which the Fourteenth Amendment is directed, has successfully insulated itself from its duty to provide effective desegregation remedies by vesting sufficient power over its public schools in its local school districts."

Marshall's personal disappointment with the decision of the majority is evident from a separate dissent he authored: "Today's holding, I fear, is more a reflection of a perceived public mood that we have gone far enough in enforcing the Constitution's guarantee of equal justice than it is the product of neutral principles of law. In the short run, it may seem to be the easier course to allow our great metropolitan areas to be divided up each into two cities—one white, the other black—but it is a course, I predict, our people will ultimately regret. I dissent."

The case made its way back to the Supreme Court in 1977 in *Milliken v. Bradley*, 433 U.S. 267. When the original trial judge died, his successor ordered the Detroit School Board to submit proposed desegregation plans. The District Court then ordered the Detroit Board and the state defendants to institute comprehensive programs in four educational components: reading, in-service teacher training, testing, and counseling.

The State of Michigan defendants sought review by the Supreme Court challenging those components. The Court concluded the District Court's decree was aptly tailored to remedy the consequences of Michigan's constitutional violation, comment-

1971: Michigan parents people picket local schools in protest of bussing. (Photo by Michael Mauney/Time Life Pictures/Getty Images)

ing, "Children who have been thus educationally and culturally set apart from the larger community will inevitably acquire habits of speech, conduct, and attitudes reflecting their cultural isolation. They are likely to acquire speech habits, for example, which vary from the environment in which they must ultimately function and compete, if they are to enter and be a part of that community."

This decade also brought the issue of affirmative action before the United States Supreme Court.

Housing issues included a 1971 case involving the Metropolitan Housing Development Corporation's application to the Village of Arlington Heights, a suburb of Chicago, for rezoning of a fifteen-acre parcel for planned townhouse units for low- and moderate-income tenants. The Village denied the application, and MHDC brought suit, alleging racial discrimination.

The Supreme Court issued its opinion in 1977 in *Arlington Heights v. Metropolitan Housing Development*, 429 U.S. 252, finding that official action does not violate the Equal Protection Clause solely because it results in racially disproportionate impact. Discriminatory intent or purpose is required, and the Village had first adopted a zoning map in 1959, when the area had been zoned R-3. The Court commented, "if the property involved here always had been zoned R-5 but suddenly was changed to R-3 when the town learned of MHDC's plans to erect integrated housing, we would have a different case."

This decade also brought the issue of affirmative action before the United States Supreme Court. Economist Gunnar Myrdal had long advocated a form of positive discrimination or affirmative action to remedy past wrongs. It was viewed as a moral and political necessity with its reasoning deeply rooted in American history. The argument was that in a country already tainted by past discrimination, if laws and opportunities were just neutral, there could never be equal protection because the effects of past discrimination would be continued. Advocates and supporters for affirmative action contended that individual assessment of specific instances of past discrimination was a hopeless task, and urged the use of quotas. They argued that whites had a chance for upward mobility by reason of their whiteness.

Haywood Burns, dean of the law school of City University of New York, noted in 1978, "Even if it involved changing the name, the accent, style of dress, getting more education, the ladder was there for them. . . . [¶] . . . Surely every white person, however free of direct implication in victimizing non-whites, is still a daily beneficiary of white dominance—past and present."[380]

Some of the solutions backed by supporters of affirmative action had been specifically avoided in the 1960s when President Johnson, fearing his 1964 civil rights bill would fall into oblivion, compromised with a key amendment that forbade racial quotas. Title VII forbade race discrimination in hiring and firing and applied to all employers of twenty-five or more workers in an industry that affected commerce. Either the Equal Employment Opportunity Commission (EEOC), an enforcement agency created by the 1964 Civil Rights Act, or the victim could bring an action in court. Historian Paul Johnson accuses one of the early heads of the EEOC of brushing aside the quota-prohibition provision in the Act by imposing quotas.[381]

Title VII forbade race discrimination in hiring and firing and applied to all employers of twenty-five or more workers in an industry that affected commerce.

When the EEOC began operation, race discrimination was epidemic in the job market.[382] Racial quotas became a way of corporate life in the 1970s. AT&T tripled its number of minority managers. Black employees at IBM increased from 750 in 1960 to 16,564 in 1980. Numerous agencies oversaw the rights of minorities, forcing employers to face a formidable bureaucratic army: The Civil Rights Commission, the Labor Department's Office of Federal Contract Compliance Commission, the Equal Employment Opportunity Commission, the Office of Minority Business Enterprise as well as departments within Justice; Defense; and Health, Education and Welfare.[383] Some accused employers of going underground with discriminatory procedures and practices that appeared neutral, but had a discriminatory impact. Eventually Title VII's range and scope reached the highest court.

The Supreme Court first legitimized a form of affirmative action in *Griggs v. Duke Power Co.*, 401 U.S. 424. An employer required either a high school education or passing intelligence tests as a condition of employment. In 1971, the Court unanimously held that discriminatory impact was an important element to be considered under the Civil Rights Act of 1964, noting "The objective of Congress in the enactment of Title VII is plain from the language of the statute. It was to achieve equality of employment opportunities and remove barriers that have operated in the past to favor an identifiable group of white employees over other employees." The opinion observes that, "diplomas and tests are useful servants, but Congress has mandated the common-sense proposition that they are not to become masters of reality."

The practical effect of the case was that employment practices that had discriminatory impact were illegal, unless they could be justified as a business necessity. When a disparate impact was shown, the burden was given to the employer to give good reason why it did what it did, or be defeated in court.

Griggs was put to the test in 1975 in *Albemarle Paper Co. v. Moody*, 422 U.S. 405. Like the employer in *Griggs*, Albemarle used two general ability tests to evaluate non-

The Court declared that hard and fast racial quotas in college admissions were unconstitutional, but allowed schools to use race as a factor to achieve a diverse student body.

verbal intelligence and verbal ability. A few months before trial, the company engaged a psychology expert to validate its tests. The Court noted the company's study focused on job groups near the top that consisted of nearly all white workers, and did not indicate the tests permissibly measured basic qualifications of new workers, concluding Albemarle did not prove the job relatedness of its testing program. The Court remanded the case to the trial court to consider whether the black workers should receive back pay.

Affirmative action in higher education came to the Court in *Regents of the University of California v. Bakke*, 438 U.S. 265, in 1978. Allan Bakke, who was white, applied to medical school at the university's Davis campus. The school reserved sixteen of its one hundred slots for minority students. Even though Bakke had higher grades and better scores than some of the minority students accepted, he was denied admission. Bakke sued for reverse discrimination. The Court declared that hard and fast racial quotas in college admissions were unconstitutional, but allowed schools to use race as a factor to achieve a diverse student body.

The Court dealt with quotas head-on in *Fullilove v. Klutznick*, 448 U.S. 448. The action was brought by a group of non-minority contractors who did business with the federal government in public works projects. The dispute arose as a result of the Public Works Employment Act passed by Congress in 1977. The Act provided for a ten percent set-aside for minority business enterprises. Non-minority contractors argued they were denied equal protection and due process rights protected by the Fifth Amendment.

Six of the justices upheld the set-asides, but for different reasons. Justices Rehnquist, Stewart and Stevens dissented. Justices Marshall, Brennan and Blackmun relied on the rationale in *Bakke*. Since the statute did not elevate any group to a status of racial superiority, the stringent test of equal protection applied to racial distinctions did not apply. However, the three justices thought a higher judicial scrutiny was needed because of the risk of imposing unfair burdens on innocent persons. They found the contractor set-asides withstood their heightened scrutiny. The remaining three Justices, Burger, Powell and White, found that Congress had the authority to legislate the set-asides under the Commerce Clause and the Fourteenth Amendment's Enforcement Clause.

1971-1980
Hollywood

IF 1970S MOVIES ARE CAREFULLY examined, one might think that Hollywood and Washington, D.C. were on different planets. Every so often, there was a hint in a film about what was going on in the law handed down by the Supreme Court. For example, blacks appear in background shots at businesses, or there is a passing reference to affirmative action. Sometimes one or two black children are in the same classroom with white children. But most films portray African Americans in a negative way during the 1970s, while the Court, no matter how far to the right it went, displayed some sensitivity to blacks, albeit in decreasing amounts. On the other hand, the sterile opinions from the Court do not provide many clues about the simmering rage found in real life, as well as on the silver screen.

The movie business was in deep financial trouble as this decade began. MGM, once Hollywood's grandest studio, even had to auction off the ruby slippers worn by Judy Garland in *The Wizard of Oz,* and *Ben-Hur*'s chariot.[384] With *Cotton Comes to Harlem* (1970), it was almost by accident the industry realized it could increase its profits in marketing directly to African American audiences by appealing to their racial emotions. Then the industry sought to increase the numbers further by seducing whites away from their television sets. This was done by making vigilante movies that appealed directly to the racial emotions of whites, and also by toning down race issues in the black movies to draw crossover audiences. In other words, Hollywood drew black audiences to the theaters by portraying whites as being racial bigots. Then it made movies to heat up white frustrations with blacks. Combining the newly lenient obscenity laws with race issues, violence and action, films drew racially mixed audiences to increase profits. Hollywood's more lasting salvation came with a new generation of filmmakers such as Francis Ford Coppola and Steven Spielberg.[385]

The sterile opinions from the Court do not provide many clues about the simmering rage found in real life, as well as on the silver screen.

The film industry sunk to an economic low of $15.8 million average weekly box office proceeds in 1971, compared to pre-World War II highs of $90 million.[386] Hollywood was by then well aware of the increasing black box office possibilities. Black Americans had been pushed into core-area ghettos of the North in a rigidly maintained system of apartheid.[387] After years of urban riots and rebellion, whites fled to the suburbs, leaving blacks behind in the cities. Centers such as downtown Atlanta and Chicago's Loop became predominately black entertainment areas.[388] Profits from a rising black box office proved irresistible to Hollywood, and the "Blaxploitation" movement took off.[389]

These films were filled with sadistic brutality, sleazy sex, racial slurs and the patois of the streets. Film critic Pauline Kael said that except when the country was at war, such racism was never seen on the screen.[390] But this time, the racism was against whites. "Whites were moral lepers, most of whom were psychotically anti-black and whose vocabulary was laced with the rhetoric of bigotry," wrote film historian Daniel J. Leab.[391] Many inferior products earned millions from black moviegoers in rundown urban theaters.[392]

The picture that launched the new style and spirit of the 1970s[393] was *Cotton Comes to Harlem*, based on a novel by black writer Chester Himes.[394] The movie portrays blacks with pride and fun. There are no apologies or condescension for cultural ways of life or black humor. Unrepentant recognition of the value of being black was given, with such lines as "Seems to me, there's a whole lot of money in just bein' black these days." The opening lines of the movie are Ossie Davis lyrics, "Ain't now, but it's gonna be, black enough for me." African robes and hats abounded. Upbeat music boomed as the screen filled with ethnic marquis proclaiming, FATHER DIVINE'S; BIG WILT'S; HOME OF SOUL FOOD; DEACON JONES-SUNDAY STYLE CHICKEN; HARLEM GRILL; EBONY SUPER MARKETS; APOLLO THEATRE.

Dissension and distinctions between blacks and whites were underscored throughout the film. White characters are seen as thugs, junk dealers, gangsters and

Profits from a rising black box office proved irresistible to Hollywood, and the "Blaxploitation" movement took off.

morons,[395] while black characters are given a much higher value. A black detective remarks to a suspect, "You steal money from white folk, that's your business. But you steal it from black folk, that's my business." And remarks such as, "Black people bein' exploited by white people." When a black witness clarified how he could identify the race of masked men, he explained, "They ran white." Another exclaimed, "Honkeys in the woodpile." A sexy and gorgeous black woman enticed a white police officer into undressing. Wearing nothing but a paper sack over his head, he ended up locked out of her apartment. Another white police official made decisions about an expected race riot in front of a grinning Richard Nixon on a wall calendar.

Cotton was a success and an unabashed moneymaker.[396] The movie cost $1.2 million to make, and grossed over $5.5 million domestically.[397] *Variety* predicted that even Southern exhibitors would want a piece of the action.[398]

Black movies sold. *Shaft* was even more successful. The film was more celebratory of blacks without running down and alienating

An Italian poster for the film, Shaft, *starring Richard Roundtree and directed by Gordon Parks, 1971. (Photo by MGM Studios/ Courtesy of Getty Images)*

whites to the extent in *Cotton*, and attracted more white moviegoers.[399] Film histori-an Donald Bogle says: "This little picture, which its studio, MGM, thought might make a little money, instead made a mint—some $12 million within a year in North America alone—and single-handedly saved MGM from financial ruin."[400] According to Darius James a.k.a. Dr. Snakeskin, eight and a half million tickets were sold, and "the result was a conventional action film for general audiences, enlivened by its Black cast members."[401]

Black pride was stressed throughout the film. Shaft was assertive and individu-alistic, and not intimidated by whites, "giving the finger" to a driver who objected to his jay-walking. His office was stylishly decorated with modern furniture and African art. He took a shower and had sex with a white woman, but obviously respected and far preferred his black girlfriend. A new handshake appeared. Characters called each other "Brother" or "Soul Brother," and black frustration was highlighted with such scenes as a taxi driver speeding away from a potential black fare to pick up a white man. When Shaft was asked whether he had any problems, he responded, "Yeah, I gotta coupla them. I was born black and I was born poor." "Just wanta find out his views on urban renewal," was another of Shaft's remarks.

Cooley High, one of the last Blaxploitation films made, is considered by some to be one of the best films of this period. While some say it mutated into something resem-bling a brainless television sitcom,[402] it managed to portray how exquisitely sad the life of a black child in the ghetto could be. In the movie, the black youths attend Edwin G. Cooley Vocational High School. All of the pupils are black. Two of the fac-ulty are portrayed, one black, one white. The white teacher is awkward and inept. Mr. Mason, the black teacher, is kind, caring and competent.

Cooley High can be compared to the contemporary white youths in *American Graffiti* (AFI's #77), which demonstrates the vastly different experiences of black and white teenagers. *Graffiti*'s school is slightly integrated, and shows just a handful of black students in crowd scenes. In both movies, the boys lash out at the police with pranks and escape by driving away. The difference is the white boys have their own cars, while the black boys joyride in someone else's car. *Graffiti*'s boys bear no conse-quences for their actions, but *Cooley*'s boys are later arrested for grand theft auto.

The Modesto, California white neighborhood in *Graffiti* is dream-come-true Americana, with the clean and well-decorated Mel's Drive-in, complete with roller-skating waitresses delivering hamburgers and milkshakes. The black neighborhood displays utter decay and hopelessness, the teen hangout being the crumbling Martha's Rib Shack, featuring soul food and pig ears, and a meat cleaver-wielding proprietor.

The white kids talk about picnics at the canyon and at the lake. The subject of jail most commonly comes up with the black kids. For the whites, it is Buddy Holly and the Beach Boys; for the blacks, it's Smokey Robinson and the Temptations. In both movies, the teenagers want their alcohol. The white boys find it difficult to obtain, while it is readily available to the black boys. *Cooley's* high school has peeling, filthy, graffiti strewn walls; its bathrooms are disgusting. *Graffiti's* school is pristine. The black kids have a dance in a crowded tenement apartment, while the whites enjoy a well-maintained gym, with a prize given to the committee who did the wonderful decorations.

In each movie, a boy receives a scholarship to college. *Graffiti's* recipient, Curt, ponders his option to refuse the scholarship and attend a local college instead, and is able to have talks with his family around the dinner table. *Cooley's* Cochise irritates his mother when he asks whether he received his scholarship letter, and accidentally finds the baby floating the letter in the toilet. Curt not only has the support of his family, community leaders in the Moose Lodge are behind him, while Cochise has no one, with the possible exception of Mr. Mason. The teacher is the only black person of authority available to any of the black kids. They have mothers, but no fathers are shown. Both boys accept the scholarship, but, while Curt is last seen at the airport leaving for college, Cochise is last seen being lowered into the ground in a coffin after being beaten to death.

Vigilante films provided a countercurrent to Blaxploitation, and sent thinly-veiled racist messages.

Vigilante films provided a countercurrent to Blaxploitation,[403] and sent thinly-veiled racist messages. Ed Guerrero says these films "seemed to transcode a large, conservative white audience's early 1970s desire to, at least on the screen, suppress the black revolt in all its manifestations and the white liberal—left social and cultural agenda built during the 1960s with the violent mechanisms of vigilante action and an aggressive criminal justice apparatus."[404]

Detective Harry Callahan is disgusted with restraints on police brutality and the constitutional rights of suspects at the same time real life politicians used the code words "law and order" to denote racial issues. One of *Dirty Harry's* most famous scenes has the intolerant, rebel cop pointing his 44-magnum at a horizontal African American armed robber at the end of a gun battle. He expended five or six bullets. "You've got to ask yourself one question," Harry's says mockingly, 'Do I feel lucky'? Well, do you punk?" The bank robber submits to the police and looks up at Harry pleadingly, "I gots to know." Harry points his magnum dead-on his captive, and shoots from an empty chamber.

Tension between the races is crudely laid out in *Walking Tall*. Set in Tennessee, the law and order action film has a character who proclaims about a black man: "I know'd him since he was a pickaninny. Hired his ol' daddy many times. Well, he got educated, see? Then he come down with that new social disease, black power. . . . I believe in equality just as much as anybody, but I don't want it forced on me."

The film industry realized that, with a toned down black-white social confrontation formula, it did not need an exclusively black film to attract the large black audiences that had saved Hollywood from financial disaster.

When a black man declines to cooperate with the police, the sheriff says, "They got eight dead niggers stretched out over there. All died from poison, rot gut whiskey made from someplace up around here. You've been shootin' your mouth off all over this county about how you want to help your people. I'm tryin' to give you a chance."

Spewing the same outrage as Harry Callahan over the rights of criminals, *Walking Tall*'s sheriff rails against suspects being released on "technicalities," such as the requirement for a search warrant and the right to counsel.

Death Wish is the epitome of vigilante films. The film takes place in New York City. Early in the film, crime statistics of fifteen to twenty-one murders a week provoke a character to remark, in code for whites to flee to the suburbs, "Decent people are going to have to work here and live somewhere else." Another says, "The underprivileged are beating our God damned brains out." "Stick 'em in concentration camps. That's what I say," is muttered. Known in the movie as ordinary man Paul Kersey, Charles Bronson single handedly reduces crime, after his wife and daughter are brutally attacked—and he is mugged by a black man. "More blacks are muggers than whites," one character states with conviction.

Blaxploitation saw its demise in the mid-1970s. Black audiences tired of the industry's cheap, endless reworkings of crime in the ghetto, and the film industry realized that, with a toned down black-white social confrontation formula, it did not need an exclusively black film to attract the large black audiences that had saved Hollywood from financial disaster. Thus, the film industry developed "crossover" films. Using the same formulaic ingredients of sex, violence and action as they had in black films, they could draw both blacks and whites.[405] For example, 35 percent of the audience for the megahit, *The Godfather* (1972 Best Picture of the Year and AFI's #3) was black, even though it had several script lines such as a mafia leader's derisive remark, "In my city we would keep the traffic in the dark people, the coloreds. They're animals anyway, so let them lose their souls."

Once Hollywood had its "crossover" formula down pat, it significantly reduced the number of films that focused on blacks, whether positively or negatively. In 1972, thirty-nine of Hollywood's 229 films were focused on blacks, but by 1977, that number was reduced to four out of 311. Later in the decade, the film industry returned to politically conservative films, often produced with slick technology. The shift to the right coincided with the formation of megamedia conglomerates that replaced the studios. The days of experimentation as a way of stimulating the market with new ideas, such as the compromising Sidney Poitier roles of the 1960s, were over.[406] Guerrero accuses the industry of deciding "that its most profitable course lay in ignoring the demands of minorities for fair representation and rebuilding its older practices and paradigms."[407]

Not considered a vigilante film, *Network* (1976, AFI's #66) delivered the same message of white discontent toward blacks. The film demonstrates mainstream Hollywood's shift to the right, along with raw antipathy toward blacks. A mentally deteriorating newscaster tells his television audience, "If there's anyone out there who can look around this demented slaughterhouse we live in and tell me that man is a not a demented creature, believe me that man is full of bullshit. I don't have to tell you things are bad out there. Everyone knows. There's a depression. Everybody's out of work or scared of losing their job. The dollar buys a nickel's worth. Banks are going bust. Shopkeepers keep a gun under the counter. Punks are running wild in the street and there's nobody anywhere who seems to know what to do—and there's no end to it. . . . We sit watching TVs while some local newscaster tells us today we had fifteen homicides and sixty-three violent crimes—as if that's the way things are supposed to be. We know things are bad. They're crazy. It's as if everything everywhere is crazy so we don't go out anymore. We sit in the house and slowly the world we're living in is getting smaller and all we say is 'Please leave us alone in our living room. Let me at least have my toaster and my TV and my steel belted radials and I won't say anything. Just leave us alone.'"

One interview on the fictional network is of an obvious Angela Davis look-alike, shown as a radical revolutionary who cavorts with criminals. The black woman attorney, with a huge curly hair-do says, "I'm Loreen Hobbs, a bad ass commie nigger," and "The Communist Party believes that the most pressing political necessity today is the consideration of the revolutionary, radical and democratic movements into a united front." She provides the network with footage of a bank robbery by a white heiress under the auspices of a black man named Ahmed Khan, leader of the Ecumenical Liberation Army. Ahmed Khan is shown at his hideout chewing fried chicken with grease dripping from his chin, while he spews filthy words. He is clearly irrational and dangerous. At the end of the movie, he brutally massacres the television newsman.

The only speaking parts for blacks are the radical woman attorney, terrorist

Ahmed Khan and a security guard who greets a white executive as he opens the door for him, sending the message that the only good black is the one who is serving whites. Numerous television audiences are shown, but the only black in any of them is the terrorist Ahmed Khan who comes to assassinate the star.

Other films reveal Hollywood's return to ignoring blacks or using them in disrespectful and stereotypical roles.

Rocky (1976 Best Picture of the Year and AFI's #78) could also be included in the group of movies that represented white anger toward blacks. In its story about a poor white man who takes on black champion Apollo Creed in the boxing ring, it featured an implied racial contest with the triumph of the white working class over blacks.[408]

White antagonism toward blacks was also demonstrated in *Star Wars* (1977, AFI's #15). The story line is a white versus black allegory that celebrates the recovery of patriarchy and militarism.[409] The fantasy has old white men in charge with clearly defined societal levels. All non-white characters were not human. "[W]hite people, particularly white males are constructed as the sole and sovereign human norm, contrasted to the 'Wookies' and an assorted myriad of exotic creatures and humanoids, especially as depicted in the film's memorable bar scene."[410] The Star Wars cantina had rules regarding "Droids." "We don't serve that kind here." White is constructed as goodness, most specifically with Princess Leia and her flowing white gown, while the nefarious Darth Vader, whose voice sounds like James Earl Jones, has black armor and a black space station.[411]

Other films reveal Hollywood's return to ignoring blacks or using them in disrespectful and stereotypical roles. The only blacks in *The Godfather* are shown as servants of a Hollywood producer in a 1945 scene. In *Chinatown* (1974, AFI's #19), the only black actor in its 1930s Los Angeles setting is a morgue attendant who callously eats and drinks over a dead body. In *A Clockwork Orange* (1971, AFI's #46), the only black actors are a few inmates in prison.

One Flew Over the Cuckoos Nest (1975, AFI's #20) is set in 1963 on a psychiatric ward. All of the ward's patients are white, and the ward doctor and nurses are white. All of the ward's orderlies are black, and at times quite savage and brutal. While there is some compassion shown blacks in the movie there is an overall negative portrayal and the sympathy is more a statement that whites thought blacks had gone too far. A television in the background of one scene has a newscaster reporting the bombing of a black church in Birmingham, Alabama, where children were killed while they were attending services. He finishes the story, "Police say the men will be held on misdemeanor charges pending full investigation."

Taxi Driver (1976, AFI's #46) refers to blacks as "spooks," "jungle bunnies" and "niggers," and one husband is livid because his wife is having an affair with a black man.

Black antipathy toward and suspicion of white police and courts, described at the turn of the century by W.E.B. DuBois,[412] was evident throughout the decade. All of the Blaxploitation and vigilante movies portray blacks as mistrusting police and having distain toward authorities. *The French Connection* (1971 Best Picture of the Year

Many more black actors appeared in 1970s movies than in previous decades. Possibly this was due to Justice Department intervention to end discrimination in the film industry.

and AFI's #70) shows police going into a black bar twice during the movie, and hatred is shown in the eyes of black patrons as they are rousted by white officers. Later, two cops beat a black dope user to get the man's drug connection from him. The main detective character warns his partner, "Never trust a nigger."

Other films were less direct, but contained the clear message that the rules are different with blacks when it comes to crime and the police. *Annie Hall* (1977 Best Picture of the Year and AFI's #31) has Woody Allen's father upset because his wife fired the cleaning woman, remarking, "She's a colored woman from Harlem. She's a right to steal from us. Who's she going to steal from, if not us?" *The Sting* (1973 Best Picture of the Year) has a scene where a woman openly talks about her life of stealing as she is the midst of telling her daughter to hurry so they won't be late for church.

Despite numerous films that suggest resentment toward African Americans, there were some movies that respectfully reflect advances made by American blacks in the 1970s. Many more black actors appeared in 1970s movies than in previous decades. Possibly this was due to Justice Department intervention to end discrimination in the film industry. In response to Justice, Hollywood instituted a job pool for minorities.[413] Black contributions to the Vietnam War were recognized in *Apocalypse Now* (1979, AFI's #28), and *The Deer Hunter* (1978 Best Picture of the Year and AFI's #79).

Three of five crew members on a small boat, the center of much of *Apocalypse*, were black, including an older crew chief who carefully watched over an eighteen-year-old black crew member. They were displayed so sympathetically that the saddest parts of the tragic film were when the younger black man was shot and the older was speared to death. In fact, when the chief died, a white crew member cleaned him up, kissed him, and performed as reverent and loving a funeral as was possible along the river in the midst of combat.

The Deer Hunter opened with scenes of blacks and whites working side by side at a small town Pennsylvania refinery, which indicated they were all members of the same union. After work, they chatted as they walked away from the plant, lunch pails in hands. The film also showed significant numbers of pitifully wounded and injured black soldiers both at an Army hospital in Saigon and a Veterans Hospital in Pennsylvania. At the Pennsylvania hospital, there was a pretty and sexy black nurse, with black doctors in the background.

Raging Bull (1980, AFI's #24) held up Sugar Ray Robinson as a boxing superstar. *Jaws* (1975, AFI's #48) had blacks in crowd scenes, a black police officer and black families on the beach. *Close Encounters of the Third Kind* (1977, AFI's #64) has few black actors, but it did manage to portray two working in jobs that indicated labor union membership. One played an air traffic controller in Indianapolis and the other was a trash collector in Muncie. *Kramer v. Kramer* (1979 Best Picture of the Year) has several scenes outside a Manhattan grammar school with parents dropping off and picking up their children, including a well-dressed black father. Even *Network* had several blacks in non-managerial, non-speaking parts at the fictional corporate headquarters.

Black actors were given special respect a few times, even if they were gone from the screen in the blink of an eye.

Black actors were given special respect a few times, even if they were gone from the screen in the blink of an eye. Perhaps departing from history, *Godfather, Part II* (1974 Best Picture of the Year and AFI's #32) has a 1901 scene showing two African immigrants, one man and one woman at Ellis Island. The woman has the only speaking black part when she states her one syllable name. It also shows a black FBI agent long before there actually were black agents in the FBI.[414] The general's orderly in *Patton* (1970 Best Picture of the Year and AFI's #89), the only black actor in the film, had better insight and judgment than the famous white man. *The Sting* managed to build the plot around a respected older black man named Luther, who taught whites the art of being a con-man, but he was shown for only a few minutes. A few other black actors played bit parts.

Family Plot (1976) was Alfred Hitchcock's last film. Sure enough, he took a final cheap shot. An amateur sleuth in search of a white man named Arthur Adamson, heir to a fortune, finds a worker with that name whose head is hidden in a ceiling when she first questions him. When he pulls out his face, the "joke" is revealed. He is black.

*Movies not discussed in text appear in endnote.[415]

1971-1980
Decade Wrap-up

IRONICALLY HOLLYWOOD CAN THANK THE Supreme Court for helping the film industry out of its financial doldrums in the 1970s. The Court's liberalization of obscenity laws indirectly contributed to the success of Blaxploitation films, allowing tolerance for the depiction of explicit sex, violence and graphic language on the screen.[416]

The Court also did a great deal to shape the lives of African Americans in society during this decade, by continuing enforcement of school desegregation, monitoring equal access to housing and forcing employers to cease discriminatory hiring. Hollywood did just as much to reflect African Americans in a negative light by reflecting them as highly sexual and prone to crime. Some movies, however, did accurately reflect advancements by blacks in America.

While the film industry was able to pull itself out of financial disaster at the expense of African American dignity, the Supreme Court lost a lot of respect among Americans during this time. From the point of view of many races, the Supreme Court had run amok. The busing cases were despised. *Miranda v. Arizona*, 384 U.S. 436, 1966, was seen as giving too much power to criminals. *Roe v. Wade*, 410 U.S. 113, 1973, was viewed as an abomination. Such cases as *Cohen v. California*, 403 U.S. 15, 1971, upholding a person's right to wear a jacket proclaiming "fuck the draft" to be free speech were considered scandalous. *Byrne v. Karalexis*, 401 U.S. 216, 1971, which upheld a ban on prosecutions for the exhibition of dirty films, was believed disgraceful.

Meanwhile, many feared the rest of the country was going to hell in a hand basket. Four Kent State University students were killed by the National Guard in 1970. Lieutenant William Calley was convicted of murder at the My Lai massacre in 1971. America lost a war for the first time. Women across the country burned their bras and stormed into universities.

Despite racial rage, discontent, and disrespect for the Court, African Americans made advancements both in the Court and the movies.

It was at this low ebb for the country, a time many white Americans were moody and rampantly discontent, that African Americans demanded their due. Rage from white America could best be summed up by the maid's lament in *Guess Who's Coming to Dinner*: "Civil rights is one thing. This here is sumpin' else."

Despite racial rage, discontent, and disrespect for the Court, African Americans made advancements both in the Court and the movies. United States Supreme Court cases stopped employers in their discriminatory tracts in several cases, thus shaping new racial workplace standards. Even with the exploitive films of decade, movies did portray blacks in the workplace in *The Deer Hunter, Network, Close Encounters of the Third Kind, Jaws, One Flew Over the Cuckoo's Nest, Taxi Driver* and *Godfather, Part II*.

The Court imposed school integration within school districts, and *Cooley High* provided a strong indication that school segregation in big, black-destination cities was alive and well. And movies did reflect at least some desegregated schools in *American Graffiti, Dirty Harry* and *Kramer v. Kramer*. Films also portrayed blacks and whites to be comrades, and even friends at times in *Apocalypse Now, The Deerhunter, Rocky* and *The Sting*.

Yet, while blacks advanced in the movies in some ways, they retreated in others. Blacks were almost never shown in a family setting, and when they were there was a strong negative overtone. In *The Sting,* there was a warm scene of a black family getting ready for church. The problem is that both parents were lifelong thieves. *Cotton's* black homes resembled houses of ill repute. A den of black terrorists was shown around their kitchen table in *Network. Cooley High* had a few in-home scenes, but, as already noted, there were no fathers and each home was the essence of poverty.

A dozen or more movies portrayed blacks involved with the police or crime, so America was not given the slightest hint by Hollywood that hardworking, decent, family-oriented African Americans existed in the 1970s. This is not to say that

America was not given the slightest hint by Hollywood that hardworking, decent, family-oriented African Americans existed in the 1970s.

Hollywood should have *always* portrayed African Americans as middle-class success stories from a pie-in-the-sky view such as television's Cosby family. Rather, Hollywood *never* portrayed African Americans as anything but dysfunctional and criminal, unless they were mere silent backdrops.

For some segment of the 1970's African American population, *Cooley High's* depiction of African Americans frequently discussing the police was, in fact, stunningly realistic. As mentioned, real life African Americans knew their chances of having law enforcement contact were disproportionately high. The movie's portraying the boys being charged with grand theft auto is in accord with the New York judges' study mentioned earlier, which showed black youths were almost always charged with grand theft while whites were only charged with unauthorized use of a vehicle.

The conditions at both fictional high schools were also quite realistic. Witness *Swann v. Charlotte-Mecklenburg*. Student populations were almost 100 percent black in some schools and 100 percent white in others. The federal court was concerned about inferior teachers in the all-black schools. Residences and public accommodations for the races were separated in *Swann*, just as they were in *Cooley's* Chicago, and Mayor Daley's real Chicago. *Swann* mentions there were racial restrictions in deeds to land, separation in public accommodations and zoning ordinances, and that black children scored far lower on standardized tests. The real case of *Milliken v. Bradley* discusses how white flight to the suburbs—just as with *Cooley* and *American Graffiti*—resulted

Low-angle shot of actor Clint Eastwood pointing his pistol in a still from the film Dirty Harry, *directed by Don Siegel, 1971. (Photo by Warner Bros./ 8Courtesy of Getty Images)*

In barraging millions of movie viewers with depictions of African Americans as criminals, Hollywood was not reflecting society; it was shaping it.

in suburban schools that had 81 percent white students. *Milliken's* inner-city schools suffered from inferior reading, in-service teacher training, testing, and counseling as compared with well-equipped white schools in the suburbs.

Since Blaxploitation movies introduced distasteful sexual scenes into popular movies, blacks were often blamed for lacking decency and causing deterioration and filth in American society. Sixties movies portrayed blacks as believing in the concept of equality for all. In some 1970s films, blacks actively discriminated against whites on the basis of race, and joined with whites in imposing ethnic discrimination on other groups. For example, Shaft called an Italian a wop after he was called a nigger. In *Apocalypse Now,* blacks were shown killing Vietnamese civilians with little cause, and referred to them as "slopes" and "gooks," as did their white comrades.

Even though the United States Supreme Court is said to have turned right in the 1970s, its rulings were consistently in favor of equal rights and opportunities for African Americans. Employers were forced to hire on an equal basis. Public schools were monitored to achieve desegregation. Schools of higher education were permitted to use race as a factor in admissions policies. When the issue was brought before it, the Court clamped down on discrimination in housing. The Court also endorsed set-asides for minority contractors.

Deciding constitutional issues is the Court's job, and Hollywood's job is making money. But most businesses are held accountable in some way, either by stockholders or regulators. With First Amendment concerns, Hollywood does not have to worry about accounting to anything but the box office. The film industry practiced no self-control in the 1970s when it pitted black and white against each other. With the exception of a few seconds of an E.R. doctor in *Dirty Harry*, not one movie studied reflected the tremendous successes of African Americans, while more than a third portrayed blacks as criminals. In barraging millions of movie viewers with depictions of African Americans as criminals, Hollywood was not reflecting society; it was shaping it. And once shaped, it perpetuated with sequels and similar story lines.

Another conclusion can also be drawn: Hollywood makes money by giving people what they want, while the Supreme Court is supposed to resist dominant opinion, especially on issues such as race. On the other hand, perhaps the Supreme Court's ordering busing and affirmative action while Hollywood served up racism and violence yields a striking lesson on just how out of touch with popular sentiment the Court had become.

1981-1990
Racial Framework

DURING THE 1980S, OUR NATION became more vast and complex. The population of the United States increased by 27,164,068 during the 1980s, as much as the population of a medium to large European country.[417] It was time for black Americans to move fully into the system.[418] Gradually, middle class black Americans left the cities for better homes and schools and lower crime rates in the suburbs. When the 1980s began, almost 40 percent of African Americans were in the economic middle class. Lower class blacks were left in concentrated intercity poverty, but not without some political power. By the end of the 1980s, African Americans served as mayors of hundreds of American cities.

Even Chicago, after two decades of rule by Richard Daley's democratic machine, elected black Harold Washington, who had impressive military and educational credentials.[419] No doubt some of the political achievements can be attributed to successful lawsuits under the Voting Rights Act. By federal law, city councils must redistrict their cities on the basis of new census data by December 1 of the year following the taking of a national census. Some people credit part of Harold Washington's success in Chicago to a federal court decision ordering the redrawing of racially discriminatory district lines.[420] Black and Hispanic plaintiffs sued the Chicago City Council for violating the Act when it drew the map of Chicago's fifty wards for voting district lines in 1981. The courts ordered the map re-drawn so that both black and Hispanic voters would have a reasonable opportunity to elect candidates of their choice.[421]

But all was not upbeat for African Americans during the 1980s. Some attributed Ronald Reagan's popularity and two presidential victories to white conservative reaction to civil rights gains. Whites ascribed labor and economic woes to advancement of blacks. According to authors James Oliver Horton and Lois E. Horton, "[t]his triumph of the right wing encouraged blatant racism and prompted more racial violence than had occurred in twenty years."[422]

Some attributed Ronald Reagan's popularity and two presidential victories to white conservative reaction to civil rights gains.

Historians Klinkner and Smith claim Reagan appealed to white racial resentments from the time he was first elected as governor of California in 1966, and that racial animosities were critical to his success at drawing "Reagan Democrats" to vote for him in both 1980 and 1984. They point out that Reagan kicked off his presidential campaign in 1980 in Philadelphia, Mississippi—a city that bore scars from the 1964 murders of three civil rights workers—with symbolisms to inflame white anger by declaring, "I believe in states' rights." They accuse Reagan of using such phrases as "strapping young bucks" and "Cadillac-driving welfare queens" in his rhetoric to appeal to white resentment of blacks. Reagan severely criticized affirmative action, and "whites were now portrayed as the chief victims of discrimination."[423]

Some even perceived affirmative action as illegal. As a Senate compromise to avoid a filibuster, the 1964 Civil Rights Act did not embrace positive discrimination. It was not until it was given the authority of the Supreme Court in the 1971 case of *Griggs v. Duke Power Company* that it received legitimacy. From the perspective of many Americans, inequality had been introduced into the law. People began pointing to statistics to show that it was only well-off blacks and Hispanics who benefited from racial preferences, at the expense of the poor of all races.

According to historian Paul Johnson, "Affirmative Action in universities led to massive lowering of admission standards in such key schools of medicine. Thus, by the early 1990s, less than half of black medical-school graduates passed their National Board Exams for medical certification, compared to 88 percent among whites."[424]

The climate in America was sometimes openly racist during this decade. In 1985, pollster Stanley Greenberg conducted a focus group of white Democrats in Macomb County, Michigan, and read a statement by Robert F. Kennedy that was sympathetic to African Americans. One responded, "No wonder they killed him." Another said, "That's bullshit." And, from a third, "I'm fed up with it." Greenberg concluded that there was no historical memory of racism in America, and no tolerance to remedy the results of past injustices.

White politicians openly played the race card. In his 1990 congressional campaign, white Jesse Helms was running behind his black challenger in North Carolina, when he ran an advertisement that showed a pair of white hands crumpling a letter as a voice-over said, "You needed that job and you were the best qualified, but they had to give it to a minority because of a racial quota."[425]

Even the Ku Klux Klan was looming above African Americans during this decade. One secured a Democratic Party primary victory in California[426] and another, David Duke, a former Nazi and Klansman, was elected as a Republican to the Louisiana state legislature in 1989, promising to oppose racial quotas, stop welfare handouts and get tough on crime. He later received substantial white support in his unsuccessful bids for the United States Senate, and then Governor of Louisiana.[427]

Affirmative action was significantly scaled back during the Reagan administrations. The budgets for the Equal Employment Opportunity Commission and the Office of Federal Contract Compliance Programs were substantially cut. President Reagan appointed staunch conservatives to leadership posts, including William Bradford Reynolds to head the Civil Rights Division at the Justice Department. Reynolds promised to fight "the battle of racial quotas, minority set-asides, and forced busing." He appointed Clarence M. Pendleton, Jr., a vigorous opponent of affirmative action to head the National Civil Rights Commission.[428] One of Reagan's nominees to the Supreme Court, Robert Bork, had written about the then-proposed Civil Rights Act of 1964 that the ban on discrimination in public accommodations entailed "a principle of unsurpassed ugliness," as it limited business owners from selecting their own customers. In 1988, Reagan vetoed a civil rights bill.[429] Justice Thurgood Marshall complained, "Reagan has done zero for civil rights."[430]

Regardless of Ronald Reagan's civil rights agenda, America loved him. Had a spare crown been available, it might have been plunked on his head. Reagan set out to restore the confidence and pride of ordinary Americans, and that is just what he did. He ended the faddish equality at the White House, and restored the Marine guard. "Hail to the Chief" was played regularly, and the imperial presidency returned. President Reagan never accepted the notion that America was in a state of decline, and did not hesitate to use the nation's armed forces in the British Falkland Islands, Grenada and Tripoli. The nation stood tall,[431] and by the end of his second term, he was a figure of nearly mythic proportions.[432]

In 1988, Reagan's successor, George H. Bush, was also accused of capitalizing on the country's racial divide by embracing the image of Willie Horton in his presidential campaign. According to Klinkner and Smith, "The 'Willie' Horton imagery served several purposes for the Republicans—it not only conjured up white fears of black crime, but also reinforced the perception of many white voters that the Democrats were overly tolerant of social deviants (read, blacks)."[433] President Bush also vetoed a civil rights bill, passed by Congress after Supreme Court decisions made it difficult to sue under the Civil Rights Act.[434]

The concept of "political correctness" swept the country in the 1980s.

The concept of "political correctness" swept the country in the 1980s. Historian and author Paul Johnson says the classic PC statement was drawn up by John Casteen of the University of Connecticut, who later became president of Thomas Jefferson's University of Virginia. It was in a 1989 student handbook. Johnson said of the handbook: "This urged black, Hispanic, and female students to report all derogatory remarks they heard to the authorities, and it ordered those administering the complaints procedure to 'avoid comments that dissuade victims from pursuing their rights' since such behavior is itself discriminatory and a violation of the policy."[435]

Johnson compares the process to the Salem witch hunts and the Hollywood blacklists, and says it caused many university teachers to lose their jobs and large numbers of students to be expelled.[436]

African Americans finally achieved significant success during this decade. Civil rights leader Jesse Jackson vied to be the presidential nominee for the Democratic Party in both 1984 and 1988.[437] Black entertainers were immensely popular during the 1980s. Bill Cosby, Flip Wilson, Diahann Carroll and Redd Foxx were popular television stars, and Quincy Jones, Tina Turner, Aretha Franklin, Whitney Houston and Michael Jackson dominated popular music.[438] Ordinary black workers also made significant advances. Four decades earlier, only 5 percent were managers or professionals, but by 1990, 20 percent were.[439] Historian Donald Bogle laments, "Perhaps it was not surprising then that many Americans frequently lulled themselves into the assumption that the races were at peace with one another, that inequities ceased to exist, that indeed America's past history of racism had vanished."[440]

1981-1990
The Supreme Court

ONCE THE SUPREME COURT CLEARLY stated in case after case that blatant and overt white supremacy would not be tolerated in the American legal system, racial discrimination issues became less clear. Many statutes were neutral on their face, but, for one reason or another, hit a particular group harder. Those issues were far more blurred and difficult for the Court to sort through. When discrimination was found, it was often enmeshed in serpentine layers, reflecting decades of local practice.

Several cases that involved affirmative action measures to remedy prior discrimination were before the Court during this decade. In 1986, in *Wygant v. Jackson Board of Education*, 476 U.S. 267, the Court considered whether the Constitution prohibits a teacher's union and a local school board from agreeing how layoffs would occur so they can preserve the effects of an affirmative action hiring policy. Non-minority teachers with seniority challenged the agreements that required they be laid off before minority teachers with less seniority. The Court held, while the end was legitimate, the means were not narrowly enough tailored, and less intrusive methods, such as the adoption of hiring goals, were available. In his dissent, Justice Marshall said the decision nullified years of negotiation and compromise designed to solve serious educational problems in the public schools of Jackson, Michigan.

An association of black and Hispanic firefighters in Cleveland, Ohio, called the

Vanguards of Cleveland, filed an action charging the city and municipal officials with discrimination on the basis of race in hiring, job assignments and promotions in the fire department. The Vanguards claimed violations under the Thirteenth and Fourteenth Amendments, and the parties were able to reach an agreement after the city admitted defeat.

The Supreme Court noted that in appropriate cases, courts may provide relief under Title VII that benefit individuals who were not victims of a defendant's discriminatory practices.

Cleveland had been defending claims of race discrimination in civil service jobs for years, including a lawsuit filed by the city's black police officers in 1972. "You don't have to beat us on the head. We finally learned what we had to do and what we had to try to do to comply with the law, and it was the intent of the city to comply with the law fully," the city's lawyer told the trial court. Accordingly, the lower court reviewed the evidence before it, found an historical pattern of racial discrimination in promotions within Cleveland's fire department and entered a consent decree requested by the parties. The court-approved settlement provided remedies for past discrimination, including reserving a fixed number of already-planned promotions for minorities.

The fly in the ointment was the local firefighter's union and the union argued the decree was entered without its consent. In *Local Number 93, International Association of Firefighters, AFL-CIO v. City of Cleveland*, 478 U.S. 501, the Court ruled in 1986 that, while the union was entitled to present evidence and objections, it did not have the power to block the decree of the lower court entered after agreement by the parties. The real issue before the Court, however, was the union's argument that the federal court lacked power under the 1964 Civil Rights Act to provide relief to individuals who were not actual victims of discrimination.

The Supreme Court noted that in appropriate cases, courts may provide relief under Title VII that benefit individuals who were not victims of a defendant's discriminatory practices. It also held that whether or not Title VII precludes forms of relief after trial did not matter, since the court entered the decree following a settlement of the parties. Justice White filed a dissent, and stated an employer may not simply decide to have a racially balanced work force and displace employees of one race to make room for employees of another. Also dissenting, Justice Rehnquist said the lower court should have been required to find that the minority firefighters who will receive preferential promotions were the specific victims of racial discrimination.

In another 1986 union case filed the same day, *Local 28 of the Sheet Metal Workers v. EEOC*, 478 U.S. 421, the Court described the impenetrable barriers to blacks who wanted jobs previously reserved for whites, and concluded beneficiaries of preferential relief need not be the actual victims of discrimination. The Sheet Metal Workers covered the New York metropolitan area. In 1964, the New York Commission for Human Rights determined the union had excluded blacks in violation of state law. In 1975, the union had been found guilty in federal court of engaging in a pattern and practice of discrimination against nonwhite workers, and ordered to end the practices by 1981. In 1982 and 1983, the union was found guilty of civil contempt, fined and ordered to follow an affirmative action plan that provided preferential treatment of nonwhites who had not been victims of discrimination.

Admission to the sheet metal four-year apprentice program was conducted on a nepotistic basis, and involved sponsorship by incumbent union members, which created an impassable blockade for nonwhite applicants. When New York City adopted a plan for the hiring of minority contractors in 1970, Local 28 was the only construction local that refused to comply. In 1974, when the union's total membership, including apprentices and journeymen, reached only 3.19 percent nonwhite workers, Local 28 stopped work rather than give in to the city's attempt to assign six minority trainees to sheet metal contractors who were working on municipal construction. In fact, Local 28 restricted its membership specifically to deny access to nonwhites. To meet increased demands for workers, it recalled white pensioners and used temporary workers from unions all over the country, but refused to use workers from a New York union comprised almost entirely of nonwhites.

The dissent from Justices Rehnquist and Burger accused the majority of expanding the remedies allowed under Title VII of the Civil Rights Act. Justice White allowed that, under some circumstances, non-victims might be permissible beneficiaries of remedies for discrimination, but did not think the record on appeal supported such a decision in this case. Dissenting in part, Justice O'Connor said she disagreed to the extent the remedy included numerical goals that were, in effect, mandatory quotas.

In 1987, the Court was presented with another entity that had a history of consistent resistance to court orders in *United States v. Paradise*, 480 U.S. 149. For almost four decades, the Alabama Department of Public Safety had excluded blacks from all positions. Twelve years after first condemning the Department for its discriminatory practices, the court noted in 1984 that of the six majors, twenty-five captains, thirty-five lieutenants and sixty-five sergeants in the Department, there was not one black, and of the sixty-six corporals, there were only four.

The trial judge fashioned a new order that said until the department complied with the court's order, that at least 50 percent of the promotions to the rank of corporal must be awarded to black troopers (if qualified black candidates were available and if the rank was less than 25 percent black). The Supreme Court affirmed the order, holding that the 50 percent promotion requirement passed its strict scrutiny test, in that it was justified by compelling governmental interest in eliminating discriminatory exclusion of blacks from positions and was narrowly tailored to do just that.

In *City of Richmond v. J.A. Croson Co.*, 488 U.S. 469, the Court found in 1989 that the city could not pass the strict scrutiny test, and also made it clear that past discrimination was a requirement for the types of plans it approved in *Wygant* and *Paradise*. Evidence showed that, although Richmond's population was 50 percent black, only 0.67 percent of its prime construction contracts had been awarded to minority businesses in recent years. The city adopted a plan that required prime contractors who were awarded municipal construction contracts to subcontract at least 30 percent of each contract to minority business enterprises. When a particular construction company was denied a waiver of the set-aside, it brought suit alleging the city's plan was unconstitutional under the Fourteenth Amendment's Equal Protection Clause.

The Supreme Court said Richmond's plan was not narrowly tailored to accomplish a remedial purpose, such as to correct the effects of prior discrimination, and denied some citizens the opportunity to compete for a fixed percentage of public contracts based only on their race, in violation of the Fourteenth Amendment.

Once African Americans landed jobs, they sometimes had to fight discrimination within the workplace. In *Patterson v. McLean Credit Union*, 491 U.S. 164, there were allegations that a black woman was subjected to taunts that blacks were known to work slower than whites and, unlike white employees, was assigned the tasks of sweeping and dusting. She brought suit under section 1981 of the 1866 Civil Rights Act. By the time *Patterson* came to the Court in 1989, President Ronald Reagan's conservative appointees had changed the Court's receptiveness to civil rights litigation.[441] The Court narrowly interpreted the Act, and concluded it covered conduct at the initial formation of the contract as well as conduct that impairs the right to enforce contractual obligations through the legal process, but it does not cover racial harassment.

The Voting Rights Act of 1965 once again came before the Supreme Court in 1982, this time from a system of at-large elections in Burke County, Georgia. The County had a population of 53.6 percent blacks, but whites had a slight majority of voting age adults, and no black had ever been elected to the county board of commissioners. Black citizens pursued a class action, and claimed violations of the First, Thirteenth, Fourteenth and Fifteenth Amendments. They argued the at-large voting scheme minimized the voting strength of minority groups by permitting the political majority to elect all representatives of the district. The county had no residency requirements, which made it possible for all candidates to reside in the "lily-white" neighborhoods.

The lower court ordered single-member district elections after it concluded that the system had been maintained for the purpose of restricting access of black residents to the electoral system. Both the Court of Appeals and the Supreme Court affirmed in *Rogers v. Lodge*, 458 U.S. 613, in 1982. Justices Powell and Rehnquist dissented, and stated there was no suggestion of discriminatory intent. Also dissenting, Justice Stevens said a rule that would invalidate all governmental action motivated by racial, ethnic or political considerations is too broad.

The Eighth Amendment prohibits cruel and unusual punishment.

This decade also saw another racially connected constitutional challenge to the death penalty by a man who was sentenced to death after he was convicted of killing an Atlanta police officer. The Eighth Amendment prohibits cruel and unusual punishment. In *McCleskey v. Kemp*, 481 U.S. 279, the *unusual* element was the focus of an argument that Georgia's death penalty was given in higher frequency when it was whites, rather than blacks, who were the victims. McCleskey offered the results of sophisticated statistical studies into evidence. The studies were of two thousand murder cases that occurred in Georgia during the 1970s, and showed that defendants charged with killing white persons received the death penalty in 11 percent of the cases, but defendants charged with killing blacks received the death penalty only 1 percent of the time. The study also revealed Georgia's death penalty had been utilized in 22 percent of cases that involved black defendants and white victims, and 3 percent of cases that involved white defendants and black victims.

The Supreme Court denied McCleskey's challenge in 1987. The Court was unwilling to accept statistical evidence of unequal treatment of the races in the criminal justice system and concluded McCleskey failed to establish that any of the decision makers in his own case acted with a discriminatory purpose. From the high Court's view, the evidence indicated a discrepancy that appeared to draw a parallel with race, not a constitutionally significant risk of racial bias affecting Georgia's capital-sentencing process in violation of the Eighth Amendment.

Underscoring claims of a lack of deliberate speed, thirty-six years after *Brown v. Board of Education*, the Supreme Court was still hearing school desegregation cases in 1990. In *Missouri v. Jenkins*, 495 U.S. 33, the federal trial court judge ordered a magnet school plan to try to attract suburban students to inner city schools with a planetarium, a twenty-five acre farm, a model United Nations, an art gallery and swimming pools. To bankroll the costly venture, the court ordered a doubling of the school district's property tax.

Missouri claimed the tax order was a states' rights issue and violated the Tenth Amendment's reservation of rights to the states, but the Court never addressed the

Thirty-six years after **Brown v. Board of Education,** *the Supreme Court was still hearing school desegregation cases.*

constitutional issue. Finding the District Court was obliged to assure itself that no alternative would have accomplished the required task, the Supreme Court sent the matter back for the trial judge to consider alternatives, such as enjoining state laws that would prevent the school district from implementing the changes.

1981-1990
Hollywood

THE WAY MOVIES WERE MADE changed substantially around this time. If the idealist screenwriter's product is ever seen on the silver screen during this decade, it is purely by accident. Louis B. Mayer and Adolph Zukor had freely planted moral lessons and values. All that changed. According to Disney chairman Michael Eisner, "I am not in business to make art films. I'm in business to return a profit to my investors."[442] This reality bode poorly for African Americans in Hollywood during the 1980s. In film, they were often separated from black cultural surroundings, plopped into white culture, and summarily desexed.[443]

While a few established screenwriters might be able to pitch a concept, most could not hope to have a script attract a producer or agent unless it was completed. And the structure of a film became formulaic: a two-hour movie with three acts consisting of a thirty-minute set-up, a sixty-minute complication or confrontation, and a thirty-minute resolution. Since each page of script translates into about one minute, the screenwriter must complete one hundred twenty pages on speculation.

In the old days, directors' jobs were workmanlike roles. With the demise of studios and the rise of independently packaged films, directors theoretically have a chance to shine. But in modern Hollywood, it takes an enormous amount of box office success for a director to be able to make films exactly as he or she wants. Producers put together a package by acquiring a story, bringing creative people together and either micromanaging the filmmaking, or relinquishing decisions to the director. It is the producer who runs up to the stage to collect the Oscar.[444]

Naturally, movies cost money to make, and whoever provides the money stands to lose the most if a film flops. Stars, other actors and special effects are expensive. Most film producers require studio financing, and can run into serious problems without it. Francis Ford Coppola was forced to mortgage his home as collateral on a loan to finish *Apocalypse Now.* Ed Guerrero says Hollywood has continually been reluctant to risk capital on productions that "stray from their proven formulas of profit and ideological containment into a deeper exploration of racial themes from a black point of view." But, Spike Lee was able to make *She's Gotta Have It* on a budget of $175,000.[445]

The structure of a film became formulaic: a two-hour movie with three acts consisting of a thirty-minute set-up, a sixty-minute complication or confrontation, and a thirty-minute resolution.

Studios became big business during the 1980s. In 1982, Coca-Cola bought Columbia Pictures, and in 1984 The Walt Disney Company set up Touchstone Pictures. In 1989, Warner Communications merged with Time-Warner Inc. and Columbia merged with Tri-Star Pictures. Then Sony bought Columbia and Tri-Star from Coca-Cola and merged with Guber-Peters Entertainment Company. After all the shuffling, there were eventually eight "majors": Disney, DreamWorks SKG, MGM, Paramount, Sony (Columbia/Tri-Star), 20th Century-Fox, Universal and Warner Bros. Miramax, New Line Cinema and Polygram are considered "mini-majors." Unlike old-time studios, modern ones usually do not produce or exhibit movies themselves. Instead, they provide the money and exercise a lot of control over the product.[446]

Big budget films with politically conservative themes transformed the film industry to treat movie-going audiences as passive spectators of escapist entertainment. Making racially sensitive films was not on movie studio plates. *Jaws* was largely responsible. It made so much money so quickly that special effects became the vogue.[447] Narrative feature films became visual and acoustic formulas and commodities because corporations could extract profit at every point of distribution and exhibition. In addition to profits from movie theaters, there were network and cable television, video rentals, and a range of commercial spinoffs such as albums, books, toys, and even theme parks. Experimentation and countercultural expression were no longer tolerated. The bean counters were not concerned about challenging the spectator to address issues of social inequality, race, gender or social change.[448]

Layers of studio employees have input about scripts. There is usually a vice president of development, a creative executive, a story editor, a story analyst and a development assistant. According to screenwriter William Goldman, "The studios try to

Unlike old-time studios, modern ones usually do not produce or exhibit movies themselves.

protect themselves now. They have all these idiots who sit in on meetings and then give you their notes. The first time this ever happened to me was *Maverick.* I'm meeting with [director] Dick Donner and Mel Gibson, and these three studio executives, Happy, Smiley, and Dopey, were sitting there taking notes. And I got a note once saying, 'We feel *Maverick* would be better if it were funnier and more exciting.' And I thought, 'Who are you people?' . . . But this happens on every movie now. Because their costs are so high, they tend to make the lowest-common-denominator movies."[449] In the 1980s, films aimed at adult audiences became scarce.

Black actors in the 1980s were rarely permitted romantic roles and frequently found themselves desexed.[450] Let's examine some Eddie Murphy films. At one point during the decade, there was no more powerful a box-office draw—with the possible exception of Sylvester Stallone—than Murphy. Originally it was Stallone who was to star in *Beverly Hills Cop* (1984). Beautiful blonde actress, Lisa Eilbacher, is the female lead. She and Murphy are platonic buddies in the film.

Historian Donald Bogle wondered if filmmakers feared Murphy's sexuality and said he felt Stallone's character would have had an affair with Eilbacher's character. The creators of the film might have feared white audience objection to a romance between Murphy and a white actress, but Bogle wonders why they didn't just substitute a black actress.[451]

In early scenes, *Beverly Hills Cop* has Murphy living in a just-above-seedy Detroit apartment. Black areas in Detroit display extreme poverty. Murphy drives a dirty, beat-up Chevy Nova and dresses as if he intends to spend the day changing oil filters. Why? Police officers are well-paid. It seems to be a subliminal message that blacks, even when hired for respectable jobs that pay good money, do not know how to use it. In the film, Murphy's character clearly has a PhD in street smarts and can outmaneuver the local, and well-dressed, Beverly Hills cops at every turn. But his crudeness is unnecessary. Every so often, when he wants to impress someone, he speaks decently and politely. Murphy's language is usually smart-aleck and filthy. Another hidden message? Blacks lack class and you can't take them anywhere. To top off his lack of style and class, Murphy is portrayed as opportunistic and dishonest at the fictional Beverly Palm Hotel. When he shows up without a reservation and is informed there are no available rooms, he pulls the race card. To quiet his loud racist accusations in the hotel lobby, he is bribed with a lavish suite at the cost of a single-room.

Black actors in the 1980s were rarely permitted romantic roles and frequently found themselves desexed.

Then, when he checks out of the hotel, he steals three terry cloth robes.

Murphy also projects poorly for blacks in *48 Hrs* (1982) where he plays the part of a convicted bank robber who is sprung from jail to assist a white cop in solving a crime. Even though it would be reasonable for a man to have sex on his mind upon release from prison, Murphy is cast as over-sexed and incapable of conducting himself—or speaking—decently. The tone is set in his first scene when he is still in prison. He looks like an idiot and is wearing headphones while squealing out lyrics. His crudeness is taken to new levels when he invites a white detective to join him on a "pussy hunt," and tells the white man his dick becomes hard if the wind blows and chides him with, "You know how close I was to gettin' some trim right now, and you fucked it up." The white man has a love interest, but the black man has no relationship with a woman. Bogle asks about the Murphy character, "Couldn't Reggie have had a wife or girlfriend he had to leave behind?"[452] When convict and the cop enter a country music bar that is flying a Confederate flag, the white audience's worst fears are manipulated when Murphy pretends he is a cop and intimidates the bar's redneck patrons. "I'm your worst nightmare," Murphy declares, ". . . a nigger with a badge."

Black actress Whoopi Goldberg also starred in several movies where blacks were cast in a negative light. She did appear in a love scene with white actor Sam Elliot in *Fatal Beauty* in 1987. When preview audiences objected to the scene, it was cut from the film. Ed Guerrero says that "with a clear understanding that black women are traditionally marked as 'fallen' or prostitutes by mainstream cinema and society," Goldberg openly protested when the scene was cut. She complained to *Jet* magazine that, "if Sam Elliot had put some money on the table after the love-making scene, it would still have been in there."[453] In its place was a non-explicit scene where a bed looks messed and the white man was in her shower in the morning. Playing a detective in *Fatal Beauty*, Goldberg, a foul-mouthed misfit similar to Murphy in *Beverly Hills Cop,* is subjected to constant taunts and disrespect from her colleagues, such as, "Hey, Rizzoli, did you ever get it doggy style?"

Fatal Beauty removes Goldberg from an African American setting. She is given a strange name for a black person and is referred to as "a pretty Italian lady" by Elliot. Instead of allowing a black person to have risen to the position of detective by working hard, the script tells the viewer she used to be a drug addict, and has her using vile language. When she is not dressed outlandishly as an undercover hooker, much of Goldberg's femininity is hidden with oversized clothes.

Goldberg is also desexed and dresses frumpishly in *Clara's Heart* (1988) where she has no romantic life and wears large clothes.[454] In *Clara's Heart*, Goldberg plays a maid, perhaps even a mammy, who lives apart from her family and friends in the home of a white family for most of the film. When she visits her black friends, the audience hears explicit sexual banter, sees a black woman grinding her pelvis at a preteen boy and is introduced to a black pimp and prostitute. When the Goldberg character tells why she did not want the young boy touching her, she reveals she was raped by her teenaged son. In the film, the boy's mother and Clara supposedly become friends, but the social norm seems to be set since the white woman is called Mrs. Hart and the black woman is called Clara. The young white boy is permitted by both his parents to be openly impolite to the black woman.

Goldberg also starred in *The Color Purple* (1985), based on black author Alice Walker's Pulitzer winning novel. The story about child molestation of black girls and submission of black women to black men begins in 1909. The film almost exclusively portrays blacks, but every so often, white characters flit by so the viewer can assess the microcosm of the black society within the larger white supremacist social order. Not one black man is portrayed as likeable. Each is either a bully, child molester, wife beater, coward, drunk or some combination thereof, which caused the NAACP to protest the film.[455]

Goldberg starred in many comedies, too, and each cut her off from the black community.[456] In *Ghost* (1990), Goldberg plays a con artist with a long criminal record.

Contemporary black unrest and violence was the subject of several movies. In *Fort Apache, The Bronx* (1981), blacks are generally portrayed as specimens in a dirty bottle. Both blacks and Puerto Ricans energetically protested the movie.[457] All blacks have either minor parts or are displayed as very bad characters. In the background of the film are black orderlies, patients, cops and nurses, but in the foreground there are black drug dealers, pimps, hookers and thieves. Donald Bogle says the Pam Grier character, a zonked-out terrorizing streetwalker, is a metaphor for the random violence that lurks in city streets.[458] A black barmaid serves up a current version of the mammy character along with the beer; full of spunk and common sense, she still knows how to take orders. The historical reluctance of African Americans to cooperate with the police is neatly summed up in the script by a police sergeant, "Up here, Captain, cops are like husbands. They're always the last to know." The story is told through the perspective of two white policemen. Viewers get to share their turmoil and angst, and see both in their homes. One interacts with his family, and both have significant relationships with women filled with sensitivity. When the riot starts, viewers are primarily invited to sympathize with the frustration of the white cops.

Colors (1988) portrays black gangsters in the "Bloods" and the "Crips" on the other side of the country. Viewers are told about six hundred street gangs with a combined seventy thousand members in Los Angeles. After a fatal drive-by shooting, an older black woman says to the cops, "I ain't seen nothin'. Just get out of my face." A white police officer is shown at home with his wife and three children, including a cuddly baby. He and his wife discuss how to butterfly shrimp for the barbeque, while another officer swings their little boy on a backyard swing set. But the only home scene for a black person shows a naked black man mounted on a black woman. Their

As major studios became more reluctant to take chances on offbeat material, independent film companies began to fill the demand for quality and experimentation.

sex is so loud and consuming, they don't hear a squad of police entering the squalid house. A scene at the Los Angeles County jail shows the entire yard filled with blacks. While a few lines throw out a bone of sympathy for the black condition ("You think America's ready to love two niggers at one time?" and "Treatin' us all like criminals right in front of our children."), the movie tells the story through the experiences and reactions of two white cops.

According to *The American Film Institute Desk Reference,* as major studios became more reluctant to take chances on off-beat material, independent film companies began to fill the demand for quality and experimentation. The reference book says, "by hook or by crook, filmmakers in the 80s managed to release a number of innovative and unusual films."[459]

Spike Lee filled in some of the industry's racial gap with such films as *Do the Right Thing* (1989). Lee's great gift is to present contemporary urban black characters who are caught up in the same sexual politics as Hollywood has always presented white characters. "Yet their frame of reference and internal rhythms spring from a distinct black cultural tradition," says Donald Bogle.[460]

Do the Right Thing has an urban black riot set in Brooklyn, similar to those in *Fort Apache, the Bronx* and *Colors.* But the build-up given by Lee is from the black perspective. Lyrics of *Fight the Power* pound from the screen during the first scene:

We've got to fight the power, get free
Elvis was a hero to most, but he never meant shit to me

Without a white slant, the viewer gets to see inside black homes, and hear blacks in the neighborhood reveal how they feel, "I'm a struggling black man tryin' to keep my dick hard in a cruel, harsh world." *Do the Right Thing* also dispels metaphors about American homogeny. A black says, "Dago, wop, ginny, garlic breath, pizza slinging spaghetti breath, Vic Damone, Perry Como, Lucado Pavaratti, solo mio, non singer, mother fucker."

An Italian says, "You gold-teethed, gold chain-wearin', fried chicken and biscuit-eatin monkey, ape, baboon, big dime, fast runnin' and jumpin' spear chuckin' 360 degree basketball dunkin' titsoon spade mooinyah. Take your fuckin' piece a pizza and go the fuck back to Africa."

A Puerto Rican says, "You little slanty-eyed me-no-speakee American, own every fruit and vegetable stand in New York, bullshit Reverend Sun Yung Moon, some Olympic '88 Korean kick boxin' son-of-a-bitch."

A white policeman says, "You goya bean-eatin', 15-in-a-car, 30-in-an-apartment, pointy shoes, reg-wearin', minuto, meata meata Puerto Rican cocksucker. Yeah, you."

A Korean grocer says, "It's cheap. I got good plice for you, Mayor Kochie. How I'm doing, chocolate egg cream-drinking, bagle and the lox, B'Nai B'rith, Jew ass-hole?"

Then Samuel L. Jackson, who plays the part of a radio announcer, breaks up the tirade with, "Yo. Hold off. Time out. Time out. Y'all take a chill. You need to cool that shit out. And that's the double truth, Ruth."

When the urban riot came, it was just as depressing as in other movies, but somehow it was more predictable and understandable. "Still, *Do the Right Thing* succeeded in other important ways. Better than any other film of the period, it touched on a great deal of the discontent and unexplained anger that was so much a part of urban life during the Reagan eighties."[461]

In the eighties, Hollywood served big budget films that were both conservative and linear. "Mainstream commercial cinema of the 1980s concentrated on manipulating the audience's response and assent to its reassuring mediations of dominant social and political values," says Ed Guerrero.[462]

Even movies that tried to be sensitive to blacks placed the setting back in history instead of contemporary times, as though the problem was one from the past. *Driving Miss Daisy* (1989 Best Picture of the Year) takes place over several decades, from 1948 to 1973. It only shows the black chauffer played by Morgan Freeman in the white world. The viewer does not see his family or friends or home, or get to know how the chauffer feels about things. Rather, the anguish is shown through the white employer, Jessica Tandy's character.

Mississippi Burning (1988) takes place during 1964, and begins with the murders of two white and one black civil rights workers who were sent to Mississippi to set up a voting clinic. One sees the torment and distress of two white FBI agents, but sees the black actors from afar in wretched poverty or attending church services. However, the film demonstrates the Southern racial apartheid system of the times. Separate but unequal facilities are shown. One bigot tells what NAACP means, "Niggers, alligators, apes, coons and possums." Another says, "The rest of America don't mean jack shit. You're in Mississippi now." Alas, not a word is said about the race of the scores of FBI agents and naval reserves who come south to solve the crimes. They're all white. Some wonder how Hollywood could make a film about the Civil Rights Movement without having any major black characters in the movie.[463]

Some wonder how Hollywood could make a film about the Civil Rights Movement without having any major black characters in the movie.

Glory (1989) is supposedly about black soldiers during the Civil War, but focuses on a young white officer. *A Soldier's Story* (1984) is set in Louisiana in 1944 in an Army barracks for black soldiers. Their motto is, "Anything you don't wanta do, the colored troops will do for you." Everyone assumes it was the Klan who murdered a black sergeant, but the murderer turns out to be another black soldier, who just happens to resemble Malcolm X in both looks and philosophy. A black captain is sent to investigate, and just as in real life during World War II, the black officer is given an entire barracks to himself, rather than being housed with white officers.

Gandhi (1982 Best Picture of the Year) was about Indians who were treated the same way Africans were treated by the English colonialists. Early scenes take place in pre-World War I South Africa. Young attorney Gandhi purchased a first class rail ticket by mail. When a white man finds him in the compartment, he orders, "Just move your black ass back to third class or I'll have your black ass thrown off at the station." Gandhi was thrown off the train. While in a city, Gandhi is taunted by whites, "Get off the pavement you bloody coon." When the British required Indians to carry identity and travel passes, Gandhi led a peaceful protest of burning the passes until the laws were changed.

Out of Africa (1985 Best Picture of the Year) is set in Kenya, East Africa in 1913, also during the period of British colonialism. All blacks are servants and laborers for the whites, and the story is told from the vantage point of a white woman. One aspect that demonstrated sensitivity toward the natives concerned a school for blacks run by a European. The slant was that education of the children rendered the wise chief obsolete, and amounted to needless interference with African culture.

Goodfellas (1990, AFI's #94) takes place from the 1940s through the 1960s and has several disparaging remarks about blacks, associating them with crime. The remarks imply how unsavory underworld figures are and excuse the viewer from responsibility for such views.

Raiders of the Lost Ark (1981, AFI's #60) has a pre-World War II African scene in which a German demonstrates extreme cruelty by pointing to the leading lady, a white woman, while stating to a black African, "If she fails to please me, you may do with her as you wish."

While the Hollywood mainstream suppressed or ignored current black issues, there was a sprinkling of popular feature films that expressed black themes and points of view.[464] Spike Lee made several other movies from the black perspective during the decade. His films have few white characters. Rather than the gun-toting, drug-dealing, pimp-whore portrayals of blacks in many movies, Lee's films show ordinary black people in everyday human conflicts.

She's Gotta Have It (1986) is told from the black female point of view. The film begins with a quote from black author Zora Neale Hurston and a warm, gentle scene of lovemaking between a black man and woman. The protagonist, Nola, remarks to a man who wants to move in with her, "What makes you think I want someone to take care of?" Nola comes from a stable family and loving parents. Her apartment is tasteful and neat, and when she serves Thanksgiving dinner, she sets a lovely table.

Rather than the gun-toting, drug-dealing, pimp-whore portrayals of blacks in many movies, [Spike] Lee's films show ordinary black people in everyday human conflicts.

The characters play Scrabble, have conversations about Jesse Jackson running for president, and insult someone by accusing him of voting for Ronnie. One comments, "The decent black men are all taken. The rest are in prison or homos."

Mo Better Blues also has the main character coming from stable, loving parents. His mother pushes him to practice his music so he can be a success. When he grows up, his home is elegantly decorated, and most of the characters are affectionate and loving toward each other. Their humor is funny and often racially tinged. A few black men taunt a co-worker for dating a white woman from France. They call her a "white bitch." The lover complains, "She's an educated woman . . . went to the Sorbonne. You guys don't know what that is." A taunter shoots back, "Yeah you get it down on 125th Street."

In another conversation, one of them tells about being whacked by his mother, who had no tolerance for white girls for her son, when, as a youth, he had a picture of Betty and Veronica on the wall of his room.

Many 1980s movies ignored or abridged the roles of blacks, or presented blacks in a negative light. Donald Bogle is very critical of one popular film: "But certainly no early 1980s film so blatantly (and perhaps cruelly) reduced (and exploited) its black stars to mere background filler as did *The Blues Brothers* (1980)."[465] *The Blues Brothers* briefly presented Cab Calloway, Ray Charles, James Brown and Aretha Franklin, but focused on two pallid, fleshy white men.

Several movies were sensitive to other groups, while ignoring blacks when attention was warranted, and some were outright insensitive to blacks. *Ordinary People* (1980 Best Picture of the Year) should have had black actors, at least in background scenes. Millions of blacks lived in Chicago in 1980, but not one is seen in Chicago-area restaurants, shopping malls, buses, a bowling alley, a high school or outdoor scenes. But one anti-Semitic remark is placed to demonstrate how cold and uncaring a character is.

Chariots of Fire (1981 Best Picture of the Year) shows a few Africans representing their countries in the 1924 Olympics, but underscores the film's sub-theme of condemning anti-Semitism. *Rain Man* (1988 Best Picture of the Year) has a black employee in a minor part, but has scenes all over the country, and should have featured at least a couple of black actors. In *Tootsie* (1982, AFI's #62), there are only a few blacks walking the streets of New York City or working on the set, and in *Terms of Endearment* (1983 Best Picture of the Year), there are scenes in Houston, Texas, Des Moines, Iowa and Lincoln, Nebraska with no black actors at all.

E.T. the Extra-Terrestrial (1982, AFI's #25) is about an adorable, hairless little dark-skinned creature who has been described as the perfect visitor since he, ". . . arrived alone, cannot reproduce, and has no intention of seeking citizenship," says Ed Guerrero.[466] Darling children abound, including a few teenagers who ride their bikes through the sky. The lone black teen in the movie is shown wearing a head band and a large chain crossed over his bare chest and appears to be a leader in acts of vandalism on Halloween night. He is the only teenager on which the camera focuses during vandalism.

Fast Times at Ridgemont High (1982) portrays several hapless, but likeable characters, but the only black featured is a large and menacing bully.

Platoon (1986 Best Picture of the Year and AFI's #83) is in a class by itself. Told from a white soldier's perspective during the Vietnam War, the film has several black actors as soldiers. All of the black characters are treated with respect, even one who feigns injury to avoid duties, but all of the main parts are played by white actors. Inferior education of African Americans is underscored when one black soldier writes "Dere Sarrah" to his girl back home. When corrected, he responds, "She don't read too good no how." When the white soldier writes home, he describes his buddies as the bottom of the barrel with two years of high school at the most.

Every position of authority is filled by a white man. When treated disrespectfully by a white, a black says to his friend, "God damn, man, you break your ass for the white man. There's no justice around here." In fact, the movie shows warmth and friendship among some of the whites and blacks. When the white protagonist reveals he left college to volunteer, a black soldier responds, "You're a crazy fucker . . . givin' up college? Volunteered?" Later he says, "Everybody know the poor always bein' fucked over by the rich. Always have. Always will." When the two are talking about drugs, the black soldier says, "Y'all be tryin' to keep the black man down—strung out on that shit." But when the fighting is at its worst, each race looks to its own for support.

A popular shoot-em-up film portrayed African Americans in the most positive light for the decade. *Lethal Weapon* (1987) set up a black man and a white man as detective buddies. The dysfunctional partner, in dire need of guidance, is the white man. The one with the stable family life, beautiful home, darling children and common sense is the black detective.

*Movies not discussed in text appear in endnote.[467]

1981-1990
Decade Wrap-up

THE PRIMARY APPROACH OF MAINSTREAM Hollywood toward race during the 1980s could best be summed up as, "Once upon a time before the Civil Rights Movement, there was racism in America, but it's all gone now." The movie industry reflected that the races were at peace with one another and America's history of racism had vanished. Secondarily, the movie industry projected African Americans in a modern version of the old minstrel shows of the nation's racist past. With more conservative justices from Republican administrations, the Supreme Court became almost as conservative as "liberal" Hollywood during the decade, but not quite.

The Hollywood establishment's slant in this decade was that racism no longer existed. Many films insulated contemporary audiences from reality and responsibility, probably on the theory that people did not want to come to the movies to feel guilty. The industry used the same tactic during the depression when it provided audiences a safe haven from reality.

Films that dealt sensitively with race issues were set in history. Their content dealt with blatant white supremacy issues that had already been clarified by the legal system, and were generally considered resolved. For example, the segregation of African Americans in the military shown in *Glory* and *A Soldier's Story* ceased to exist after President Truman's Executive Order was implemented. Overt interference with the voting rights of African Americans, as was shown in *Mississippi Burning*, was curtailed by Congress's Voting Rights Act of 1965. The chauffer in *Driving Miss Daisy* would have been able to find a restroom after both Congress and the Supreme Court acted on public accommodations issues in the 1960s. *Gandhi*'s travails, and similar scenes of colonialism shown in *Out of Africa*, were England's fault, so that was safe territory for Hollywood. The racist remarks in *Raiders of the Lost Ark* and *Goodfellas* were okay since they were set in times long ago, and because everybody hates Nazis and the Mafia.

Gandhi's travails, and similar scenes of colonialism shown in Out of Africa, were England's fault, so that was safe territory for Hollywood.

Several films focused on the white man's perspective and angst over racial problems, rather than on the black man who suffered from them. Essentially, Hollywood avoided dangerous racial areas that were too close to America's real 1980s problems, permitting its audiences to murmur "tsk, tsk" while munching on popcorn.

Unlike Hollywood movies, Supreme Court cases recognized that problems still existed. In *Local 28 of the Sheet Metal Workers v. EEOC*, the Court described the impenetrable barriers to blacks who wanted construction jobs reserved for whites, and concluded the historical problem of nepotism would continue, even for blacks who had not been discriminated against, unless relief was granted. Similarly, in *Local 93, International Association of Firefighters*, the Court permitted the lower federal court to implement hiring policies for fire fighter positions on the basis of race, even though the beneficiaries had not been actual victims of discrimination. A comparable order was approved for hiring police officers in *United States v. Paradise*. In *Rogers v. Lodge*, the Court affirmed a lower court's order that changed residency requirements for political candidates in a county that had 53.6 percent blacks, where no black had ever been elected to the county Board of Commissioners.

Movies with contemporary settings either ignored racial subjects or portrayed them as a joke. For example, Nick Nolte used racially derogatory phrases to Eddie Murphy in *48 Hrs.* and Whoopie Goldberg was the recipient of numerous racial slurs in *Fatal Beauty*. Both black characters treated the barbs as jokes and retorted with vulgar comebacks. Often, black actors were portrayed as flawed. Even when the insults were unspoken, they were there nonetheless. Goldberg is dressed like a clown in most of her movies. For example, in *Ghost*, she wears bright blue long johns and a shell necklace to bed, and outrageously loud, baggy clothes during the day.

E.T. the Extra-Terrestrial and *Fast Times at Ridgemont High* briefly show a black character, but they make him a heavy. *Clara's Heart* has Whoopie Goldberg the victim of incest. In *Fatal Beauty*, she is a reformed drug addict. In *Ghost*, she is a con artist with a long criminal record. Eddie Murphy steals the hotel's bathrobes in *Beverly Hills Cop*. Blacks are also cast as major criminals in *Fort Apache, the Bronx* and *Colors*. *The Blues Brothers* appropriates black culture and minimizes major black talent.

Sometimes the degrading racial references and parody of the decade surpasses in vulgarity the minstrel shows of the nation's racist past. Blacks are portrayed to conform to white expectations. Criminal roles remained the most plausible for blacks in many movies.[468] "You can take 'em out of the ghetto, but you can't take the ghetto out of 'em," bemoans Donald Bogle.[469] Racism is used as a running gag throughout several movies.[470]

Historian Ed Guerrero refers to the appropriation and representation of African Americans as "neominstrelsy." "Dan Aykroyd and John Belushi, clad in black suits,

Sometimes the degrading racial references and parody of the decade surpasses in vulgarity the minstrel shows of the nation's racist past.

shades, and stingy-brim hats—the trappings of urban bluesmen—and performing antics, add up to a sort of an updated symbolic blackface of the 1980s."[471] About Eddie Murphy sitting in prison wearing headphones in *48 Hrs.*, Guerrero says, "Here, at the beginning of the narrative, the white middle-class spectator is positioned to see someone they can reflexively feel superior to, a black convict and a compulsive fool who is literally contained by society's walls and bars."[472] Regarding the scene where Eddie Murphy impersonates a cop in the redneck country music bar, he says, "Murphy's scene is deceptive; it seems to depict a reversal of black-white power relations and to contradict the racial order of the film, which inscribes whites in the subordinate position. But the scene actually makes the argument that if blacks were to attain institutional authority, and by implication social equality, they would behave as brutally to whites as they have historically been treated by them."[473]

It could be said that back in Washington, the Supreme Court was as conservative as "liberal" Hollywood in some respects. Hollywood blew off Whoopi Goldberg's racial harassment in *Fatal Beauty*. By giving her thick skin, she one-upped her harassers every time. In *Patterson v. McLean Credit Union*, a black woman worker was subjected to taunts that blacks were known to work slower than whites. The Supreme Court ruled the 1866 Civil Rights Act did not cover racial harassment. Congress quickly amended the statute to cover allegations such as Patterson's, so the Court's ruling could have been referred to as strict statutory construction.

Regarding school desegregation, Hollywood portrayed all-white suburban schools as the norm. *Ordinary People*'s high school scenes show only white students.

Fast Times at Ridgemont High and *E.T. the Extra-Terrestrial* have only a few black students. The Court did not step in to eradicate school desegregation and approve the

A 1990 opinion poll of black New Yorkers conducted by the **New York Times** *and CBS found that 64 percent of blacks who responded felt drugs and urban violence were part of a white conspiracy to eliminate blacks.*

lower federal court's program to integrate inner-city schools by attracting students from the suburbs. But in *Missouri v. Jenkins*, the lower court clearly went beyond *Brown*'s dictate to remove segregation from the nation's public schools.

A few independent filmmakers managed to accurately portray African Amercians in movies. Spike Lee is the finest example. In *She's Gotta Have It*, the characters discuss current politics, including how they exercise their votes. The film includes dialogue about the disproportionate number of black prison inmates, a topic similar to an argument before the Supreme Court around the same time. In *McCleskey v. Kemp* there was a contention the death penalty was administered with higher frequency when it was whites, rather than blacks, who were murdered. Black urban frustrations are explored in *Do the Right Thing*, which ends with a quote about nonviolence from Martin Luther King, Jr.[474] Black sexual conundrums and motivations to succeed are the main topics in *Mo Better Blues*.

Ed Guerrero says, "Lee has been able almost singlehandedly to make films about black life, rendered from a black point of view, that are popular with a general audience. Thus he has opened vast opportunities, new audiences, and markets to black films and black filmmakers.[475]

Oliver Stone's *Platoon* depicts several uneducated, but incredibly smart and likeable black soldiers, which sadly demonstrates the results of a lack of equal educational opportunities. The remark about drugs and whites "tryin' to keep the black man down" reflected fears and beliefs of African Americans. A 1990 opinion poll of black New Yorkers conducted by the *New York Times* and CBS found that 64 percent of blacks who responded felt drugs and urban violence were part of a white conspiracy to eliminate blacks.[476]

Steven Spielberg's *The Color Purple*, while it has nothing good to say about black men, does explore the then-current hot topic of black feminism, which emerged long after white women burned their bras. During slave times, black men were not accorded the customary familial authority of men in patriarchal societies. According to authors James Oliver Horton and Lois E. Horton, "During the centuries of struggle for freedom and justice, the complexities of gender roles complicated the relationships between black men and women and even the operation of civil rights organizations."[477] Spike Lee's *She's Gotta Have It* delves into black feminism, too.

As the twentieth century entered its last decade, the United States Supreme Court continued to remove legal obstacles to equal opportunities for the races. Reactionary mainstream Hollywood looked backward. Had it not been for the independents, virtually all 1980s movies would have moved race issues to ancient history, or portrayed African Americans in what Ed Guerrero calls the modern version of blackface.

Zooming in . . .

A Close-up Look at Blacks and Crime

WHETHER OR NOT BLACKS ARE unfairly and disproportionately targeted by the police and the courts is not known. But many people believe it is a fact that a higher percentage of blacks are convicted of crimes than whites. They attribute this to racism within our justice system rather than a higher propensity for blacks to commit crimes.

The film *Crash* presented the situation well. Two young black men resented that a white woman showed fear when she saw them. Her husband, a white prosecutor, lamented after they robbed the couple at gunpoint, "Why did they have to be black guys?" Later in the movie, a successful black man, convinced white police targeted both law-abiding and law-breaking black men, protected one of the thugs from the police while telling him, "You embarrass me. You embarrass yourself."

Traditionally blacks have had good reasons to distrust the police. After the Civil War, blacks tried to enjoy their new rights. As an outgrowth of the patrols during slavery, and in response to advances made by blacks, the Ku Klux Klan organized in the South. As night riders and assassins, Klan members roamed around intimidating and killing blacks.[478] The Ku Klux Klan maimed, lynched, murdered, raped and terrorized blacks. Even after the Thirteenth, Fourteenth and Fifteenth Amendments were adopted, the perpetrators of these crimes and civil rights violations went unpunished by state and local authorities.[479]

W.E.B. Du Bois said the police system of the South was designed to control black men, and it was tacitly assumed that every white man was a member of the police. He said the first and almost universal device was to use the courts as a means of re-enslaving blacks. Blacks came to look upon courts and the police as instruments of injustice and oppression, and upon those convicted as martyrs and victims. When a real black criminal appeared and was convicted, blacks refused to believe the evidence of white witnesses or the fairness of white juries. Thus, DuBois said, "the greatest deterrent to crime, the public opinion of one's own social caste, was lost, and the criminal was looked upon as crucified rather than hanged."[480]

Blacks came to look upon courts and the police as instruments of injustice and oppression, and upon those convicted as martyrs and victims.

Time after time, blacks were unfairly arrested and convicted in the South. One frightening example occurred on the night of September 30, 1919 when a number of black people had assembled in church and were attacked and fired upon by a group of white men. In the disturbance that followed, a white man, Clinton Lee, was killed. Shortly after the arrest of the black men, a white mob marched to the jail for the purpose of lynching them, but was prevented by the presence of United States troops.

Phillips County, Arkansas, had a strong black majority,[481] yet blacks were excluded from juries in the county. An all-white grand jury indicted the black defendants, who were tried before an all white male jury. During the trial, a crowd threatened anyone who interfered with the desired result. Counsel did not speak with the defendants, seek a change in venue, challenge members of the jury, request separate trials, call witnesses for the defense or call the defendants, themselves. The black men were sentenced to death after a forty-five-minute trial.[482, 483]

In 1955, Emmit Till, a fourteen-year-old from Chicago, was visiting relatives in Mississippi when, on a dare, he squeezed a white woman's hand and whistled at her. His naked body, almost beyond recognition, was pulled from a river three days later. The white woman's husband and his half-brother were the killers. They were tried and acquitted of the murder by a jury of twelve white men after sixty-seven minutes of deliberation.[484]

Regardless of racism, the Great Migration of blacks from South to North combined with welfare programs, vast social changes, decrease in respect for authority and the breakdown of many family units had a tremendous effect on the black crime rate. The arrest rate of black males between the ages of thirteen and thirty-nine rose by 49 percent between 1966 and 1974.[485]

The arrest rate of black males between the ages of thirteen and thirty-nine rose by 49 percent between 1966 and 1974.

Du Bois's 1903 observation about blacks not believing that other blacks really committed crimes proved to be visionary, but the concept has expanded to blacks who refuse to convict, even when they believe a black defendant is guilty. This is because they believe blacks are unfairly targeted for arrest and prosecution. In preparation for trying cases in modern courtrooms, rookie prosecutors are taught that black jurors refuse to convict black defendants who they know are guilty.[486]

When District of Columbia Mayor Marion Barry was tried for fourteen drug charges, the trial judge remarked it was the strongest government case he had ever seen. Yet the black jury convicted Barry on only one of the counts. Some African Americans remarked they "thought that the jury, in rendering its verdict, jabbed its black thumb in the face of a racist prosecution."[487]

Jury nullification of black criminals is actively advocated. African American former federal prosecutor turned law professor Paul Butler says: "My thesis is that, for pragmatic and political reasons, the black community is better off when some nonviolent lawbreakers remain in the community rather than go to prison. The decision as to what kind of conduct by African-Americans ought to be punished is better made by African-Americans themselves, based on the costs and benefits to their community, than by the traditional criminal justice process, which is controlled by white lawmakers and white law enforcers."

Professor Butler gives examples of racism in the criminal justice system by pointing to the extraordinary rate of incarceration of black men, Scottsboro Boys cases, history of criminalization of drug use, administration of the death penalty, use of race in the 1988 presidential campaign, beating of Rodney King and acquittal of his police assailants, disparities between punishments for white-collar crimes versus punishments for other crimes, more severe penalties for crack cocaine users than for powder cocaine users, and police corruption. About the O.J. Simpson case, he says its "racist police officer who was the prosecution's star witness and the response of many white people to the jury's verdict of acquittal" also provide examples of racism in the justice system.[488]

Another challenge for prosecutors is the "Stop Snitchin'" campaign. In Pittsburgh, a witness called to testify about three men on trial for conspiring to kill him was ejected from an Allegheny court because he was wearing a T-shirt that said STOP SNITCHIN'. Prosecutors were forced to withdraw charges against the three defendants. The following day, during the sentencing phase of a federal drug case, an assistant U.S. Attorney paused to show the judge two T-shirts vilifying witnesses who gave prosecutors information about a cocaine kingpin. One shirt had a photograph of a witness, an admitted drug dealer who eventually won a reduced sentence for cooperating with authorities. Above his image and a photo of another cooperating witness were the words NO SNITCHING ALLOWED. On the opposite side, it read NIGGAS JUST LOOKING FOR A DEAL and, once again, STOP SNITCHIN.[489]

In 1997, the U.S. Sentencing Commission found that, while most of the nation's crack users were white, 88 percent of those convicted of federal crack offenses were black.

The Boston Globe stated fear and social norms against snitching are factors in witnesses' reluctance to testify.[490] Baltimore officials say that witness intimidation hampers efforts to convict criminals and about one-quarter of 2004's gun cases were dropped because of direct or perceived threats against witnesses.[491] According to a *Texas Law Review* article, another remarked, "When young men and women see rappers refuse [to cooperate], they think it's cool. How do we tell them, 'we'll support you,' when they see that?"[492]

Of course, for every action there is a reaction. Some prosecutors try to modify hearsay rules, arguing that exclusion of out-of-court statements because of hearsay creates a huge incentive to make witnesses disappear.[493] After drug dealers produced a DVD called *Stop Snitching*, in which they threatened to kill anyone who testified against them, the Baltimore Police Department responded with their own DVD, *Keep Talking*, which mentioned the arrests of three of the drug dealers featured in the gang's video.[494]

In 1997, the U.S. Sentencing Commission found that, while most of the nation's crack users were white, 88 percent of those convicted of federal crack offenses were black.[495] Currently, blacks are arrested for felony-level offenses at rates significantly greater than their proportion in California's population.[496] And black defendants are the most likely to receive prison sentences for felony offenses. Black defendants with no prior record are the most likely to receive prison sentences for violent offenses while white defendants are the least likely.

The police are aware there is a disparity in arrest and conviction rates. San Diego Chief of Police Jerry Sanders observed: "Whole communities get very upset when they see that pretty soon everybody that they love has been arrested, and I think that creates far more problems. The issue is one of community trust. If you're relying on the public to assist you in just about any way, and if you're stopping people in communities of color, and your stops are out of sync with the way they are in every other community because you're simply stopping people because you think they may look suspicious, we found that it's awfully difficult for those communities to support and trust the efforts of what the police are doing."[497]

The ACLU expects that increased post-9/11 powers of the police to invade the privacy of U.S. citizens will eventually weigh heavily on African Americans. It points out the Federal Bureau of Investigation undermined and spied on many blacks, including the Rev. Martin Luther King, Jr., during the Civil Rights Movement.[498] It claims that if blacks are considered by the police to be more likely to commit crimes, they will be stopped and investigated more than whites, and the crime rate among blacks will increase. They also claim if the police concentrated their efforts on white citizens, they would find an increased rate among whites as well.[499]

For many years the United States Supreme Court has required that police officers give specific facts to justify stopping people. The Court has clearly stated that the Constitution prohibits selective enforcement of the law based on race.[500] Someone's presence in a high crime area is not a sufficient reason.[501] An officer's suspicion—or a hunch—are not enough either.[502]

The ACLU expects that increased post-9/11 powers of the police to invade the privacy of U.S. citizens will eventually weigh heavily on African Americans.

The Supreme Court struggled with several arguments that African Americans were unconstitutionally sentenced to death in America. In *Furman v. Georgia*, 408 U.S. 238, 1972, the Court struck down the death penalty under the cruel and unusual punishment clause of the Eighth Amendment in three cases involving African Americans. They all were sentenced to death, two in Georgia and one in Texas. Justice William Douglas said capital punishment was disproportionately applied to the poor and socially disadvantaged. He pointed out that when this country was founded, there was no developed prison system, and death, not a unique punishment, was routinely accepted by society. Thereafter, Georgia quickly redrafted its death penalty statute. By the time a case under the new statute made its way to the high court, Justice Douglas had retired. In *Gregg v. Georgia*, 428 U.S. 153, 1976, a changed Court voted to uphold the constitutionality of the death penalty.

In *McCleskey v. Kemp*, 481 U.S. 279, 1987, Warren McCleskey, a black man, unsuccessfully argued that Georgia's death penalty statute was administered in a racially discriminatory manner in violation of the Eighth Amendment. McCleskey offered numerous statistical studies into evidence demonstrating that blacks were disproportionately executed in Georgia. The studies revealed Georgia's death penalty had been utilized seven times more in cases with black defendants and white victims, than in cases with white defendants and black victims. The Court denied McCleskey's challenge, saying he failed to establish that any of the decision makers in his case acted with discriminatory purpose, and that the evidence indicated a discrepancy that

While the Supreme Court regularly ruled on cases involving arguments of ill-treatment of African Americans in the criminal justice system and examined state statutes and practices for discriminatory intent or purpose, blacks were frequently portrayed as criminals in films after 1970.

appeared to correlate with race, rather than a constitutionally significant risk of racial bias that violated the Eighth Amendment.

In 1994, Justice Blackmun took the unusual step of writing a dissent in a capital case, *Callins v. Collins*, 510 U.S. 1141, even though the majority denied a writ without writing an opinion. Stating he would "no longer tinker with the machinery of death," Blackmun announced he was against the death penalty because it was not administered in a racially equal manner. He noted that *Furman* sought to eliminate what remained of racism and the effects of poverty in capital sentencing, but that bits of racism remained. Bruce Edwin Callins was shortly put to death by lethal injection at the Texas state prison in Huntsville.

While the Supreme Court regularly ruled on cases involving arguments of ill-treatment of African Americans in the criminal justice system and examined state statutes and practices for discriminatory intent or purpose, blacks were frequently portrayed as criminals in films after 1970. *Cotton Comes to Harlem* (1970) shows black characters as every type of criminal, from murderer to con artist. Film after film has African Americans involved with crime, and alienated from the rest of America.

Dirty Harry Callahan points a 44-magnum at a horizontal black armed robber at the end of a gun battle. Harry mocks and taunts the man, then smiles and points his magnum on his captive and shoots from an empty chamber.

In *A Clockwork Orange* (1971), the only black actors are inmates in prison. *The French Connection* (1971) twice shows police going into a hostility-filled black bar. Hatred is shown in the eyes of the patrons, leaving the impression that white men without badges would be in deep trouble inside. Later, the main detective warns his partner, "Never trust a nigger." In *Walking Tall* (1975), the sheriff accuses a black man of shooting off his mouth about wanting to help his people, and asks him for help in solving a crime that resulted in the death of eight blacks. In frustration, the sheriff demands cooperation, "I'm tryin' to give you a chance."

Death Wish (1974) has a chilling scene of two black men who follow Charles Bronson into a subway tunnel, where they pull knives on him, and another scene where he is mugged by a different black man. Then, at a cocktail party, someone spouts crime statistics of fifteen to twenty-one murders a week, which provoke a character to remark, in code, for whites to flee to the suburbs.

Blacks are terrifying in *Network* (1976). They are portrayed as radical revolutionaries or irrational and dangerous criminals who spew filthy language. *The Godfather* (1972), *Goodfellas* (1990), *Annie Hall* (1977), and *The Sting* (1973), all include accusations that involve blacks and crime in their dialogue, even though the accusations are not integral to the plots.

A comparison of *Cooley High* (1975) and *American Grafiti* (1973) demonstrates the different ways Hollywood treated black and white teenagers during the 1970s. The white boys find it difficult to obtain alcohol, while it is readily available to the black boys. In both movies, the youths lash out at police. *Graffiti*'s white kids bear no consequences for their lark, but *Cooley*'s black kids are arrested for grand theft auto.

In *Fort Apache the Bronx* (1981) African Americans are associated with every level of crime. Beautiful black actress Pam Grier plays a savage hooker who slices the necks of her white customers. Black gang violence in *Colors* (1988) is bone chilling. Just about every black man in *The Color Purple* (1985) is a child molester or wife beater.

Even supposedly innocent and fun movies, such as *E.T. the Extra-Terrestrial* (1982), unnecessarily place African Americans in a sordid light. And, instead of portraying Eddie Murphy as just a funny cop in *Beverly Hills Cop* (1984), he is shown stealing terry cloth robes from a hotel. *Ghost* (1990) portrays Whoopi Goldberg as a swindler, and *Clara's Heart* (1988), where she serves as a maid and child care worker, tells us she had an incestuous encounter with her teenage son.

Black moviemakers got into the act, too. While most of Spike Lee's *Do the Right Thing* (1989) portrays African Americans sensitively, Lee ends his film by having almost every black in the film engage in vandalism. John Singleton's *Boyz N the Hood* (1991) begins with startling statistics on the extent of violence among black men. The film has a pitiful scene with two young black kids being taken off in a patrol car as the neighbors watch. *Mo Better Blues* (1990) viewers must watch Denzel Washington undergo a severe beating by other black men.

Devil in a Blue Dress (1995) has a black business owner ready and willing to engage in crime. In *Rising Sun* (1993), black residents of Los Angeles are shown eager to engage in crime when black actor Wesley Snipes leads Japanese pursuers into a black residential section of the city. He arranges for the local hoods to "detain" his pursuers, explaining, "Rough neighborhoods may be America's last advantage." When white teenagers want to buy drugs, they proceed immediately to the black section of an Ohio city in *Traffic*, 2000.

Jackie Brown (1997) is supposed to be a comedy. Indeed, it is funny. But it sure is scary in its treatment of African Americans, holding the entire race out to be feared for its violence. Black actor Samuel L. Jackson, who plays an arms dealer, remarks, "When them Hong Kong flicks came out, every nigger in the world had to have a 45 and they ain't want one, they want two cause all those niggers wanta be the killer." When another character confides he faces up to three years in prison, Jackson retorts, "Three years! That's an old crime. Man, they ain't got room in the joint for all those niggers out here killin' people now. How they gonna find room for you?" Shortly thereafter, Jackson shoots the other character.

> *We do not know the extent racial profiling plays in targeting African Americans for prosecution, but we definitely know both that it is a problem and that Hollywood perpetuates the belief that blacks are natural born criminals.*

In 2001, *Training Day* shows black actor Denzel Washington as a consummate cop-gone-wrong, comfortably committing crimes right along with the criminals in areas inhabited by violent black gangs.

Recent movies also match blacks with violent natures, even when the story has nothing to do with blacks and violence. *Inside Man* (2006) explains a problem in a relationship between a black detective and his black girlfriend. The problem stems from the fact that her seventeen-year-old brother has just been convicted of his third felony. The detective explains that one of the crimes was a violent robbery. Later in the film, for no apparent reason, an eight-year-old black boy explains a computerized animation game to an adult white man who is mystified with the violence portrayed. One animated black man in the game shoots another black man while shouting, "Kill dat nigga!"

We do not know the extent racial profiling plays in targeting African Americans for prosecution, but we definitely know both that it is a problem and that Hollywood perpetuates the belief that blacks are natural born criminals. The United States Supreme Court has been writing about racial profiling for decades. When two black defendants argued they did not want police officers stopping cars based on the race of the occupants, conservative Justice Scalia wrote: "We of course agree with petitioners that the Constitution prohibits selective enforcement of the law based on considerations such as race."[503]

But not the film industry. In popular movies, moviemakers still use blacks as if they were props. Just as they show expensive furniture to indicate an elegant home, they use black actors to depict a high crime location. During the same decades the justices have been struggling with racial issues to rid the law of inequality, Hollywood has continually damned the entire African race by routinely displaying blacks as being prone to crime.

1991-2000
Racial Framework

AMERICA IN THE 1990S WAS a middle class country. Most people had at least a high school diploma, and almost a third had a college degree. A majority of Americans owned their own home, and many owned stocks and bonds. Blue collar work was shrinking fast. By 1996, higher education was touching more than half of the nation's young people. Of those receiving higher education, 9.2 percent were black, 5.7 percent Hispanics, 4.2 percent Asian and women of all races composed 52 percent of the whole. At the same time, 12 percent of the population was below poverty level, with an overclass and an underclass drifting further and further apart. Black urban poor were particularly hard hit.[504] The average CEO was making 157 times the amount of a shop worker.[505]

In April 1992, the whole nation watched in fear as Los Angeles burned, after four white police officers, who were captured beating a black man on videotape, were acquitted by an all-white jury. "Very much in the same way that the 1950s lynching of Emmett Till or the 1960s assassination of Dr. Martin Luther King, Jr. marked defining moments in African America's ongoing struggle for racial justice, the stark videotape, the acquittal of the four white police officers, and the uprising that followed it marked a consciousness-shaping moment for a new generation of Americans."[506] Los Angelinos rioted for four days. Authors James Oliver Horton and Lois E. Horton say there were thirty-eight deaths, four thousand arrests, thirty-seven hundred buildings destroyed and damage estimated at five hundred million dollars.[507]

Racial tensions in the country continued. The Hortons say there were accusations that some whites perpetrated racist beliefs and reinforced stereotypical notions about blacks. A popular book published in 1994, *The Bell Curve* stated there were important connections between race and intellect, and suggested African Americans were genetically limited and best suited for society's lower-level jobs.[508] Some blacks made similar claims about whites.

Even though President Clinton was supportive of liberal positions on social issues, his economic practices caused concern in black America. In 1995, black unemployment was twice the level of whites.

Professor Leonard Jeffries, head of the Afro-American Studies Department at City College, New York, taught that whites were biologically inferior to blacks, and that white genes were deformed in the Ice Age, producing an inadequate supply of melanin. This deficiency supposedly made white people capable of appalling crimes. All the while, black genes were enhanced by the sun.[509]

Louis Farrakhan's Nation of Islam published a book in 1991, *The Secret Relationship Between Blacks and Jews*, which charged that Jews financed the slave trade. Blacks and Hasidic Jews were pitted against each other as tensions grew in a section of Brooklyn that same year.[510]

Pat Buchanan won a substantial white "protest vote" against George Bush in the early 1992 presidential primaries and the applause of delegates at the Republican National Convention.[511] But Bill Clinton won the 1992 presidential election with only 43 percent of the popular vote, as blacks voted for him in overwhelming numbers.[512] Clinton came from a modest family and rose through academic achievements as a Rhodes Scholar at Oxford and a Yale Law School graduate.[513] Even though he was supportive of liberal positions on social issues, his economic practices caused concern in black America. In 1995, black unemployment was twice the level of whites.[514]

Clinton focused on the need for more police to combat urban crime, and was criticized for reinforcing conservative assumptions that African Americans were more likely to be criminals."[515] In fact, there *had* been a rapid rise in crime. In 1993, 1.3 million Americans were victims of gun related crimes. By mid-June 1994, America's prison population exceeded one million, double the population of ten years earlier. In the year ending June 30, 1995, the prison population grew by nearly nine percent, the largest increase in American history. A high percentage of convictions in some cities, such as Los Angeles, were of black defendants.[516]

Historians James and Lois Horton explain that in poorer African American urban neighborhoods, unemployed people's vulnerability to crime and drug addiction is debilitating. They point out that many young black males have a choice between zero

There was a split among African American leaders and organizations when the first President Bush nominated Clarence Thomas to replace Justice Thurgood Marshall on the United States Supreme Court.

and the drug trade, and that laws punish crack users and dealers particularly severely. "They are more likely to be sent to jail and to receive longer sentences, for example, than cocaine users, who are more likely to be middle class and white." A 1990 survey revealed that 67 percent of college-edu-cated American blacks either believe or would not dismiss the possibility that the availability of crack in the inner cities is a systematic plot against black communities.[517]

There was a split among African American leaders and organizations when the first President Bush nominated Clarence Thomas to replace Justice Thurgood Marshall on the United States Supreme Court. On one hand, they were proud to have a continued black presence on the Court, but on the other hand they feared Thomas's conservative views. When Professor Anita Hill accused Thomas of sexual harassment, the split worsened. Nonetheless, the Senate confirmed Thomas after contentious discussions.[518] A very popular black appointment by President Bush was General Colin Powell as chair of the Joint Chiefs of Staff.[519]

The difference in black versus white marriage rates was small until the 1960s. By the 1990s, only 38 percent of black women aged 15 to 44 were married, while 58 per-cent of the white women in the same age group were. There was a huge rise in unmar-ried mothers during the same time. In 1960, there were seventy-three thousand never married mothers, and by 1990, there were 2.9 million. Unmarried motherhood has been far more common among blacks than among whites. In 1960, 24 percent of black children were born to unmarried mothers compared to 2 percent of white children. By 1991, the percentage of births to unmarried mothers was 68 percent of black births and 18 percent for whites. The alarming acceleration in births to unmarried mothers was probably the biggest factor in persuading Congress to end the Aid to Families with Dependent Children program. In August, 1996, Clinton signed the Welfare Reform Act which diminished a fundamental part of the welfare structure.[520]

Many also perceived the result of the murder trial of O.J. Simpson as a racially determined verdict.[521] Television cameras displayed pictures of jubilant blacks and disbelieving whites. There were discussions about the historical treatment of blacks by the police and the courts, and disagreements over justice were heated. In the midst

After all the racial turmoil of the twentieth century, it seems ironic that by the end of the century many scholars agreed that race is a social construction, and not biological.

of the controversy, Louis Farrakhan conducted a Million Man March on Washington to show disappointment that the Civil Rights Movement had not brought true equality to African Americans.[522]

Political correctness continued. It included an attack on the English language, along with an assertion that minorities had a right to be taught in their own language. Seen as a form of dumbing down of America was a 1997 proposal by the School Board of Oakland, California that "Ebonics" be recognized as a distinct language and used for teaching purposes. The word was compounded from the words ebony and phonetics, and was given to black street speech. For example, "What's up?" became "Sup?"[523]

News coverage of crimes was racially imbalanced. Many more black men were casualties of crime than were perpetrators, but their victimization did not attract the media spotlight—especially on local television news programs—the way their crimes did. Some claim the media paid far more attention when whites and women were victims of crime.[524]

In response to America's racial discord, President Clinton called for Americans to hold conversations on racial issues. Clinton appointed Professor John Hope Franklin to head a commission on race. It was an interesting choice. The respected scholar has apparently always believed in the American Dream. He remembers accompanying his lawyer-father to court when he was six years old. The judge asked the little boy about his future plans and he replied, "I intend to be the first Negro president of the United States when I grow up."[525]

After all the racial turmoil of the twentieth century, it seems ironic that by the end of the century many scholars agreed that race is a social construction, and not biological. In fact, earlier in the century, a person might have changed race by simply crossing state lines, since states defined race differently. In Texas, Tennessee and Alabama a person with any African ancestry was a Negro, but in other states, persons with just one sixth or one eighth African ancestry were considered white. Virginia used to draw racial distinctions between Caucasians and American Indians, unless the Indian ancestry could be traced to Pocahontas.[526]

Resentment of affirmative actions programs was pervasive. In California, Proposition 209 passed by a substantial majority in the 1996 election. Phrased similarly to the 1964 Civil Rights Act, it amended the California Constitution to prohibit the use of quotas by California state institutions. A similar initiative passed in Washington in 1998.[527]

1991-2000

Supreme Court

MUCH CHANGED BESIDES THE CENTURY by the end of this decade. Attempts at fulfilling *Brown*'s "all deliberate speed" mandate were abandoned. Efforts at affirmative action, even by the federal government, would have enormous difficulty passing constitutional muster.[528] The Court would apply the strict scrutiny test to racial classifications used by state governments in redistricting plans. And the Supreme Court decided criminal defendants, as well as prosecutors, were prohibited from selecting juries on the basis of race.

The 1990s Court put the 1954 Court's vision in *Brown v. Board of Education* into updated perspective. The *Brown* decision focused on race being the "sole" basis for segregation. Forty years later, issues such as urban sprawl, private schools and demographics raised modern concerns that were not considered in 1954.

School busing efforts of the variety that had become prevalent once segregation was eradicated were dealt a heavy blow in 1992 in *Freeman v. Pitt*, 503 U.S. 467. Post-1970s federal courts, alert to the detrimental effect of segregation, attempted to stamp out segregation by increasing the educational benefits offered in cities and enticing whites to attend metropolitan public schools. The Court ruled that district courts need not continue shuffling children around when segregation resulted from independent demographic shifts. Only segregation that is a product of state action justifies federal court's intervention for structural reform of schools. So, societal or actual segregation was not enough to continue with federal reforms.

Brown efforts ended when *Missouri v. Jenkins*, 515 U.S. 70, returned to the Court in 1995. Five years earlier when the case, 495 U.S. 33, first came to the Supreme Court, Missouri argued the federal trial judge violated the Tenth Amendment's reservation of powers to the states. Ducking the Constitutional issue, the Court unanimously disapproved the order that Missouri raise its property tax to finance construction of an inner-city school to attract white students from the suburbs. The Court held, while the end was legitimate, the means were not narrowly enough tailored, and less intrusive methods, such as the adoption of hiring goals, were available. When the case returned in 1995, Missouri argued all remnants of the formerly segregated school system were gone. The circuit court gave some indication the remedies would remain in place until students achieved scores to the level of the national standard.

Chief Justice Rehnquist, who wrote the opinion for the court,

Actor Denzel Washington, who portrays Rubin "Hurricane" Carter in the motion picture The Hurricane, *arrives December 14, 1999 with his wife, Paulette, to the Los Angeles premiere of the film. The movie is based on the true story of professional boxer Carter's twenty-year fight to prove his innocence after he was convicted of a triple homicide. (JIM RUYMEN/AFP/ Getty Images)*

sided with Missouri. Justice Thomas indicated it was offensive that the lower courts aimed to solve school problems in the largely black district by luring white children into the schools. The Court sent the case back for the lower court to determine whether all traces of segregation had been eliminated.

The Supreme Court reversed course regarding minority set-asides in federal construction contracts in 1995 in *Adarand Constructors v. Pena*, 515 U.S. 200. Special consideration to the federal government regarding color conscious preferences had been given fifteen years earlier in *Fullilove v. v. Klutznick*, 448 U.S. 448, when six justices, differing sharply in their reasoning, upheld a 1977 statute passed by Congress that mandated set-asides. The *Adarand* Court did not completely denounce the concept of set-asides. Rather, it sent the matter back to the lower federal court to determine whether the federal program was narrowly enough tailored and applied only to individuals who were victims of past discrimination, rather than all minorities. Now, even the federal government would have to survive the Court's strict scrutiny test with regard to racial classifications.

> *In all likelihood, politics will **always** be the predominate factor and race will **never be** the predominate factor in redistricting.*

Justice Scalia wrote, "In the eyes of government, we are just one race here. It is American." Calling the federal program paternalistic and citing the Declaration of Independence, Justice Thomas was even more adamant: "As far as the Constitution is concerned, it is irrelevant whether a government's racial classifications are drawn by those who wish to oppress a race or by those who have a sincere desire to help those thought to be disadvantaged."

The 1990s Supreme Court also added an extra requirement to voter redistricting plans by ruling the strict scrutiny test applied to these as well. But in trying to apply that concept, there was a problem. The Voting Rights Act of 1965 tells state legislatures they must take race into account when they draw redistricting maps after each census. The stakes are very high in these cases since redistricting results in control over the state legislature for the next ten years. In 1993, in *Shaw v. Reno*, 509 U.S.630, the Court said the non-minority plaintiff who brought the suit had stated a cause of action, since race played too great a role in the redistricting plan. So, it seemed that the case just did not survive the strict scrutiny test. Yet in *Miller v. Johnson*, 515 U.S. 900, 1995, the Court said strict scrutiny was only used when race was the *predominant* factor in redistricting. In all likelihood, politics will *always* be the predominate factor and race will *never* be the predominate factor in redistricting. Income, education, race and occupation are good predictors about how a person will vote. Race is used by politicians as a proxy for how the person is likely to vote, so in the end, race is part of a political goal. Even if the plan does trigger strict scrutiny, the state has a defense of compliance with the Voting Rights Acts, but only if it would have been subjected to litigation for failure to comply with the Act.

From the wide attention given to both the trial of four California police officers who were captured on video beating a black man named Rodney King, and the murder trial of black celebrity O.J. Simpson, the public was acutely aware during this decade that the racial composition of juries is significant. The Supreme Court was also concerned with the issue. In 1986, the Court had issued an opinion in *Batson v. Kentucky*, 476 U.S. 79, that held the Equal Protection Clause in the Fourteenth Amendment meant *states* could not eliminate prospective jurors based on race. This issue arises from the use of peremptory challenges by lawyers on both sides during jury selection. Before *Batson*, prosecutors routinely used challenges to shape a jury based on race.

In 1992, the case of *Georgia v. McCollum*, 505 U.S. 42, arrived at the Supreme Court. Three white owners had been tried for assaulting two black customers of a dry cleaning establishment. The prosecutor requested the trial judge order that the defense attorneys not use their peremptory challenges to exclude blacks from the jury. Georgia courts declined to extend the *Batson* precedent to apply to defense attorneys, so the prosecutors appealed to the Supreme Court. The 1992 opinion extended *Batson*, stating the Constitution also prohibits criminal defendants from engaging in purposeful discrimination based on race.

1991-2000
Hollywood

ACCORDING TO SCREENWRITER WILLIAM GOLDMAN, "I think the 90s are by far the worst decade in history. I can't come up with the ten best movies of the 90s. I think each decade's been worse since the 30s. It's not just the studio thing. We don't know why, but talent tends to cluster. I believe right now is a time of low talent not just in the movies, but in all the arts."[529]

Considering only mainstream Hollywood, the industry's treatment of African American issues confirms Goldman's statement. Mainstream directors and producers continued to demean African Americans during the 1990s. But despite the usual racially hateful film, a number of movies produced during this decade by African American directors show the more positive side of blacks. Numerous black actors proved to be stars during the 1990s.

Old racist messages that whites should be afraid of blacks, black men want to have white women, and slavery was not all that bad were still alive and well in mainstream Hollywood movies at the end of the twentieth century. The film industry's most offensive portrayals of African Americans during this decade are *Rising Sun* (1992), *Jackie Brown* (1997), *Traffic* (2000), and *The Patriot*, (2000).

In *Rising Sun*, black actor Wesley Snipes plays a Los Angeles detective. In Michael Crichton's novel, on which the film was based, the detective was a white man. Snipes,

Old racist messages that whites should be afraid of blacks, black men want to have white women, and slavery was not all that bad were still alive and well in mainstream Hollywood movies at the end of the twentieth century.

usually a larger than life persona, shrinks appreciably as he plays next to white Sean Connery. Connery is clearly in charge, except in one scene when the two attempt to evade Japanese pursuers. Snipes takes over by driving his car into a black ghetto, and arranges for black hoodlums to scare the pursuers, which they do with terrifying dispatch. Snipes offhandedly remarks, "Rough neighborhoods may be America's last advantage." The scene was not in Crichton's novel, and appears to have been added to give Snipes' part a racial significance.

The film hints a black man was used, not because the part could have been played by a black actor or a white one, but because the black man knew about thugs. Additionally, moviemakers did not "waste" an opportunity to scare whites by reminding them how frightening some black neighborhoods can be.

Traffic might have been worse than *Rising Sun* in its ridicule of African Americans. A pretty rich white girl is hooked on drugs. In a blatant attempt to shake up the audience with the danger of black neighborhoods, the girl searches a black ghetto for a fix, and ends up in a room with a muscular naked black man who will give her a fix and have sex with her. The scene is similar to the hated black Reconstruction Governor Lynch who tries to force the white girl to marry him, and requires the Ku Klux Klan to stop him in *The Birth of a Nation*. Hollywood continues to remind people of the racist message that black men covet white women.

The Patriot provides a 21st century time machine jolt back to *The Birth of a Nation*, *Uncle Tom's Cabin* and *Gone With the Wind*. The screen tells viewers the year is 1776 and the place is South Carolina. Sentimental music. Pastoral scenes. All the black workers are smiling and happy on the plantation. They love their master, Mel Gibson. Worse yet, the film tells viewers the black laborers are all free men working the land, minimizing the historical fact that during the 1700s, 89 percent of slaves in the colonies were living in the South.[530] The film almost denies the very existence of slavery in the heart of Dixie.

Forrest Gump (1994 Best Picture of the Year and AFI's #71) is also as a comedy. It succeeds. The film is very funny. Forrest is mentally backward, but gifted with a naïve and basic common sense, and amazing good luck. Viewers are told Forrest has an I.Q. of seventy-five. But no such explanation is given for the main black character, Bubba, who is portrayed just as dim-witted as Forrest.

Unforgiven (1992 Best Picture of the Year and AFI's #98) challenges perceptions about the old West. It is difficult to believe a black man was living in the late nineteenth century West without anyone noticing his race. Black actor Morgan Freeman plays opposite Clint Eastwood. Both own little farms and when they take off in search of outlaws, Eastwood says, "He's my partner. He don't go, I don't go." Later, concern is shown about giving Freeman his share of the reward money, but no indication is given that a black man is being beaten because of his race when the Freeman character is bound and whipped to death. Dialogue explains, "This is what happens to assassins around here." History was probably rewritten a little for *Unforgiven.*

Fear of black men being too close to white women was implied in several films of the decade. In James Patterson's novel *Kiss the Girls* (1997), John Grisham's novel *The Pelican Brief* (1993), and Walter Mosley's novel *Devil in a Blue Dress* (1995), the men have love affairs with the female in the book. When Hollywood adapted the books to the screen, it eliminated the love scenes. In *Devil in a Blue Dress*, light skinned Jennifer Beals plays the leading lady, who passes for white in the story. Still, the film industry was afraid to have Denzel Washington too close to her. Author Walter Mosley learned the browner Washington could not kiss Beals in the movie because of the studio's fear the picture would "lose Alabama." "Maybe," he said, "Denzel could *think* about kissing her. He's a good actor."[531]

> *Throughout the 1990s, African Americans managed to significantly extend their influence over the production of movies.*

Besides the deletion of a love affair between a darker man and lighter woman, *Devil*'s story demonstrates how white men are afraid to have black men near white women. When a white woman speaks with Denzel Washington, a white man panics and calls to his friends, at which point the whites attack Washington. Both *The Pelican Brief* and *Kiss the Girls* place the men and women in hotel rooms together, but nothing more than camaraderie and a father/daughter relationship takes place.

Throughout the 1990s, African Americans managed to significantly extend their influence over the production of movies. *Boyz N the Hood* (1991) was directed by black director John Singleton. Singleton's need to attract a crossover white audience could be an explanation for the bone chilling statements shown as text on the screen when the movie begins, "One out of every twenty-one Black American males will be murdered in their lifetime. . . . Most will die at the hands of another Black male. . . . South Central Los Angeles, 1984." On the other hand, it could have been the director's way of reminding everyone who the victims of crimes really are.

That appeal to a black audience is sought is not in doubt. Reminiscent of a wall calendar that bears a photograph of President Richard Nixon in the Blaxploitation film *Cotton Comes to Harlem*, *Boyz* shows Reagan/Bush posters being used for target practice. An alarming scene reveals the lack of relevance of an elementary school teacher's lesson on Thanksgiving and the Pilgrims to a class of black students. In another scene, a black crime victim is shown waiting over an hour for police to arrive, only to have the officers refuse to write a report. A scene where two young black boys are hauled off in a patrol car for stealing is disturbing and disquieting. The next time we see the children it is seven years later. It looks as though they were locked up the entire time.

Singleton does not use *Boyz* as an apology for black males from poor neighborhoods. In fact, he seems intent to point out how unsavory, uncouth and unstructured some can be. Several times characters point out that someone lacks motivation or ambition. Most of the language used in casual conversations among the youths is gratuitously filthy. When the food is served at a barbecue, the teenage boys push ahead of the girls in line.

It is not clear whether the movie's treatment of women is intended to illustrate the attitudes of African American men toward African American women. The film portrays a sad state of affairs for black women, and focuses on one black man, underscoring his virtues to such an extent that viewers likely mused about recommending him for canonization.

The most positive portrayal of black women, on the other hand, is as ineffectual and incapable of dealing with family problems. For example, the protagonist's mother admits she cannot handle her son, does not appear to try very hard to change things and turns the child over to his father's care. Most of the teenaged girls are depicted as shallow and dim. One mother shows open preference for one son and hostility toward another. A different mother, a drug addict, allows her dirty, diapered baby to run unattended in the street. Since there was no counter balancing of the mother's situation, such as showing what role the baby's father had in bringing up the child, it appeared the portrayal was misleading, and not intended as an illustration. Another hint there was women hating involved was revealed in a scene where a black man meets his former wife at an upscale restaurant she selected. It is obvious that he is resentful of her success. White movie directors would probably not have dared display such blatant distrust and open hostility toward black women.

A film specifically intended to be about black women, *Waiting to Exhale*, 1995, is based on a novel by black author Terry McMillan. Four black women are longtime friends. The book delved into the women's juggling of careers and families, as well as men, but the film superficially portrays their problems with men. Their concerns about black men preferring white women and black men being in prison are discussed, but not to a meaningful extent.

Film director John Singleton provides a history lesson about racism in America from an African American perspective in *Rosewood*. The movie depicts a real incident in Florida in 1923 when an entire town of black people was massacred after a white woman falsely reported she was beaten by a black man. The difference between Singleton's movie and other renditions of the historical plight of African Americans is that he tells the tragedy through the massacre's victims, and not a white person. Singleton makes viewers share in the horror, but he does not shun whites or make them the enemy. The film shows the often seen refusal and fear of blacks to cooperate with the police. A black woman is asked if she saw anything. In fact, "Aunt Sarah" saw a white man beat the woman, but she tells the sheriff, "No, Mr. Ellis. I ain't seen nothin'."

Hammering home how the system cannot be trusted, *Rosewood*'s screen text states at the end of the film, "In 1993, seventy years after the massacre, the Florida House of Representatives granted reparations to the Rosewood families, spearheaded by Philomena's son, Arnett Doctor. The success of the case was due largely to the sworn testimony of several SURVIVORS, who were children at the time of the events, and to the deposition of one WHITE citizen who testified on behalf of the victims. [¶] The official death toll of the Rosewood massacre, according to the state of Florida is eight—two WHITES and six BLACKS. The survivors, a handful of whom are still alive today, place the number anywhere between forty and one hundred fifty, nearly all of them AFRICAN AMERICAN."

Devil in a Blue Dress, based on a novel by a black author, tells a story through the eyes of the black protagonist. Besides Hollywood's fear of having black men too close to white women, as discussed above, the film highlights blacks' fear and distrust of the police. When Denzel Washington is at the police station, he remarks, "The game of cops and niggers," while being beaten by two white policemen. Later, he finds himself driving Jennifer Beals—who he does not yet realize is "passing"—past a patrol car, and shakes his head with fear on his face and remarks, ". . . in the middle of the night, in a white neighborhood, with a white woman in the car. . . . "

A Time to Kill, 1996, is a story about a black man who takes the law into own hands after his little girl was raped and beaten by two depraved white crackers. The story within the story, however, is the black man's inherent distrust in the justice system.

The quintessential story from an African American's mouth about disgust and disrespect for the white man's system is Spike Lee's *Malcolm X*. Another twist about the white man's distress over black men and white women is shown when Denzel Washington's *Malcolm X* character remarks, "Because so many black women have been raped by the white man, the black man can't wait to get his hands on the white man's prize—the white woman." According to the movie, Malcolm X had a long affair with a white woman. In the midst of it, he says to her, "When you gonna holler rape?" Later, Malcolm and a black friend, along with their white girlfriends, are arrested for burglary. It was the first offense for all of them. The white women are sentenced to two years in prison, while the black men are sent away for eight to ten years. One man whispers to the other, "Our crime was sleeping with a white girl."

During his early years, Malcolm has his hair straightened (to look "whiter") until an acquaintance asked, "What makes you ashamed of being black?" Perhaps the saddest part of the film is a young Malcolm sitting behind his school desk with his white teacher standing over him dashing his dreams, "A lawyer is no realistic goal for a nigger." As an adult, when Malcolm works at a job that society finds acceptable for a black man (an attendant on a train), a white passenger praises his services as a piece of lemon meringue pie is placed before him, at which point Malcolm fantasizes about shoving the pie into the passenger's face. Later, Malcolm tells his followers that "X" is the unknown in mathematics, and Muslims substitute "X" for their slave name because they don't want the slave name and don't know their real name.

Malcolm X deals with the black/police issue, too: "They traded those white sheets for police uniforms. They traded those blood hounds for police dogs." The film criticizes the American system with such statements as: "Even if you get out, you're still in prison." and "We didn't land on Plymouth Rock. Plymouth Rock landed on us." When the plot reveals Jackie Robinson joined the Brooklyn Dodgers, the retort is, "White men throw us a bone and we're supposed to forget four hundred years of oppression."

The Hurricane (1999) was also based on a true story. Just like Malcolm X, Ruben "Hurricane" Carter survived a difficult childhood. As did Malcolm, Carter explained his last name was his slave name that was given to his forefathers by slave owners. Also like Malcolm, Ruben Carter was sentenced to prison and was placed in lengthy solitary confinement, until he followed prison rules. The movie is painful to watch, as an innocent man spends twenty-two years in prison, primarily because a white policeman hated him.

Amistad (1997) can be compared with *Rosewood* (1997). Both are about historical and little known true incidents of racism in America. Both are sensitive to the tyranny against blacks in America. But *Amistad* focuses on the young white lawyer who represents escapees from a slave ship in 1839 who are claimed as property, salvage and goods by numerous whites, rather than the blacks themselves. Nonetheless, the film provides an excellent revelation of important issues. In spite of the fact that seven of the nine Supreme Court justices were slave owners, the black men prevailed. It may be due to Steven Spielberg's fame and success—and also his sensitivity—that such a movie was made at all.

Philadelphia (1993) is the story of a white man who is an attorney. He sues his silk stocking law firm after he is fired when the firm discovers he has AIDS. Denzel Washington is a plaintiff's lawyer hired to represent him. While the film is not explicitly about an African American, it contains several racial issues. The race of the plaintiff's lawyer does not add too much to the movie except that a black man can hold the same kind of bias about homosexuals as a white man. More significantly, Denzel Washington's race demonstrated that many roles can be played by any competent actor, regardless of race.

One of the witnesses in the movie's trial, a secretary in the law firm, is also an African American. She explains that a partner at the firm complained her earrings were too ethnic. He wanted her to wear something more American, and she told him the earrings were American, African American. A remark by the AIDS victim's mother is telling in that it demonstrates the struggle of African Americans has been understood and applauded by white America. After the man with AIDS is fired, he discusses whether or not to file suit against his former employer. In encouraging her son, the mother says, "I didn't raise my kids to sit on the back of the bus. You get up and fight for your rights."

Conflict between two non-white groups was sensitively depicted in the non-mainstream 1992 film, *Mississippi Masala*. The story begins in Uganda in 1972 when an Indian family, including a mother, father and their young girl, along with many Asians, is expelled. "Africa is for Africans, black Africans," a character states. The next scenes show the little girl, grown up and sexy, hence "masala" or spicy, and living in Mississippi. Racism within the Indian culture is displayed when the girl, dark skinned, is being considered as a wife for wealthy Harry Patel. One of the Indian women states, "You can be dark and have money. You can be fair and have no money. But you cannot be dark and have no money and expect to get Harry Patel." Lucky for her, the "masala" does not want Harry Patel. She wants Denzel Washington, the local man who owns a carpet cleaning business. And there the trouble begins.

Before the two young people get together romantically, a few of her Indian relatives try to talk Washington out of bringing a lawsuit over a traffic accident. "All us people of color must stick together." When the romance is revealed, the Indians go berserk and Washington explodes, "You and your folks can come down here from God knows where and be about as black as the ace of spades and as soon as you get here, you start acting white and treating us like we your doormats. I know that you and your daughter ain't but a few shades from this right here," as he points to his face.

Masala sensitively portrays Indians as victims of discrimination by Africans and then turns the tables by having the Indians practice racial discrimination against

African Americans without having learned any lessons from their own experiences as victims of racism. The story leaves the viewer wondering whether or not we are all racists at our cores. The film ignores Hollywood's taboo regarding miscegenation, and the two walk off into the sunset together.

Other films provided opportunities for strong, talented African American actors to display their abilities. *Enemy of the State* (1998) lent a vehicle to Will Smith, Regain King and Lisa Bonet to show what they could do. Smith, portrayed as a successful lawyer who lived in a beautiful Washington D.C. home with his wife and son, proved to be a leading man, sympathetic and susceptible to harm, but very bright and imaginative at the same time. Smith's role did not require him to be a super jock; he does not have a filthy mouth. His character manages to disagree without displaying an attitude. And most of all, he is very funny. King was also funny and convincing as his wife. She was strong willed, but soft and vulnerable at the same time, unlike many other roles played by African American women. Bonet, who played the part of the other woman, demonstrates she is more than just a pretty face.

Murder at 1600 (1997) gave Wesley Snipes a chance to carry a serious film while appearing dignified and smart, although he was not allowed to get too close to his beautiful blond sidekick. Morgan Freeman ran circles around Brad Pitt in *Se7en* (1995), although Pitt was smart enough to follow along and give Freeman center stage. Eddie Murphy displayed how outrageously funny and tender and talented he can be all at the same time in *The Nutty Professor* (1996). Samuel L. Jackson, although also not allowed anything more than a chaste kiss with the beautiful white woman, was clever and entertaining in *The Long Kiss Goodnight* (1996).

Whoopi Goldberg was funny and a definite star in *Sister Act* (1992). She played a cabaret singer who goes into hiding by posing as a nun. The film managed to eliminate the black actress's race from her role, a feat that appeared somewhat awkward in one scene in particular. Gangsters were searching for the Goldberg character among a group of nuns in a casino, yet no one thought to describe her as the black one.

*Movies not discussed in text appear in endnote.[532]

1991–2000
Decade Wrap-up

THE UNITED STATES SUPREME COURT put the brakes on *Brown*'s school desegregation mission. It also all but stopped minority set-asides for construction contracts and made voting rights cases more difficult to win. Meanwhile, Hollywood utilized techniques from 1915's *The Birth of a Nation* by keeping black men at arm's length from white women, delivered the racist message that whites should be afraid of blacks and continued to put America's racism into historical settings. At the same time, non-mainstream filmmakers produced some racially sensitive movies.

Throughout the 1990s, Hollywood continued with its obsession of keeping black men away from white women. *Devil in a Blue Dress, The Pelican Brief, Kiss the Girls, The Long Kiss Goodnight* and *Murder at 1600* stand as exhibits of the industry's fixation.

Movies such as *Traffic, Rising Sun* and *Jackie Brown* have scenes calculated to make whites afraid of blacks. Hollywood makes money fanning racial tensions. With its portrayal of happy blacks on the plantation in *The Patriot*, the film industry in the year 2000 sent the same messages it did in *The Birth of a Nation*: blacks need to be controlled and blacks are happy when they are controlled by whites. The film industry, mainstream and non-mainstream, did produce movies dealing with racial issues during the 1990s. *Amistad* was set in 1839. *Rosewood* was set in 1923. *Devil in a Blue Dress* was in the late 1940s. *Malcolm X* took place from the 1940s through the 1960s. *The Hurricane* began in the 1940s and continued through the 1980s. None dealt with con-

Hollywood makes money fanning racial tensions.

temporary racial issues, although *The Hurricane* was close in time. But that film "cheated" some by pretending to be based on a true story while placing a fictionalized 1930s racist cop in the 1960s through the 1980s.

The industry did what it does best in making *The Hurricane*. A screen disclaimer at it's beginning puts the viewer on notice that significant deviations from the truth were taken. In real life, a courageous federal trial judge, Haddon Lee Sarokin, ordered Rubin "Hurricane" Carter's release, eloquently explaining his reason, "There is a substantial danger that our society, concerned about the growth of crime, will retreat from the safeguards and rights accorded to the accused by the constitution. The need to combat crime should never be utilized to justify an erosion of our fundamental guarantees. Indeed, the growing volume of criminal cases should make us even more vigilant; the greater the *quantity*—the greater the risk to the *quality* of justice."

Eddie Murphy was honored for his role in Beverly Hills Cop *on October 31, 1995. (Photo by Ron Galella/ WireImage)*

The judge found two basic deficiencies in Carter's murder conviction. The prosecution appealed to racists on the jury by arguing that Carter and his codefendant, who were both black, were motivated to murder total strangers solely because they were white. Second, the prosecution did not disclose exculpatory evidence to the defense. In real life, New Jersey prosecutors unsuccessfully tried to have Carter reincarcerated after Judge Sarokin's ruling.[533] Carter's case ended on January 11, 1988, when the United States Supreme Court denied review.[534]

Instead of adhering to the true story, which is compelling, Hollywood chose to liven it up by including a maliciously racist white cop. The fictional movie version does not make much sense. The racist cop begins a personal vendetta against a cute eleven-year-old black boy with a stutter. "A nigger with a knife," the cop murmurs. The script required the man to keep the hatred fire burning for decades, including inducing witnesses to lie. Instead of pointing out defects within the criminal justice system, the film points to one man, letting the system off the hook. Movie audiences were allowed off the hook too, since most believe modern police departments have rid themselves of overt racists. Had viewers been told the system was at fault, they might not have returned to the snack stand or the movie theatre.

Time will tell, but the Court's reigning-in civil rights cases may be its way of declaring that legal impediments under the Fourteenth Amendment have been successfully removed.

In a way, Rubin "Hurricane" Carter's real case was perfect for the 1990s atmosphere when racial biases of jurors were on everyone's mind. Most of the world talked about little else during the O.J. Simpson trial. And the U.S. Supreme Court ruled in the 1992 case of *Georgia v. McCollum*, which involved three whites who were tried for assaulting two blacks, that defense attorneys cannot use peremptory challenges to exclude blacks from the jury. The Court said the Constitution prohibits criminal defendants from engaging in purposeful discrimination based on race.

Time will tell, but the Court's reining-in of civil rights cases may be its way of declaring that legal impediments under the Fourteenth Amendment have been successfully removed, and the Court will continue to monitor to assure they are never again implemented. Regarding Hollywood, time will also tell. But while the mainstream film industry continues to pretend there *is* such a thing as a "Southern Box Office," non-mainstream moviemakers, including many nonwhites, have managed to produce significant and important works that are both entertaining *and* sensitive to racial issues, and many African Americans have shown themselves to have noteworthy talent.

Many nonwhite producers, directors and actors have succeeded over the last century, and this must be viewed in context with the many significant Supreme Court cases. Each case lifted a barrier that blocked the success of these creative people. It can't be a coincidence.

Zooming In . . .

A Close-up Look at How Hollywood Revised History to the Detriment of Blacks

SINCE THE BEGINNING OF THE film industry, Hollywood has made misrepresentations about blacks, their status and their achievements. A few times the misrepresentations might have been well-meaning, but generally they seemed to be efforts from moviemakers to relieve audiences from feeling guilty. Slavery was portrayed as a gentle institution. Achievements by blacks were shown to be won long before they actually were, which minimized the grief and turmoil suffered. Probably the worst technique was to show discrimination and racism through individual rabid racists, rather than reveal the depth of prejudice and bias that actually existed.

It started with *The Birth of a Nation*. Blacks were cast in a negative light while whites were shown to be tolerant and suffering at the hands of blacks. Text on the silent screen told the audience that slave masters were "kindly" and that slaves were given long breaks when doing chores. Puppies and kittens played on the laps of the master and his family.

After the Civil War, when blacks tried to exercise their rights, whites were shown disheveled and emaciated, suffering from the ineptness of blacks. In one scene that depicted a black South Carolina Legislature in action, one legislator is shown picking his toes while another is drinking alcohol from a bottle, as a third gnaws on a meaty bone. At a voting station, blacks are shown cheating by voting more than once while whites are deprived of their right to vote at all.

When the film *Uncle Tom's Cabin* was released in 1927, blacks expected white audiences to gain an understanding of the black man, as seen through Harriet Beecher Stowe's eyes. They hoped it might finally eliminate the caricature the black man had acquired in years of gauche roads shows.[535] But how unlike Stowe's book the film turned out to be. Hollywood eliminated the author's sensitive treatment of slavery and inserted an often happy and sometimes comical existence for blacks.

The film had the same "Swanee River" music that played at the South Carolina plantation of the Camerons in *The Birth of a Nation*, but here the text on the screen reads, MR. AND MRS. SHELBY, WHOSE GENTLE RULE OF THE SLAVES WAS TYPICAL OF THE SOUTH. Harriet Beecher Stowe's book identifies Eliza as "a young quadroon woman,"[536] but the only indication in the film that Eliza is associated with other slaves is that the silent screen text says so. The other slaves are dark, bear silly smiles, eat watermelon, and display a need for serious dental work. But Eliza's and little Harry's quarters have flowered wallpaper, upholstered chairs, portraits hanging on the walls, lovely curtains and carved wooden furniture.[537] Uncle Tom and his family live in a cabin. While the other slaves are dressed in rags, Eliza and Harry wear nice clothes and Eliza's hair and make-up are perfect.

Topsy, the young slave girl is mischaracterized in the movie. The film gives her a comic appearance, and she appears to be a white boy in black face with a steel wool wig. But it is more than her appearance that the film changed. In the book she is a sympathetic character, who shows signs of neglect and abuse.[538] Yet the movie has a comical woman beating Topsy for stealing. The scene is funny as Topsy jumps up and down, as though the flogging is harmless. But moviemakers reduced the humanity and sensitivity of the book by making the child a jester and a thief, and relieved audiences from having to worry that slaves were mistreated.

By the time *Gone With the Wind* was released in 1938, Hollywood had further romanticized its rendition of slavery with its beautiful opening scenery and music over the rolling statement: THERE WAS A LAND OF CAVALIERS AND COTTON FIELDS. HERE IN THIS PRETTY WORLD, GALLANTRY TOOK ITS LAST BOW. HERE WAS THE LAST EVER SEEN OF KNIGHTS AND THEIR LADIES FAIR, OF MASTER AND OF SLAVE . . . LOOK FOR IT ONLY IN BOOKS FOR IT IS NO MORE THAN A DREAM REMEMBERED . . . A CIVILIZATION GONE WITH THE WIND.

As Melanie looks over the idealized plantation scene, she remarks: "It is our world, wanting only to be graceful and beautiful." Throughout the film, slaves are shown as being treated with compassion. After the war Ashley complains about Scarlett mistreating convicts who are hired to work in her lumberyard. Scarlett points out he had not been so particular about owning slaves. Ashley replies, "That was different. We didn't treat them that way. Besides, I'd have freed them all when father died if the war hadn't already freed them.' Thus, with one sentence, *Gone With the Wind* wiped away the need for the Civil War to free the slaves.

Possibly the most despicable portrayal of slavery was in the 2000 film *The Patriot*. The movie is loosely based on the real life of Revolutionary War fighter Francis Marion, known as "The Swamp Fox." The story begins in 1776 with the same idyllic scenes of a South Carolina plantation as in *The Birth of a Nation*. Disregarding historical realities, *The Patriot* shows actor Mel Gibson's black field hands as being free, minimizing the historical fact that during the 1700s, 89 percent of slaves in the colonies were living in the South. So happy are the field hands, they volunteer to return to help Gibson rebuild his plantation after the Revolutionary War. Filmmakers would have its viewers believe The Swamp Fox freed his slaves. In fact, the real Francis Marion was not only a slaveholder, he is said to have raped his female slaves.[539]

Military service by blacks in America's armed forces has also been seriously misrepresented by Hollywood.

Military service by blacks in America's armed forces has also been seriously misrepresented by Hollywood. Hundreds of thousands of African Americans served in the Revolutionary, Civil, and Spanish-American wars; and in World Wars I and II. Yet Hollywood's early portrayal of blacks in the military was misleading. *Yankee Doodle Dandy*, a patriotic 1942 movie solute to songwriter and entertainer George M. Cohan that starred James Cagney, included a tribute to all who served America in its wars. Blacks were excluded from all military routines. The only blacks shown were grateful former slaves who sang spiritually around the Lincoln Memorial. Even though the first hero of World War II was an African American sailor stationed at Pearl Harbor, *From Here to Eternity* (1955), a film that showed Americans at Pearl before, during and after the Japanese attacked it on December 7, 1941, ignores the presence of blacks in the military. On the morning of the attack, African American Dorie Miller, a mess attendant on the USS Arizona, pulled a wounded captain to safety, seized a machine gun and shot down at least four Japanese planes. For his bravery, Miller received the Navy Cross, and became America's first war hero in World War II.[540] Dorie Miller had to wait until the twenty-first century to be recognized by Hollywood in the film *Pearl Harbor*.

For some of the historically inaccurate Hollywood renditions, it is possible some of the filmmakers had "pure" intentions. Perhaps some democratically inspired producers and directors were overly anxious to include African Americans to make up for earlier wrongs. Thus, some socially conscious directors such as Eliza Kazan, who portrayed black and white stevedores working side by side at a time when unions were racially segregated, and Francis Ford Coppola, who had Africans entering through Ellis Island just as Europeans did, intended to convey a shared experience by all Americans. But such misinformation also sent the message that African Americans had equality in some parts of American society much sooner than a particular gain actually happened.

President Truman signed Executive Order 9981 on July 26, 1948, which called for equal treatment and opportunity for all persons in the armed forces.

In *Judgment at Nuremberg* (1961) the screen tells viewers of a trial in Nuremberg in 1948. Throughout the film, military guards are present in the courtroom, and several are black. In fact, in 1948, the Army was still segregated. It was not until 1954 that segregation and discrimination were eliminated from the armed services.[541] President Truman signed Executive Order 9981 on July 26, 1948, which called for equal treatment and opportunity for all persons in the armed forces. But the order did not call for the end of segregation in the military.[542]

When it might have ruined the mood to show segregation or lack of equal job opportunities, Hollywood punted. *The Greatest Show on Earth* (1952 Best Picture of the Year) shows muscular, hard-working black men every time tents are raised or lowered. Yet they are never seen mingling among the carneys or when the circus is operating. But the white characters who are part of the set-ups and tear-downs are also circus entertainers, and seen throughout the movie. In scenes when fans are watching the circus, Hollywood did not show any segregated seating sections. Instead, blacks were scattered throughout crowds going into the circus tent, but were not seen inside.

A particularly insidious tactic of Hollywood was to deflect blame from the real culprit, racism across America, and place it on the back of one vile racist, with whom no one could possibly identify. In that way, the audience, likely feeling superior to the racist wretch, could sit back and munch popcorn during the entertainment.

Pinky (1949) is about the daughter of a black washerwoman who passes for white. When she returns to her hometown in the South to stay with her grandmother, after graduating from nursing school in the North where she enjoyed the privileges of the white world, she is subjected to the cruel treatment specifically reserved for blacks. A nasty white woman and her family are portrayed as the cause of Pinky's problems.

Pinky was sympathetic to blacks to a point, but the overall message was more negative than positive. First, Pinky was played by a white actress instead of a black one, possibly to try for audience identification, a technique used in *The Birth of a*

Nation where whites in blackface played the speaking parts. In *Pinky*, local authority figures—doctor, lawyer and judge—sided with Pinky when she was the defendant in a lawsuit. This unrealistic plot sent the false message that blacks had the same legal protections as whites. In the real South, had authority figures turned their backs on white folk, there would have been problems. In fact, in the novel, written by Cid Ricketts Sumner, Pinky won her lawsuit just as she did in the movie, but the Ku Klux Klan burned down the mansion Pinky inherited from the white woman, which is a more believable ending than that dished out by Hollywood, which showed Pinky using her inherited property as a hospital for black patients.[543]

In *No Way Out* (1950) Sidney Poitier plays Dr. Luther Brooks, whose felon patient, Johnny Biddle, dies while the doctor tries to save his life. Brooks then faces a charge from the dead man's bigot brother that the "nigger doctor" murdered Biddle. According to historian Daniel Leab, "Once again racism is relegated to the lower classes, to the Biddles and the other slum inhabitants, one of whom spits at Brooks when he tries to treat a white injured in the race riot."[544]

> **With the use of subtle techniques, Hollywood covered up actual conditions in America so its audiences could enjoy the show without guilt.**

In *The Hurricane* (1999) Hollywood places blame for the plight of an incarcerated African American on a bigoted police officer, rather than on a system that permitted racist tactics. One bad cop is shown as the cause for "Hurricane" Carter's troubles. The movie is painful to watch, as Carter spends twenty-two years in prison because a white policeman hated him.

In real life, the prosecution was permitted to appeal to racist penchants of the jury and didn't turn over exculpatory evidence to the defense. Instead of telling the truth—that the justice system sometimes permits racism—Hollywood placed the blame on a fictional racist white police detective.

Thus has Hollywood revised history to the detriment of African Americans, always minimizing their ordeal. Slavery was shown as a kind and gentle institution, and rights have been falsely portrayed as existing during times they were withheld. With the use of subtle techniques, Hollywood covered up actual conditions in America so its audiences could enjoy the show without guilt. When a wrong occurred, the movie took the blame off the system and placed it on a miserable individual instead.

2001-2009
Racial Framework

THE TWENTY-FIRST CENTURY ARRIVED to witness a continuing racial divide in the United States. Two-thirds of blacks believe racism is an ongoing problem in America while two-thirds of whites believe it is not. Social Science research demonstrates beyond debate that discriminatory attitudes and behavior still exist and a large percentage of bias and prejudice, and the resulting discriminatory behavior, is due to unconscious factors.[545]

In August 2005, the entire world watched in horror as Hurricane Katrina destroyed significant portions of Louisiana and Mississippi. Television screens showed stadiums full of stranded African Americans with thirsty babies and hungry families. In 2006, the Human Rights Committee of the United Nations issued stinging conclusions regarding the human rights conduct of the United States during the emergency: "The Committee, while taking note of the various rules and regulations prohibiting discrimination in the provision of disaster relief and emergency assistance, remains concerned about information that poor people and in particular African-Americans, were disadvantaged by the rescue and evacuation plans implemented when Hurricane Katrina hit the United States of America, and continue to be disadvantaged under the reconstruction plans."[546]

African Americans tend to view the stranding of blacks during Katrina a result of continuing racism in the United States. Then Senator Barack Obama has similarly declared that the inadequate response to Katrina was not the product of overt racism, but rather "the continuation of passive indifference."[547]

In 2007, we saw the exoneration of three lacrosse players from Duke University after they were falsely, and publicly, charged with sexually assaulting an African American woman. That was the same week radio shock jock Don Imus was publicly criticized for making derogatory remarks about black women athletes from Dartmouth. The next week, *60 Minutes* ran a segment about black rock stars who support a form of noninvolvement by discouraging members of the black community from cooperating with the police, even when they are victims of crimes. In June 2007, the House of Representatives voted 422 to 2 to pass a bill called the Emmett Till Unsolved Civil Rights Crime Act. The bill would authorize up to $13.5 million a year for investigations into cold case killings during the Civil Rights era.[548]

> *African Americans tend to view the stranding of blacks during Katrina a result of continuing racism in the United States.*

Critical Race Theory is a scholarly analysis that provides understanding of legal debates concerning civil rights strategies and is taught mostly by black academics. Legal authorities in the twenty-first century, however, question the bases for CRT's premise.[549] Former executive director of the NAACP, attorney Derrick Bell, is one of those credited with creating the model. The theory is critical of the Civil Rights Movement as it presumes the white man will not make a change unless it is helpful to him.[550] The theory disagrees with the idea that laws are or can be written from a neutral perspective. For example, a commitment to "free speech" may seem like a neutral principle, but CRT theorists say it is not. They point out that saying one is committed to allowing free speech for the Ku Klux Klan is also saying that the freedom to say hateful things is more important than the right to be free from the humiliation that hate speech entails. CRT advocates are highly suspicious of liberal agenda measures such as affirmative action, and maintain that standards and institutions created by and fortifying white power should be resisted.[551]

Critical Race Theory writing and lecturing is characterized by frequent use of first person storytelling and narrative. One of Derrick Bell's best-known stories is "The Space Traders." Aliens from outer space visit this country and promise wealth in the form of gold, environmental-cleansing material, and a substitute for fossil fuels. If their offer of riches in exchange for taking every black person in America back to their home in outer space is accepted, another century of prosperity for the nation is guaranteed. In a referendum vote, Americans opt for the trade by a 70 to 30 percent

Critical Race Theory is a scholarly analysis that provides understanding of legal debates concerning civil rights strategies.

vote. The story ends with twenty million silent black men, women, and children—including babes in arms—standing on a beach at gun point by guards, and then herded onto space ships.[552]

Another phenomenon has also emerged in the new century. On September 12, 2001, Americans looked at each other in wonderment as Palestinians and other groups paraded, sang and clapped the day after thousands of our people were killed by terrorists. "Why do people hate us?" was a common query. As a result, there has been a new emergence of community identity among all Americans in the wake of 9/11.[553]

2001-2009
The Supreme Court

THE DIFFERENCE BETWEEN CONSERVATIVE AND liberal appointments to the United States Supreme Court is making huge differences in the opinions issued by the Court in the twenty-first century. Liberal and less conservative justices were inclined to level the playing field in relation to African Americans. But more conservative justices tend to be color blind and give no special treatment on the basis of race, although some regard is given on the basis of diversity.

In 2003, the Supreme Court revisited the law school admissions issue it ruled upon in 1978 in the case of *University of California v. Bakke* (438 U.S. 265). In the earlier case, a medical school at the University of California reserved sixteen out of one hundred openings for minorities. The *Bakke* decision produced six separate opinions, none of which commanded a majority. Justice Powell, who announced the Court's judgment, provided a fifth vote for invalidating the set-aside program, and also for reversing the state court's injunction against any use of race whatsoever. In the part of his opinion that was joined by no other Justice, Powell expressed his view that attaining a diverse student body was the only interest asserted by the University of California that survived scrutiny. Grounding his analysis in academic freedom, Justice Powell emphasized the nation needs diversity far broader than just ethnic and racial origin.

In *Grutter v. Bollinger* (539 U.S. 306), 2003, white law school applicants claimed they were denied admission due to a race-conscious admissions policy at the University of Michigan. The policy requires admissions officials to evaluate applicants, not only on their grades and tests scores, but also on all available information, including a personal statement, letters of recommendation and an essay that describes how each applicant will contribute to law school life and diversity. Michigan's policy does not define diversity solely in terms of racial and ethnic status, but it does state the school is committed to diversity with special reference to the inclusion of African-American, Hispanic and Native-American students.

In its divided opinion, written by Justice O'Connor, the Supreme Court held that the University of Michigan's policy was narrowly tailored to serve its compelling interest in obtaining the educational benefits that flow from a diverse student body, and did not violate the Equal Protection Clause of the Fourteenth Amendment. Chief Justice Rehnquist, joined by Justices Scalia, Kennedy and Thomas dissented. They said that the University of Michigan was using numbers just as the University of California did in 1978. They pointed out that in 1995, when 9.7 percent of the applicant pool was African-American, 9.4 percent of the admitted class was African-American. By 2000, when only 7.5 percent of the applicant pool was African-American, 7.3 percent of the admitted class was African-American. The dissent said the correlation is striking and that the tight correlation between the percentage of applicants and admittees of a given race must result from careful race-based planning and suggests the law school used a formula. The Chief Justice accused the law school of admitting members of selected minority groups in proportion to their statistical representation in the applicant pool.

Justice Powell emphasized the nation needs diversity far broader than just ethnic and racial origin.

Meanwhile, in another case heard at the same time, *Gratz v. Bollinger* (539 U.S. 244) involving University of Michigan's undergraduate admissions policy, several white would-be undergraduates filed a class action lawsuit. Their claims were the same as those made against the law school. They sought compensatory and punitive damages and asked the courts to require that Michigan's admissions policy be race neutral. It was undisputed that the university considered African Americans, Hispanics and Native Americans to be underrepresented in the school and admitted virtually every qualified applicant from these groups. The admissions policy automatically distributed twenty points, or one-fifth of the points needed to guarantee admission, to every person the university considered to be an underrepresented minority applicant solely because of race. The Court found that because the policy was not narrowly tailored to achieve the university's interest in diversity, the policy violates the Equal Protection Clause. The Court also noted that Michigan's undergraduate admissions policy made race decisive and did not meet Justice Powell's criteria, which did not mean that any single characteristic automatically ensured a specific and identifiable contribution to a university's diversity.

The *Gratz* case was sent back to the trial court for the class action to proceed. In January 2007, the University of Michigan announced the plaintiffs had dismissed their suit for a small settlement.

In another race-based policy case, heard in 2005, the Supreme Court reversed and sent it back to the trial court because the policy was not narrowly enough tailored. In *Johnson v. California* (533 U.S. 499), Garrison Johnson was an African American inmate in the California prison system. The California Department of Corrections racially segregates prisoners based on a rationale that its segregation policy prevents violence caused by racial gangs. The Court said the appeals court should have held California to the higher standard of strict scrutiny and required the department of corrections to demonstrate that the policy was narrow enough to serve a compelling state interest. It also pointed out that all other states, as well as the federal government, manage their prisons without resorting to racial segregation. The Court noted it had rejected the notion that separate can ever be equal or neutral fifty years earlier in *Brown v. Board of Education* (347 U.S. 483). The Johnson case was sent back to the trial court for the Department of Corrections to demonstrate that its policy is narrowly enough tailored.

The hot button issue of minority set-asides in government contracts was once more considered in 2003 in *Concrete Works of Colorado, Inc. v. City and County of Denver* (507 U.S. 1027). We will probably be hearing more about it in the future. Remember that in the 1989 case of *City of Richmond v. J.A. Croson Co.* (488 U.S. 469), the Court found that the city of Richmond could not pass the strict scrutiny test, and made it clear that past discrimination was a requirement for preferential public contracts based on race. In *Croson*, the Supreme Court said Richmond's plan was not narrowly tailored to remedy the effects of prior discrimination, and denied some citizens the opportunity to compete for a fixed percentage of public contracts based solely upon their race, in violation of the Fourteenth Amendment.

In the 2003 Denver case, Justice Scalia plainly stated that Denver fell short. He said that preferences are presumed unconstitutional and when they are used, it becomes the government's burden to prove that it is acting on the basis of a compelling interest in rectifying racial discrimination. Ultimately, the Court voted to deny a hearing involving Denver's use of racial preferences in public contracting. Justice Scalia, critical of the lower court for permitting racial preferences for "mere might-have-been racial discrimination," dissented, and Justice Rehnquist joined, stating the appeals court ignored Crosen's requirement that the government prove that it is remedying the discrimination and that the Supreme Court should once again hear the issue.

One might think that by the twenty-first century, old-fashioned racial intimidation, cross-burning and the Ku Klux Klan would be gone from America. One would be wrong. In *Virginia v. Black* (538 U.S. 343), the Supreme Court ruled on a cross burning case in 2003. Two basic constitutional concepts butted head to head when one of the defendants raised a First Amendment defense.

> *One might think that by the twenty-first century, old-fashioned racial intimidation, cross-burning and the Ku Klux Klan would be gone from America. One would be wrong.*

The Ku Klux Klan held a rally during which speakers made negative statements about blacks and Mexicans. One speaker said he would love to randomly shoot blacks. At the conclusion of the rally, the crowd circled around a twenty-five- to thirty-foot cross. The cross was between three hundred and three hundred fifty yards from the road. According to the sheriff, the cross "then all of a sudden . . . went up in a flame." As the cross burned, the Klan played "Amazing Grace" over the loudspeakers.

Virginia's statute, which did not target cross-burning on the basis of race, color or creed, said: "It shall be unlawful for any person or persons, with the intent of intimidating any person or group of persons, to burn, or cause to be burned, a cross on the property of another, a highway or other public place. Any person who shall violate any provision of this section shall be guilty of a Class 6 felony. [¶] Any such burning of a cross shall be prima facie evidence of an intent to intimidate a person or group of persons."

In its analysis, the Supreme Court discussed the history of cross-burning from a fourteenth-century Scottish ritual to the first cross-burning in the United States in celebration of the lynching of Leo Frank. It also discussed the use of cross-burnings as a means of intimidation in the 1930s, 1940s and 1950s. The Court said that, while the burning of a cross in this country is a symbol of hate, it is not always done to intimidate. Sometimes it is a ritual to symbolize group solidarity or as a statement of group ideology.

Showing just how imprecise some of our constitutional rights can be, the Court noted that invoking a sense of anger or hatred is not enough to ban cross burnings. The Court quoted Gerald Gunther: "The lesson I have drawn from my childhood in Nazi Germany and my happier adult life in this country is the need to walk the some-

The Court affirmed that the usual protections given to corporate owners are alive and well.

times difficult path of denouncing the bigot's hateful ideas with all my power, yet at the same time challenging any community's attempt to suppress hateful ideas by force of law."

Because the statute banned cross burning without also requiring an intent to intimidate, the Supreme Court found Virginia's law to be unconstitutional. The way the statute was worded, it banned an expression of speech without requiring the State to prove it was done for an illegal purpose.

Discrimination in housing is also still present America. An African American woman and white man, Emma and David Holley, claim they were discriminated against when they attempted to purchase a house in California. Witnesses said the sales agent referred to them with racial invectives and said they were a salt and pepper couple. The Supreme Court decided in *Meyers v. Holley* (537 U.S. 280), 2003, that while the couple could sue the employer of the sales agent, a corporation, they could not sue the broker under whose real estate license the sales agent was operating. The Supreme Court explained that traditional rules make employers explicitly liable for the acts of their employees and agents in the scope of their employment or agency. That meant it was the employer (the corporation), and not the owner of the corporation, who could be sued. So the Court affirmed that the usual protections given to corporate owners are alive and well.

The issue of excluding black jurors from jury panels overshadowed the death conviction of Thomas Joe Miller-El. The Supreme Court carefully examined the jury selection process in Miller-El's Dallas, Texas trial and reversed his conviction because ten of the eleven blacks called to serve on the jury were excused by prosecutors. The Court began its examination by stating it had previously decided in *Batson v. Kentucky* (476 U.S. 792), 1986, that a defendant may make a case of discriminatory jury selection by showing all the facts that indicate a prosecutor's conduct was discriminatory.

The Court had little difficulty in finding the discriminatory nature of the prosecutors' conduct in Miller-El's case in 2005 in *Miller-El v. Dretke* (545 U.S. 231). Not only were 91 percent of the potential black jurors who were questioned excused, but the prosecutors asked potential black jurors different—and more graphic, and trick—questions than the bland questions they asked potential white jurors. Dallas had an old manual that outlined the reasons prosecutors should exclude minorities from juries, and the notes kept by prosecutors during jury selection demonstrated they were considering race. Plus, Texas law permits either side to shuffle the cards bearing the names of potential jurors. So, when a number of black members moved to the front row, the prosecutors called for a shuffle, and several of the blacks went to the back where there was less likelihood they would be called for questioning.

The NAACP's Legal Defense Fund's June 15, 2006 newsletter said of the reversal of Miller-El's conviction and death sentence: "The Court thus reaffirmed its commitment to ending racial bias in jury selection and acknowledged that the only way to put the history of racial discrimination in criminal justice behind this country is to acknowledge its reality."

In *Johnson v. California* (545 U.S. 162), an African American defendant was found guilty of murder and assault on a nineteen-month-old baby. He argued the prosecutor violated *Batson* when no explanation was given for excusing three potential jurors who were African American. At trial, defense counsel argued that the prosecutor had no reason, other than race, to challenge the African American jurors. The trial judge did not ask the prosecutor to explain his rationale for excusing the potential jurors, and instead found that Johnson had failed to establish his case.

After winding its way through California and federal courts, the case ended up in the Supreme Court in 2005. The Supreme Court expressed dismay at the way California handled *Batson* issues. The Court said when it issued *Batson*, it assumed the trial judge would have all of the relevant circumstances, including the prosecutor's explanation, before deciding if it was likely that the challenge was improperly motivated. The Court said it didn't intend the defendant's requirement of showing purposeful discrimination to be so difficult. A defendant should not have to persuade the trial judge that the challenge was the result of purposeful discrimination when the defendant couldn't possibly know all the facts. The trial judge should have required the prosecutor to provide a race-neutral reason for excusing the African American jurors once the defendant had produced enough evidence to permit the trial judge to determine that discrimination occurred. The Court sent the case back to the trial court for retrial.

The holdings in Miller-El's and Johnson's cases did not indicate the Court was sending a message to prosecutors that they could not excuse African American jurors from a jury by using peremptory challenges. In 2006, in *Rice v. Collins* (546 U.S. 333), a Los Angeles jury convicted Steven Martell Collins, an African American male, of possessing cocaine for purposes of distribution, and subjected him to sentencing under California's Three Strikes law. During the trial, the prosecutor struck a young African American woman, juror number 16, from the panel of potential jurors. Collins argued to the trial judge that the woman was excused because of her race.

As a race-neutral explanation for striking Juror 16, the prosecutor said she had rolled her eyes in response to a question from the court, that she was young and might be too tolerant of a drug crime, and that she was single and lacked ties to the community. The trial judge did not see any rolling of the eyes but noted the prosecutor had also challenged a young white juror. The Court of Appeal affirmed, noting

Juror 16's youth was sufficient reason for the challenge, and that the potential juror's demeanor was an additional reason.

The Supreme Court of California refused to grant Collins' request to review his case. Collins then pursued relief in the federal courts. The federal trial judge denied relief, but the federal appeals court said it was unreasonable to credit the prosecutor's race-neutral reasons for striking the African American woman from the jury. The Supreme Court reversed the federal appeals court and Collins' conviction stands. The Court said the state trial court's decision to credit the prosecutor's race-neutral explanation for the strike in response to defendant's *Batson* challenge did not constitute an unreasonable determination of the facts in light of the evidence.

A 2008 Louisiana conviction was reversed when the Supreme Court concluded a prosecutor's explanation for excusing all five potential jurors who were African American was pretext. The Supreme Court centered its decision around one of the potential jurors, a college student, a man who the prosecutor said looked nervous and might want to return a lesser verdict to avoid a penalty phase so he could get back to school sooner. In *Snyder v. Louisiana* (128 S.Ct. 1203), the Court noted it was not always possible to judge nervousness from a written record, but said the explanation about time constraints was implausible because the prosecutor accepted white jurors whose time concerns were at least as serious as the college student's.

School vouchers remain an important issue. In 2002, the Supreme Court decided *Zelman v. Simmons-Harris* (536 U.S. 639), a case involving a school voucher program in Ohio. The program provided tuition aid for certain students in the Cleveland City School District, the only covered district, to attend participating public or private schools of their parent's choosing and tutorial aid for students who chose to remain enrolled in public school. Both religious and nonreligious schools in the district participated. Tuition aid was distributed to parents according to financial need, and where the aid was spent depended solely upon where parents chose to enroll their children. In the 1999-2000 school year, 82 percent of participating private schools had a religious affiliation, and 60 percent of the students were from families at or below the poverty line.

Prompting the voucher program was a recognition of the "crisis of magnitude" that existed in the Cleveland public school system, with only 10 percent of ninth graders able to pass a proficiency test, and more than two-thirds of high school students failing to graduate. The program passed with the strong support of inner-city minorities, who saw it as a way to escape failing urban schools. African American parents strongly supported school choice, "with 60 percent saying they would switch their children from public to private school if money were not an obstacle." (551 U.S. 701)

Some think the *Zelman* decision may end up mattering less than many thought it would. The reasons for this are that issues of stricter standards, and accountability of faculty of public schools, came to the forefront with the federal government getting involved with public schools within the states (536 U.S. 639).

Opinions in two school cases, *Parents Involved in Community School Dist No.1 v. Seattle School District* and *Meredith v. Jefferson County Board of Education*, filed on June 28, 2007, concerned the problem of too many students who wanted to attend the same school within particular school districts (551 U.S. 701). The Court said neither a high school nor an elementary school could justify using racial classifications in student assignment plans when there were more requests for slots in the schools than the schools could accommodate. The Court said the way to stop discrimination on the basis of race is to stop discriminating on the basis of race. It found that race was being used to achieve diversity in the schools, not as one factor among others, but as a decisive factor in and of itself, and such a procedure violates the Equal Protection Clause of the Fourteenth Amendment.

> *The Court said the way to stop discrimination on the basis of race is to stop discriminating on the basis of race.*

In cases involving education, housing, jury selection, government contracts and prisons, the Court sent the same message. Decisions should be made based on reasons other than race. An Indiana statute that required voters at polling places to show a government issued photo identification to vote was challenged in *Crawford v. Marion County Election Bd.* (128 S.Ct. 1610). One study showed that African Americans were four to five times less likely to have government-sanctioned photo identification than whites. The Court held that Indiana's interests in the integrity and reliability of the electoral process were sufficiently weighty to support its requirement for photo identification of voters.

2001-2009
Hollywood

SO FAR, FILMS OF THE twenty-first century are both the same and different. They are the same in that in typical Hollywood cowardly fashion, the film industry challenges racism from a historical perspective. These challenges might have been courageous had they been closer in time to the events portrayed. Of course, the same tired stereotypical violent black man is still being shown. But some films are different. A handful of popular films send a message to African Americans that their future is in their own hands. Another handful treats the races as if they are equal.

Ray, for which Jamie Fox won the 2004 Best Actor of the Year, showcased the incredible talent of the incomparable Ray Charles. The film openly deals with the unfairness blacks faced in a segregated America, but does so late in the game. Charles was shown to be very savvy in contract negotiations. His ambivalence about success, while at the same time wanting to support the Civil Rights Movement, was shown when Charles finally relented and refused to play in a segregated theater. White Atlanta fans were portrayed as selectively discriminatory—as much of the country was in the 1960s—as they eagerly awaited Charles's astonishing talent inside a theater that would not admit black patrons. Had the movie been made a few decades earlier, it could have helped smooth the rough road African Americans had.

The story behind *Glory Road* (2006) revolves around a college basketball team.

Without funds to attract talented white players, a 1965 Texas coach recruits more black players than usual. Based on a true story, the film tracks the successes, failures and challenges the integrated team faces. The movie is typical of the way Hollywood treats controversial issues. That is, it ignores them when it might do some good in guiding people toward tolerance. *Glory Road* does finally get around to telling the story when acceptance by the American people is a foregone conclusion. Nonetheless, the movie shows how talented black and white players successfully interacted and how the black players raised their self esteem with success.

Far From Heaven is a 2002 film set in the 1950s. A gorgeous Connecticut white woman falls in love with her black gardener when her hidden-in-the-closet homosexual husband ignores her. The film tries to deal with racial prejudice, but fails in that there is no explanation as to how the black gardener managed to emerge into a racist society with such elegance, education, sensitivity and success. Nor does it explain how the white woman existed without any racial prejudice in the midst of a community full of it.

A handful of popular films send a message to African Americans that their future is in their own hands. Another handful treats the races as if they are equal.

Chicago (2003 Best Picture of the Year) is a musical comedy set in the 1920s and makes no pretense of being historically accurate. Black men and white women sensuously dance together, in a manner that would have resulted in a lynching in the real America of the 1920s. With a twist from other films, the prison guard is a black woman and is just as twisted and crooked as prison guards often are portrayed, and the prisoners are white women.

Doubt (2008) is set in the Bronx in 1964. A mother superior is concerned that a priest is molesting the only African American pupil in a Catholic school. The most shocking part of the film is the twelve-year-old's mother's reaction when the nun reveals her suspicions. The mother is willing to have the possible molestations continue just so her son can receive a good education and some personal attention, which is a pathetic commentary on the quality of education available to 1960's blacks.

Training Day (2001) is awful in its portrayal of a black policeman. He is shown in the same scary role as Eddie Murphy was in *48 Hrs* when he says to a group of bar patrons, "I'm your worst nightmare . . . a nigger with a badge." *Training Day* is about police corruption and abuse. The bad man in the movie, a police undercover officer, is played by Denzel Washington—who won the Best Actor of the Year award for his performance. Washington plays a callous, sociopathic killer. He refers to a white recruit as his nigger. He shoots it up in residential neighborhoods, searches a house

In the new century, Hollywood films have started to place blame for the condition of blacks in America on blacks themselves.

after showing a menu from a Chinese restaurant instead of a search warrant and kills without apparent concern. The film represents Hollywood's tried and true formula for both frightening white people and making them feel superior to "primal" blacks.

Gladiator, which won the 2001 Academy Award for Best Picture of the Year, indirectly dealt with the modern race issue. Set in ancient Rome, it showed Russell Crowe as Maximus, a military hero taken into slavery. So, it was subtly revealed that at one point in time, slavery and race did not go hand in hand.

In the new century, Hollywood films have started to place blame for the condition of blacks in America on blacks themselves. Some popular movies are now telling blacks to pull themselves up by their own bootstraps.

The most obvious of this type of film is *Coach Carter* (2005). The film deals with the lack of accountability of some African Americans in taking responsibility for their own situation. Based on a true story, the coach refuses to permit his high school basketball team to play unless all players attend classes and maintain passing grades, as they promised they would do when they signed a contract with the coach at the beginning of the season. The coach teaches that part of growing up is making one's own decisions and living with the consequences. He attempts to guide players toward winning at basketball, and in life, by encouraging them to study and to go on to college. What is most interesting is that some of the parents and school officials argued against the coach's approach, but the kids went along with the coach and got their grades up to snuff.

Dreamgirls (2006), for which Jennifer Hudson won the 2007 Best Supporting Actress of the Year, is not quite as obvious in its message, but it is there nonetheless. Three young black girls, talented, energetic and wholesome, soar to success as singers. With an almost exclusive black cast, some of the parts portray evil and greedy scoundrels and others are selfish, immature and self-centered. Most have high morals. The movie shows that, as in all the races, there are good and evil people, and there are self-centered and over-indulgent people. One of the messages is that blacks cannot automatically trust other blacks.

Crash (2006 Best Picture of the Year) has essentially the same message with an added one. It exposes the prejudices, biases, misconceptions and vulgarities of all races, including black people. No one race or ethnic group is shown in an exemplary way. Yes, African Americans are targeted for "driving while black," but so does the movie target Hispanics when a black cop keeps calling his partner Mexican and she corrects him and says she is half Puerto Rican and half El Salvadorian. The black cop remarks how amazing it is that all these diverse cultures get together in America and every one of them parks their cars on the middle of their lawn.

A post-9/11 "we're all in the same boat" theme is seen in some twenty-first century films. These films either say sayonara to racism or simply assume it's a relic of the past.

A black social worker is also revealed to be bigoted and vengeful when she won't give approval for medical care for a white cop's father. The cop tells her that his sick father started as a janitor and saved to buy his own business and hired twenty-five black people as his employees, but lost his business when the city awarded his contract to a minority-owned company. The black woman is so furious she refuses to approve the medical expenses for the obviously sick father. In this way, *Crash* tells blacks they have to take responsibility for being as racist as everyone else.

At the same time, *Crash* displays a great deal of sensitivity to blacks. A well-educated black man with a high paying job in the movie industry is dressed down because he is hesitant to tell a black actor to talk "more black." The actor was supposed to say "don be talking bout dat," but said, "I told you not to talk to me about that." The black executive does his best to follow the rules at work and in other parts of his life, but after an emasculating interaction with a white police officer, he loses his temper.

Gran Torino (2008) was similar to *Crash* in that it portrayed different races preying and intimidating others. But the story took a more positive path when its characters sought common ground.

The Departed won Best Picture of the Year in 2007. It has almost nothing to do with African Americans and is about the Irish mafia in Boston. But in an almost throw-away remark, a lead character, played by Jack Nicholson, makes a crack about African Americans while discussing how twenty years after Irishmen could not get a job, there was one in the White House: "That's what the niggers don't realize. If I got one thing against the black chappies, it's this: no one gives it to you. You have to take it." Clearly, the message was that blacks should take upon themselves the responsibility for their own successes and failures.

The Pursuit of Happiness (2006) is about an African American man who has no education and no future. But he does have ambition and a dream of being happy. Based on a true story, it follows the frustrating and successful endeavors of a single 1970s father as he tries for the brass ring. The film gives the clear message that nothing is handed to a person and that hard work is necessary for success.

A post-9/11 "we're all in the same boat" theme is seen in some twenty-first century films. These films either say sayonara to racism or simply assume it's a relic of the past.

Antwone Fisher (2002) places blame for some black problems on whites, but at the same time recognizes the responsibility of the black protagonist to face the racial issue without using it as an excuse and get on with his life. A young man is close to mental collapse because of the cruel physical and sexual abuse he underwent as a child at the hands of black women. The blame is placed on whites when the young man is told to read a book called *The Slave Community*, which explains how blacks learned to view beatings as the normal way of life during slavery. The film sends the message that the man has to pull himself out of his circumstances and succeed on his own, without using racial prejudice as an excuse.

Halle Berry won the 2002 Best Actress of the Year award for *Monster's Ball*. It is a deeply insightful film regarding both blacks and whites. The father of a white prison guard is portrayed as an old fashioned bigot. He hates blacks. The son chases two pre-teen black boys from his property by shooting two rifle shots into the air, but his actions are not coming from bigotry as much as loyalty to his father. When the father of the black boys confronts the officer about his actions, the officer half-heartedly defends his actions, almost whimpering, "They were on my property," which displays his racial ambivalence.

Sensitive interactions between blacks and whites are shown, and the film does not set up either race as being good or bad. Rather, each is revealed in shades of grey. The prison guard and a black woman find each other, after each loses a son. But the guard's father ridicules and insults his son's black lover. As if symbolically calling a halt to racism, the guard moves his father to a nursing home so the lovers will not be impaired by the father's dated and dreary racial perspective. After examining the miserable workings of both the black and the white family, the film seems to say it's time to see whether or not a black/white family may be a little more successful.

The Last King of Scotland (2006) won the 2007 Best Actor of the Year award for Forest Whitaker. Set in 1970 Uganda, a young Scottish doctor finds himself over his head when he accidentally becomes an advisor to the charming and mad Idi Amin. It is apparent the Scot, who presumes himself to be farther up the evolutionary scale, is no more civilized than the Ugandans. Early on, when asked if there are monkeys in Scotland, he quips that if there were, the Scots would probably deep-fry them. But in a tense scene amidst a crowd of Ugandans around a wailing cow, it is the Scot who can't stand the animal's loud sounds, and brutally and needlessly shoots and kills it. At one point, Amin and the Scot demonstrate similar perversity when they talk about lusting after married women, remarking how passionate they are.

2004's Best Picture of the Year, *Million Dollar Baby*, was filled with close-ups of relationships among three different people, two of them white and one black. All three displayed affection, respect and loyalty toward the others. There was not a hint of racial tension among them. The only racism exhibited was the use of the "N-word" by a mentally challenged young man, a technique that sent the message that it would

While films in the new century do have some of the same stereotypes, they also have portrayals of people based on who they are rather than simply what color they are.

take someone retarded to spew the poison of racial hatred. On the other hand, the film portrayed a black boxer as being unnecessarily cruel to the slower white man, once again sending the message there are evil people in all races.

Gone Baby Gone (2007) shows that a small white child is better off with a black family than with her biological white family. *No Country For Old Men* (2007, Best Picture of the Year 2008) portrays a black motorist who picks up a white hitchhiker as the sanest and safest of the two. *Juno* (2007) has blacks and whites side-by-side on a high school campus and a doctor's office. *Michael Clayton* (2007) does the same thing: lawyers, secretaries, cops and bystanders are both black and white. *Atonement* (2007) depicts black and white war buddies as intensely loyal to each other.

American Gangster (2007) is interesting in the way it portrays real-life black criminal Frank Lucas during the 1960s and 1970s. He is played by Denzel Washington. Historically, Hollywood showed black criminals as lowlifes. Although Frank Lucas is vicious at times, he is fastidiously neat and dignified in his speech and dress. And he's a gifted and shrewd, albeit crooked, businessman.

It's hard to miss the story similarities between *Home of the Brave* (2006) and 1946's *The Best Years of Our Lives*. Both feature three returning soldiers. Both show soldiers whose jobs were taken by someone else while they were gone, other soldiers who try to cope with lost limbs, how excess drinking plagues returning soldiers, and how difficult it is for military families to understand their soldiers when they come home. But, while the 1946 film has three white men, the 2006 version has a white man, a black man, and a white woman. In both films the soldiers respect and depend on each other and relate better to each other than to non-military people.

While films in the new century do have some of the same stereotypes, they also have portrayals of people based on who they are rather than what color they are. It is not that Hollywood types are more enlightened than they used to be. Rather, it seems to be an indication that America is finally more enlightened than it used to be.

2001-2009
Decade Wrap-up

GRANTED, THE 1960's SUPREME COURT opinions and popular Hollywood movies came from a liberal perspective, and the 2000 to 2009 opinions and movies come from a more conservative one. Nonetheless, the two periods have common elements. The 1960's decade will always be in a class by itself in that Hollywood films and United States Supreme Court cases went hand-in-hand during that decade. But, the films and opinions of the very early part of the new millennium also track each other to a certain extent. Recent films and High Court opinions more often than not recognize the equality of the races, and each tells everyone they have an equal chance. It's just up to them whether or not they take that chance.

It is hard not to recognize the impact of 9/11 on Hollywood movies. As Americans realized many countries all over the world resent us and hold us in distain, they banded together more, and Hollywood projected that phenomenon. Several popular movies portrayed Americans of all races acting together as equals in ways not much shown prior to 9/11. *Million Dollar Baby* and *Monsters' Ball* had blacks and whites, side by side, in the same boat trying to find success and happiness. *Crash* showed all races doing bad things to other races because of prejudice. It sent the message we are all the same; none of us are all good and none of us are all bad. We all basically want to do good—and we all fail at times.

Because of court decisions, and the election of an African American President, the relevancy of Critical Race Theory has been called into question. The Supreme Court's conservative justices apparently hold the concepts in a liberal agenda, including affirmative action, in the same low regard as CRT advocates. In *Parents Involved in Community School Dist No.1 v. Seattle School District* and *Meredith v. Jefferson County Board of Education*, filed on June 28, 2007, the Court clearly said it did not tolerate different treatment on the basis of race. The opinion assumes everyone is equal and everyone has a fair shake at entry into coveted schools.

Several popular movies portrayed Americans of all races acting together as equals in ways not much shown prior to

On the other hand, the opinion in *Virginia v. Black*, the case in which the KKK argued, and the Court held, it had a right under the First Amendment to express itself by burning a cross, the Supreme Court ruled in a way CRT theorists say is discriminatory to blacks. According to Critical Race Theory, the Court would have made a value judgment that freedom of expression is more important than the right of African Americans to be free from reminders of the humiliation, pain and stigma of slavery.

Hollywood indirectly got into the Critical Race Theory act, too, by portraying stories of blacks succeeding on their own. The message in *The Departed* was clear. Blacks were told to take upon themselves the responsibility for their own successes and failures when Jack Nicholson said, "If I got one thing against the black chappies, it's this . . . no one gives it to you. You have to take it."

All in all, Hollywood has been far more progressive regarding African Americans during the twenty-first century than it was during the twentieth. Blacks and whites are often portrayed on an equal footing. Blacks are not shown as violent freaks or losers quite as often, and are shown taking charge of their own destinies. The Supreme Court has continued on its course to rid the law of any direct or indirect discrimination. While liberals believe the court should permit more affirmative action to compensate for past discrimination, conservatives believe there has been enough extra help given and from here on, it's up to the individual to carve his or her own destiny out of equal opportunity.

That's a Wrap

FOR THE FIRST FEW DECADES of the twentieth century, both the Supreme Court and Hollywood operated with passive racist philosophies. As the South persisted in maintaining bits of slavery by denying African Americans the vote and due process in its courts, the Supreme Court began to intervene. The high court issued numerous peonage, voting and criminal procedure cases, all to the benefit of America's black citizens. As Hollywood persisted in its racist course, the two institutions parted ways. At the same time, the movie moguls were still in place. While the moguls often acted insensitively and did not challenge national or regional prejudices, they did not overtly try to harm blacks on the screen. Meanwhile, the Supreme Court moved steadily, albeit still sometimes reluctantly, toward *Brown v. Board of Education*.

During much of the 1960s, the two institutions temporarily shared the same course of fairness and equality toward black Americans. When Hollywood's fortunes changed in the late 1960s, with the popularity of television and moves to the suburbs, the movie industry blatantly and actively appealed to white Americans' biases and prejudices to attract them back to movie houses. This change in direction coincided with the demise of the studio system. Nothing but the bottom line dictated what appeared in mainstream movies. Black-bashing was profitable for big business Hollywood.

Had it been lucrative for the film industry to portray blacks as the majority of them exist in American society, that is, as employed homeowners with families, Hollywood probably would have done so. Alas, it was not profitable. So the industry took the low road and opted for pseudo recognition of the advancements of African Americans by showcasing an occasional black doctor or lawyer. But its token portrayals of black successes were shown with a negative black backdrop. African Americans were often shamefully displayed as vulgar, as objects of fear or grasping for an unfair advantage over everyone else.

Nothing but the bottom line dictated what appeared in mainstream movies. Black-bashing was profitable for big business Hollywood.

The Supreme Court cases that had the most profound positive effect on American society were those related to housing. In *Buchanan v. Warley*, 245 U.S. 60, 1917, and *Harmon v. Tyler*, 273 U.S. 668, 1927, the Court invalidated ordinances that segregated neighborhoods by race on the ground they interfered with property rights protected by the due process clause of the Fourteenth Amendment. The cases were probably decided to protect white property owners, but they got the ball rolling.

In the 1948 restrictive covenant cases (*Shelley v. Kraemer*, 334 U.S. 1.), the Court removed the government's protection of restrictive covenants, and rendered unenforceable property deeds that restricted who could purchase property in the future. After that, in case after case, the Court refused to tolerate purposeful racial discrimination. W.E.B. Du Bois's sentiments in *The Souls of Black Folk* (about taking a man by the hand and looking frankly into his eyes and having a cigar or a cup of tea together, and how that would mean more than legislative halls or magazine articles and speeches) harkens back. How important it is that people share experiences. As long as races were kept apart in segregated neighborhoods, they could never partake in that cup of tea together. Also central to the significance to the housing dilemma is Martin Luther King's observation that while a court can declare rights, it cannot deliver them. So for the delivery of the rights, the races had to drink that cup of tea together. And the only way that would happen would be for them to see each other day-to-day on an equal footing. Once housing was available to everyone on the same basis, people could wave when they got home from work, see each other at the grocery store, and stand in the same line at the neighborhood bank.

While the Court demonstrated unswerving intolerance toward racial restrictions in housing, for several decades Hollywood rarely showed integrated neighborhoods in its films. On the other hand, all-black neighborhoods were frequently shown in movies such as in *Cotton Comes to Harlem* (1970), *Cooley High* (1975), *she's gotta have it* (1986), *Clara's Heart* (1988), and *Ghost* (1990).

All-white neighborhoods were also common in films such as in *Kramer v. Kramer* (1980), *Ordinary People* (1980), *Raging Bull* (1980), *E.T. the Extra-Terrestrial* (1982), and

Terms of Endearment (1984). Techniques used in films after 1970 to avoid depicting housing for blacks included *Rocky* (1975), which portrayed an all-white neighborhood but had black actors in and in front of the gym and at busy commercial areas. *Fatal Beauty* (1987), and *Rising Sun* (1993), showed the inside of the home of the black character, but not the outside neighborhood. In *48 Hrs.* (1982), Eddie Murphy's home was prison. In other movies, such as *Fast Times at Ridgemont High* (1982), and *Tootsie* (1982), the few black actors were shown at school or work, but not at home. It was not until late in the century, such as in the 1988 film *Lethal Weapon*, that black families were portrayed living in a nice home. Even then, Hollywood found it necessary to send the message the family lived in a black neighborhood by showing a black jogger running outside the home at the beginning of the film. *Enemy of the State* (1998), finally, had the main characters, a black family, living in a lovely and love-filled home in an integrated neighborhood.

> *Had it been lucrative for the film industry to portray blacks as the majority of them exist in American society, that is, as employed homeowners with families, Hollywood probably would have done so.*

Hollywood continued to portray blacks in a harmful way through the end of the twentieth century, though its methods became more subtle as the century grew to a close. But the Court was not swayed from its direction toward equality, at least as far as white supremacy was concerned. The Court was unrelenting in examining both federal and state statutes and practices for purposeful discrimination, as well as discriminatory intent or purpose. It routinely measured whether or not legitimate ends were sought by the least intrusive means.

For many, the United States Supreme Court is considered to be one of the most stodgy, slow and conservative institutions in America. By contrast, an institution viewed as one of the least reactionary and most liberal is the Hollywood film industry. Yet throughout the twentieth century, the Supreme Court was at least as equally as advanced—and usually more advanced—than Hollywood in recognizing and acting upon the achievements and advancements of African Americans.

When then-Senator Obama gave his speech about race in Philadelphia on May 18, 2008, he said: "I am the son of a black man from Kenya and a white woman from Kansas. I was raised with the help of a white grandfather who survived a Depression to serve in Patton's Army during World War II and a white grandmother who worked on a bomber assembly line at Fort Leavenworth while he was overseas. I've gone to some of the best schools in America and lived in one of the world's poorest nations. I am married to a black American who carries within her the blood of slaves and slave-owners—an inheritance we pass on to our two precious daughters. I have brothers, sisters, nieces, nephews, uncles and cousins, of every race and every hue, scattered across three continents, and for as long as I live, I will never forget that in no other country on Earth is my story even possible. It's a story that hasn't made me the most conventional candidate. But it is a story that has seared into my genetic makeup the idea that this nation is more than the sum of its parts—that out of many, we are truly one."

The day after President Obama was inaugurated, CNN's Anderson Cooper and PBS's Gwen Eifel chatted about whether or not we are now in a "post-racial environment."

The Supreme Court has declared the rights of all Americans. For decades Hollywood did little to help deliver them to African Americans. But as all America turns the racial page, Hollywood has little choice but to get in step.

THE END

Endnotes

1 E.g. see, Michael J. Klarman, "The Plessy Era," The Supreme Court Review, 1998, p. 387.

2 In this work, "Hollywood" is used in its broadest generic context, and refers to popular films seen by the American public.

3 Loren Miller, "Hollywood's New Negro Films," The Crisis, November, 1934; January, 1938.

4 Los Angeles Times, September 25, 2002.

5 Neal Gabler, An Empire of Their Own, Anchor Books, Doubleday Publishing Company, 1988, p. 7.

6 Ibid.

7 Merriam-Webster, Webster's New Biographical Dictionary, Merriam-Webster, Inc., 1983, P. 425.

8 Melinda Corey and George Ochoa, Editors-in-Chief, The American Film Institute Desk Reference, Dorling Kindersley Publishing, Inc., 2002, p. 426.

9 Thomas Cripps, Hollywood's High Noon, The Johns Hopkins University Press, 1997, p. 27.

10 Thomas Cripps, Slow Fade To Black, Oxford University Press, p. 64.

11 Neal Gabler, An Empire of Their Own, supra, pp. 202-203.

12 Id., p. 216.

13 Ibid.

14 Id., p. 120.

15 Ibid.

16 Id., p. 216.

17 National Association for the Advancement of Colored People.

18 Loren Miller, "Hollywood's New Negro Films," The Crisis, November, 1934.

19 Marshall Frady, Martin Luther King, Jr., Viking Penguin Press, 2002, p. 106.

20 Paul Johnson, A History of the American People, Harper Collins Publishers, 1998, pp. 447-448.

21 E.g., see Thomas Cripps, Black Film As Genre, Indiana University Press, 1979.

22 Thomas Cripps, Black Film As Genre, supra, pp. 14-15.

23 Thomas Cripps, Slow Fade To Black, supra, p. 37.

24 Three Hitchcock films were unavailable: "The Pleasure Garden," 1925; "Downhill," 1927; "Waltzes From Vienna," 1933. Many of Hitchcock's early films were made in England, but they were very popular in the U.S.A.

25 Thomas Cripps, Slow Fade To Black, supra, Preface.

26 Marshall Frady, Martin Luther King, Jr., supra, p, 1.

27 Lisa Aldred, Thurgood Marshall, Black Americans of Achievement, Chelsea House Publishers, 1990, p. 22.

28 William W. Freehling, "The Road to Disunion," Oxford University Press, 1990, p. 124.

29 Ibid, at 136; "The Migration or Importation of such Persons as any of the States now existing shall think proper to admit, shall not be prohibited by the Congress prior to the Year one thousand eight hundred and eight, but a Tax or duty may be imposed on such Importation, not exceeding ten dollars for each Person." (United States Constitution, Article III, Section 9, Clause 1.)

30 United States Constitution, Article IV, Section 2, Clause 3. Runaway slaves.

31 Stephen E. Ambrose, Personal Reflections of an Historian, Simon & Schuster, 2002, p. 62.

32 Joseph J. Ellis, *Founding Brothers*, 2002, Vintage Books, A Division of Random House, p. 240.

33 Paul Johnson, *A History of the American People, supra*, pp. 447-449.

34 *Id.*, pp. 416-419.

35 Fred Rodell, *Nine Men*, Random House, 1955, pp. 111-115.

36 Walter Ehrlich, *The Oxford Guide to United States Supreme Court Decisions*, edited by Kermit L. Hall, 1999, Oxford University Press, p. 278.

37 W.E.B.Du Bois, *Writings, The Souls Of Black Folk*, first published in 1903, The Library of America, Library of Congress Catalog Card Number: 86-10565, 1986, p. 360.

38 *Id.*, p. 501.

39 Arthur Bestor, "The American Civil War as a Constitutional Crisis," 69 American Historical Review (1964), p. 219-234.

40 *Id.*, p. 219-234.

41 Booker T. Washington, *Up From Slavery*, by first published in 1901, Bibliobazaar, 2007, p. 31.

42 William Nelson, *The Fourteenth Amendment*, 1988, Harvard University Press, p. 43.

43 13th Amendment (1865)

Section 1. Neither slavery, involuntary servitude, except as a punishment for crime whereof the party shall have been duly convicted, shall exist within the United States, or any place subject to their jurisdiction.

Section 2. Congress shall have power to enforce this article by appropriate legislation.

14th Amendment (1868)

Section 1. All persons born or naturalized in the United States, and subject to the jurisdiction thereof, are citizens of the United States and of the State wherein they reside. No State shall make or enforce any law which shall abridge the privileges or immunities of citizens of the United States; nor shall any State deprive any person of life liberty, or property, without due process of law; nor deny to any person within its jurisdiction the equal protection of the laws.

 Section 2. Representatives shall be apportioned among the several States according to their respective numbers, counting the whole number of persons in each State, excluding Indians not taxed. But when the right to vote at any election for the choice of electors for President and Vice President of the United States, Representatives in Congress, the Executive and Judicial officers of a State, or the members of the Legislature thereof, is denied to any of the male inhabitants of such State, being twenty-one years of age, and citizens of the United States, or in any way abridged, except for participation in rebellion, or other crime, the basis of representation therein shall be reduced in the proportion which the number of such male citizens shall bear to the whole number of male citizens twenty-one years of age in such State.

Section 3. No Person shall be a Senator or Representative in Congress, or elector of President and Vice President, or hold any office, civil or military, under the United States, or under any State, who, having previously taken an oath, as a member of Congress, or as an officer of the United States, or as a member of any State legislature, or as an executive or judicial officer of any State, to support the Constitution of the United States, shall have engaged insurrection or rebellion against the same, or given aid or comfort to the enemies thereof. But Congress may by a vote of two-thirds of each House, remove such disability.

Section 4. The validity of the public debt of the United States, authorized by law, including debts incurred for payment of pensions and bounties for services in suppressing insurrection or rebellion, shall not be questioned. But neither the United States nor any State shall assume or pay any debt or obligation incurred in aid of insurrection or rebellion against the United States, or any claim for the loss of emancipation of any slave; but all such debts, obligations and claims shall be held illegal and void.

Section 5. The Congress shall have power to enforce, by appropriate legislation, the provisions of this article.

15th Amendment (1870)

Section 1. The right of citizens of the United States to vote shall not be denied or abridged by the United States or by any State on account of race, color, or previous condition of servitude.

Section 2. The Congress shall have power to enforce this article by appropriate legislation.

44 Michael J. Klarman, "The Plessy Era," *supra*, p. 325.

45 Stephen E. Ambrose, *Personal Reflections of an Historian*, *supra*, p. 68.

46 Arthur Bestor, "The American Civil War as a Constitutional Crisis," *supra*, p. 219.

47 William Nelson, *The Fourteenth Amendment*, 1988, *supra*, p. 43.

48   Stephen E. Ambrose, *Personal Reflections of an Historian*, *supra*, p. 62.

49 Booker T. Washington, *Up From Slavery*, *supra*, pp. 61-62.

50 Booker T. Washington, *Up From Slavery*, *supra*, pp. 63, 65, 66.

51 Lisa Aldred, *Thurgood Marshall, Black Americans of Achievement*, *supra*, p. 13.

52 Graham, "Fourteenth Amendment," Stanford Law Rev., Dec., 1954, p. 11.

53 W.E.B.Du Bois, *The Souls Of Black Folk*, *supra*, pp. 376, 379, 385.

54 W.E.B.Du Bois, *The Souls Of Black Folk*, *supra*, p. 367.

55 *Id.*, p. 385.

56 *Id.*, p. 390.

57 *Id.*, pp. 485-486.

58 *Id.*, pp. 486-490.

59 *Id.*, p. 494.

60 *Id.*, p. 496.

61 Fred Rodell, "Nine Men," *supra*, p. 159.

62 *Ibid.*

63 Graham, "Fourteenth Amendment," *supra*, p. 37.

64 Walter F. Pratt, Jr., *The Oxford Guide to United States Supreme Court Decisions*, edited by Kermit L. Hall, 1999, Oxford University Press, p. 239.

65 Michael J. Klarman, "The Plessy Era," The Supreme Court Review, 1998, p. 342.

66 *Graham*, "Fourteenth Amendment," *supra*, p. 37.

67 "No persons shall . . . be deprived of life, liberty, or property, without due process of law. . . ." [United States Constitution, Amendment V.]

68 Fred Rodell, *Nine Men*" *supra*, p. 147.

69 *Id.*, p. 148-150.

70 Ward E.Y.Eliott, *The Oxford Guide to United States Supreme Court Decisions*, edited by Kermit L. Hall, 1999, Oxford University Press, p. 334.

71 Fred Rodell, *Nine Men*, *supra*, p. 176.

72 At page 544-545

73 Michael J. Klarman, "The Plessy Era," *supra*, p. 312-313.

74 Booker T. Washington, *Up From Slavery*, *supra*, p. 177.

75 Michael J. Klarman, "The Plessy Era," *supra*, p. 320.

76 *Ibid.*

77 Neal Gabler, *An Empire of Their Own*, *supra*, pp. 104-105.

78 W.E.B.Du Bois, *The Souls Of Black Folk*, *supra*, pp. 475, 476.

79 Lisa Aldred, *Thurgood Marshall, Black Americans of Achievement*, *supra*, p. 14.

80 David M. Tucker, "Miss Ida B. Wells and Memphis Lynching," Alexa Denson Henderson and Janice Sumler-Edmond, Editors, *Freedoms Odyssey, African American History Essays from Phylon,*, Clark Atlanta University Press, 1999, p. 411.

81 When he was freed, he had only one name, Marshall. The Union Army told him he needed two names, so he added Thoroughgood. Lisa Aldred, *Thurgood Marshall, Black Americans of Achievement*, *supra*, p. 22-23.

82 *Id.* pp. 23-24.

83 *Id.* pp. 12, 21.

84 Lawrence M. Friedman, *American Law in the Twentieth Century*, Yale University Press, 2002, p.114

85 Paul Kens, *The Oxford Guide to United States Supreme Court Decisions*, edited by Kermit L. Hall, 1999, Oxford University Press, p. 161.

86 Michael J. Klarman, "The Plessy Era," *supra*, p. 335.

87 Michael J. Klarman, "The Plessy Era," *Id.*, p. 387.

88 Paul Johnson, *A History of the American People*, *supra*, p. 691.

89 Neal Gabler, *An Empire of Their Own*, Neal Gabler, *supra*, p. 5.

90 Lawrence M. Friedman, *American Law in the Twentieth Century*, *supra*, pp. 115-116.

91 *Id.*, pp. 121.

92 Michael J. Klarman, "The Plessy Era," *supra*, p. 386.

93 Paul Bergman, Michael Asimow, *Reel Justice, The Courtroom Goes to the Movies*, Andrews and McMeel, a Universal Press Syndicate Company, 1996, p. 226. The remark was found in a discussion of, "They Won't Forget," a 1937 movie based on the 1915 Leo Frank Trial.

94 Lawrence M. Friedman, *American Law in the Twentieth Century*, *supra*, pp. 118.

95 *Id.*, p.117.

96 Philip A. Klinkner with Rogers M. Smith, *The Unsteady March*, The University of Chicago Press, 1999, pp. 110-111.

97 *Id.*, pp. 111-113

98 *Id.*, pp. 113-115.

99 Michael Klarman, "Neither Hero Nor Villain: The Supreme Court, Race, and the Constitution in the Twentieth Century," Chap. 2: "The Progressive Era," Oxford University Press, 2003, p. 108

100 *Ibid.*

101 Lawrence M. Friedman, *American Law in the Twentieth Century*, *supra*, p. 115.

102 Lawrence M. Friedman, *American Law in the Twentieth Century*, *supra*, pp. 121-122.

103 Thomas Cripps, *Slow Fade To Black*, *supra*, pp. 6, 9.

104 Thomas Cripps, *Slow Fade To Black*, *supra*, p. 29.

105 Harold Brackman, *The Attack on "Jewish Hollywood": A Chapter of Modern American Anti-Semitism*, Oxford University Press, Modern Judaism 20.1, February 2000.

106 Thomas Cripps, *Slow Fade To Black*, *supra*, pp. 41-69.

107 Thomas Cripps, *Slow Fade To Black*, *Id.*, p. 54.

108 Philip A. Klinkner with Rogers M. Smith, *The Unsteady March*, *supra*, p. 110.

109 *Ibid.*

110 Thomas Cripps, *Hollywood's High Noon*, *supra*, p. 30.

111 Thomas Cripps, *Slow Fade To Black*, *supra*, pp. 43-44.

112 Lawrence M. Friedman, *American Law in the Twentieth Century*, *supra*, p.117.

113 James Baldwin, *The Devil Finds Work*, The Dial Press, 1976, p. 45.

114 Thomas Cripps, *Slow Fade To Black*, *supra*, p. 69.

115 Thomas Cripps, *Hollywood's High Noon*, *supra*, p. 30.

116 Fredrickson, G. M., *Racism: A Short History*, Princeton University Press.

117 Hodes, *White Women, Black Men*, (Yale University Press, 1997), 28-31.

118 Novkov, "Racial Constructions: The Legal Regulation of Miscegenation in Alabama, 1890-1934," 20 Law & Hist. Rev. 225, 228.

119 Tsosie, "The New Challenge to Native Identity: An Essay on 'Indigeneity' and 'Whiteness,'" !8 WAUJLP 55, 57, 61.

120 Novkov, "Racial Constructions: The Legal Regulation of Miscegenation in Alabama, 1890-1934," 20 Law & Hist. Rev. 225, 226.

[121] Wiltse, Jeff, *Contested Waters*, p. 25

[122] *Id.*, pp. 78, 79

[123] *Id.*, pp. 3, 78, 82, 86.

[124] Oh, "Interracial Marriage in the Shadows of Jim Crow: Racial Segregation as a System of Racial and Gender Subordination," 39 UCDLR 1321, 1324.

[125] 163 U.S. 537

[126] 106 U.S. 583

[127] 287 U.S. 45

[128] 294 U.S. 587

[129] 388 U.S. 1

[130] Donald Bogle, *Toms, Coons, Mulattoes, Mammies & Bucks*, The Continuum International Publishing Group Ltd., 2001, p. 285.

[131] *Id.*, p. 369.

[132] Norment, Ebony, Nov. 1999.

[133] Neal Gabler, *An Empire of Their Own, supra*, pp. 43-44.

[134] Philip A. Klinkner with Rogers M. Smith, *The Unsteady March, supra*, p. 123.

[135] *Ibid.*

[136] Thomas Cripps, *Slow Fade To Black, supra*, p. 116.

[137] Philip A. Klinkner with Rogers M. Smith, *The Unsteady March, supra*, pp. 124-125.

[138] Michael J. Klarman, "The Racial Origins of Modern Criminal Procedure," 99 Mich.L.Rev.48, p.76.

[139] Thomas Cripps, *Slow Fade To Black, supra*, p. 117.

[140] Paul Johnson, *A History of the American People, supra*, p. 705.

[141] Lisa Aldred, *Thurgood Marshall, Black Americans of Achievement, supra*, p. 34.

[142] Thomas Cripps, *Slow Fade To Black, supra*, p. 152.

[143] Marshall Frady, *Martin Luther King, Jr., supra*, p. 12.

[144] Philip A. Klinkner with Rogers M. Smith, *The Unsteady March, supra*, p. 125.

[145] Michael J. Klarman, "The Racial Origins of Modern Criminal Procedure," *supra*, p. 50.

[146] *Id.*, p. 52.

[147] *Id.* p. 58.

[148] Michael J. Klarman, *From Jim Crow to Civil Rights,* Oxford University Press, 2004, p. 121.

[149] Paul Bergman, Michael Asimow, *Reel Justice, The Courtroom Goes to the Movies, supra*, p. 226.

[150] Thomas Cripps, *Slow Fade To Black, supra*, pp. 115-118.

[151] Melinda Corey and George Ochoa, Editors-in-Chief, *The American Film Institute Desk Reference, supra*, , p. 38.

[152] Thomas Cripps, *Slow Fade To Black, supra,* p. 119.

[153] *id.*, pp. 119-120.

[154] Melinda Corey and George Ochoa, Editors-in-Chief, *The American Film Institute Desk Reference, supra*, pp. 40-45.

[155] Thomas Cripps, *Slow Fade To Black, supra*, pp. 135, 142, 151, 153, 169.

[156] *Id.*, p. 144.

[157] Paul Johnson, *A History of the American People, supra*, p. 704-705.

[158] Thomas Cripps, *Slow Fade To Black, supra*, pp. 150, 152.

[159] *Id.*, pp. 160-161.

[160] Harriet Beecher Stowe, *Uncle Tom's Cabin*, Signet Classic, Penquin Putnam, Inc., 1998, p. 8.

[161] Mrs. Stowe merely says Eliza and Harry stayed in "a neat little apartment." *Id.*, p. 19.

[162] Id at pp. 259, 265.

163 Id. at p. 262.

164 Movies during this decade in the four categories which are not discussed in the text are:

Wings

1927-1928, Best Picture of the Year

Winner of the first academy award ever given for Best Picture of the Year, the story is about World War I. It is a sad commentary on how old men decide the fates of younger men who are wounded and killed in battle. Ethnicity is extremely important to this plot. One character named Herman Schwimpf is required to prove his patriotism over and over, since others suspect he will side with the Germans. Another man is referred to as "Irisher" and one as "Dutchman."

The Gold Rush

1925, AFI's #74 of the Top 100 American Films

Charlie Chaplin portrays life in the Yukon, where food is in such short supply, he eats the sole of his shoe. It is his soul as well as his body that is lonely, until he strikes gold and becomes a multi-millionaire.

The movie makes the point that clothes don't make the man. While aboard a ship headed back home, he is asked to pose for a photograph while wearing the mining outfit he wore when he was desperately poor. In a touching scene, the girl he loves not knowing he is now rich, attempts to pay his passage fare when a ship's hand thinks he is a stowaway.

Easy Virtue

1927, Directed by Alfred Hitchcock

The film displays the strict rules by which 1920s conduct was dictated. When evidence is offered at a divorce case that an attractive woman, who has a drunkard for a husband, is alone in a room with another man, the jury finds "conclusive proof of misconduct." Later, while vacationing on the Mediterranean, the woman meets another man and marries. When the second husband brings home his new wife, his father remarks, "Funny, I thought you would be dark and foreign looking."

The Farmer's Wife

1928, Directed by Alfred Hitchcock

A widower decides it is time to re-marry. But the candidates he selects are either not interested or unsuitable. There was nothing in this very funny silent film which was significant for this work.

Blackmail

1929, Directed by Alfred Hitchcock

A young woman, who has a detective boyfriend, ends up in the apartment of another suitor. He tries to force himself on her, and she stabs him with a nearby knife.

The sacrifice of a man low down on the social scale to shield a woman who killed a man to protect her virtue, is endorsed in this film. It was shot entirely in London, so the lack of blacks in the movie is probably not unusual.

Broadway Melody

1928-1929, Best Picture of the Year

Two sisters try to make it on Broadway. The boyfriend of the sensible one falls in love with the sexy one.

No black actors appear in this film. Nonetheless, there is some significance to this research in that the movie displays both intolerance and a willingness for Hollywood to take a cheap shot at a person's physical disability. The stage manager is presented as being very effeminate. A male character pats the stage manager's cheek and says, "You sweet little cutie." A female character tells the stage manager she is sure he prefers the color lavender. Throughout, a booking agent with a stutter is constantly used as a source of fun and mockery.

165 Thomas Cripps, *Slow Fade To Black, supra*, p. 6.

166 *Id.*, p. 11.

167 *Id.*, pp. 148, 169.

168 Lisa Aldred, *Thurgood Marshall, Black Americans of Achievement, supra*, p. 35.

169 Philip A. Klinkner with Rogers M. Smith, *The Unsteady March, supra*, p. 125.

170 James Oliver North and Lois E. Horton, *Hard Road To Freedom*, Rutgers University Press, 2001, p. 252.

171 *Id.*, pp. 249-255.

172 *Ibid.*

173 *Id.*, pp. 254-256.

174 Lisa Aldred, *Thurgood Marshall, Black Americans of Achievement, supra*, p. 41.

175 *Id.*, p.51.

176 Philip A. Klinkner with Rogers M. Smith, *The Unsteady March, supra*, p. 126.

177 James Oliver North and Lois E. Horton, *Hard Road To Freedom, supra*, p. 256.

178 Philip A. Klinkner with Rogers M. Smith, *The Unsteady March, supra*, p. 126.

179 Nicholas Lemann, *The Promised Land*, Vintage Books, 1992, p. 24.

180 Philip A. Klinkner with Rogers M. Smith, *The Unsteady March, supra*, p. 133.

181 *Id.*, p. 132.

182 *Id.* pp. 126-129, 135.

183 *Id.* p. 130.

184 *Id.* p. 129.

185 Thomas Cripps, *Slow Fade To Black, supra*, p. 264.

186 Philip A. Klinkner with Rogers M. Smith, *The Unsteady March, supra*, pp. 130-131.

187 Johnpeter Horst Grill and Robert L. Jenkings, "The Nazis and the American South in the 1930s: A Mirror Image?," J. of Southern History, Vol. LVIII, No. 4, November 1992, p. 675,

188 Philip A. Klinkner with Rogers M. Smith, *The Unsteady March, supra*, pp. 136-137.

189 Johnpeter Horst Grill and Robert L. Jenkings, "The Nazis and the American South in the 1930s: A Mirror Image?," *supra*, p. 669.

190 Michael J. Klarman, "An Interpretive History of Modern Equal Protection," *supra*, p. 222.

191 Melinda Corey and George Ochoa, Editors-in-Chief, *The American Film Institute Desk Reference, supra*, pp. 50, 51, 53, 56, 59.

192 *Id.*, pp. 51, 54, 56. 59.

193 Thomas R. Cripps, "The Myth of the Southern Box Office: A Factor in Racial Stereotyping in American Movies, 1920-1940," in *The Black Experience in America: Selected Essays 116*, Curtis and Gould, 1970, pp. 116, 120, 139, 140.

194 *Ibid.*

195 *Ibid.*

196 Thomas R. Cripps, "The Myth of the Southern Box Office,: A Factor in Racial Stereotyping in American Movies, 1920-1940,"*supra*, pp., 116, 120-128,

197 Thomas R. Cripps, "The Myth of the Southern Box Office: A Factor in Racial Stereotyping in American Movies, 1920-1940," *supra*, pp. 116, 120, 121, 123, 124, 126, 127, 128, 130, 139.

198 *Id*, pp. 130, 131, 132, 139, 141.

199 James Baldwin, *The Devil Finds Work, supra*, p. 21.

200 John Haag, "Gone With the Wind in Nazi Germany," The Georgia Historical Quarterly, Vol. LXXIII, No. 2, Summer 1989, p. 296.

201 Thomas Cripps, *Slow Fade To Black, supra*, p. 124.

202 Daniel J. Leab, *From Sambo to Superspade*, Houghton Mifflin Company, 1975, p. 107.

203 Donald Bogle, *Toms, Coons, Mulattoes, Mammies & Bucks, supra*, , p. 59.

204 Id. at p. 360.

205 Melinda Corey and George Ochoa, Editors-in-Chief, *The American Film Institute Desk Reference, supra*, p. 59.

206 Ed Guerrero, *Framing Blackness*, Temple University Press, 1993, pp. 15, 17.

207 John Haag, "Gone With the Wind in Nazi Germany," *supra*, pp. 279, 282, 283, 288, 294, 296,

208 Ed Guerrero, *Framing Blackness, supra*, p. 16.

209 Films in four categories not discussed in text are:

Frankenstein

1931, AFI's #87 of the Top 100 American Films

A mad scientist fools around with Mother Nature, and a monster is created. Eventually he escapes. Bloodhounds leading men with torches chase Frankenstein through the dark night, ending at an old windmill which is set on fire. The chase is similar to Eliza's in *Uncle Tom's Cabin*. The last scene shows the burning windmill, with its pedals straight up and down, looking much like a burning cross.

The Skin Game
1931, Directed by Alfred Hitchcock

Class issues abound in this Hatfield/McCoy-type drama. Two families: one, the Hillcrists (headed by the Squire), are gentry. The other, the Hornblowers, are middle class and newly rich. A member of the Squires family brags "We've been here since Elizabeth." Hornblower claims no ancestors and no past but "just the future." The families disagree over the development of land sold by the Squire to Hornblower. When the squabble is over, the Squire remarks, "When we began this fight, we'd clean hands. Are they clean now? What's gentility worth if it can't stand fire?"

Number Seventeen
1932, Directed by Alfred Hitchcock

This has to be one of Hitchcock's worst. It is a dumb murder mystery in an empty house. There was nothing in this film which was significant for *Race Results*. It was shot entirely in London, so the lack of blacks in the movie is probably not unusual.

Grand Hotel
1931-1932, Best Picture of the Year

The entire story takes place in a hotel in Berlin. Rich and wish-they-were-rich guests come and go. A beautiful ballerina falls in love with a jewel thief.

The most elegant dining room in the hotel advertised, but did not show a jazz band, which could be heard in the background. The main character described a disreputable man as "the black sheep of a white flock." There were no black actors in the movie, but this is hardly surprising at this time in Germany. Otherwise, the movie was insignificant for *Race Results*.

Cavalcade
1932-1933, Best Picture of the Year

The first and second scenes are New Year's Eve, 1899 and the death of Queen Victoria, symbolic of the new century's bringing changes. Two families are portrayed, one the owner of the large London home, and the other the servants downstairs. The head of each family shares the common experience of serving in the Boar War, foretelling the blurring of the classes. By the end of the movie, the son of the rich family falls in love with the servant's daughter, who has the upper hand in the relationship.

When discussing their children, the mother of the poor family warns, "Things aren't what they used to be, you know. No. It's all changing." The mother of the rich family states forlornly, "Something seems to have gone out of all of us, and I'm not sure I like what's left."

The Man Who Knew Too Much
1934, directed by Alfred Hitchcock

A family vacationing in Switzerland stumbles upon a spy scheme. The child is kidnapped to keep the parents from divulging the plot.

As with many of Hitchcock's villains, the principal villain, Peter Lorre, was dark skinned. He was a young German refugee, and appeared suspicious with his thickly-accented words and actions.

The 39 Steps
1935, directed by Alfred Hitchcock

A man meets a girl who is up to her neck in intrigue. She is killed, and when he is wrongly accused of her murder, he sets out to clear himself.

The scenes are set in England and Scotland, so the lack of blacks in the film is not unusual. In one scene the male lead is handcuffed to the female lead. He makes a crack about her being the "white man's burden."

Sabotage
1936, directed by Alfred Hitchcock

A woman is unknowingly married to a traitor, who is eventually exposed. Hitchcock continued with his apparent suspicion and disdain of anyone different or foreign. The villain is swarthy and gloomy-looking with thick, dark eyebrows and a heavy distant accent, obviously not English.

Secret Agent
1936, Directed by Alfred Hitchcock

The British Secret Service fake the death of a master spy and "bury" him. He is then given a new name and sent undercover to hunt German agents in Switzerland.

There was nothing in this film which was significant for *Race Results*. It was shot entirely in Europe, and set during World War I with only a few Americans in the cast, so the lack of blacks in the movie is not unusual.

Snow White and the Seven Dwarfs
1937, AFI's #49 of the Top 100 American Films

Regarding the apple, which is blackened from the poison, the wicked queen covers the blackness with a brilliant red color, and says:

"Look . . . on the skin
The symbol of what lies within."

Bringing Up Baby
1938, AFI's #97 of the Top 100 American Films

An anthropologist (Cary Grant) falls in love with a socialite (Katherine Hepburn). Silly, zany, fun-filled film was irreverent to all. There were no blacks actors in the film, and it contained nothing significant for *Race Results*.

The Lady Vanishes
1938, Directed by Alfred Hitchcock

An older British woman disappears on a train in Europe. A younger British woman tries to find her, and no one believes there ever was an older woman.

This film contains a number of cheap shots about ethnicity. One of the characters is a magician named "Doppo." He is first referred to by the female lead as "the little dark man." To set up the joke, the magician introduces himself, not by stating his name, but by saying he is of Italian citizenry. Later, the male lead remarks about the man's large nose. After a scuffle between the magician and the male lead, the lead appears to become faint. When he is asked if he is okay by the female lead, he waves his hand back and forth under his nose and explains, "Garlic. I'll be alright in a minute."

Displaying outrageous elitism, the movie has two remarks implying the superiority of the English. One character abandons her part in a conspiracy by explaining about the victim of a kidnapping, "You never said the old girl was English." A later comment is "But this is murder, and she was an English woman."

The Wizard of Oz
1939, AFI's #6 of the Top 100 American Films

The ideal life among the Munchkins and in Emerald City is enjoyed only by white people. No blacks appear in the cast. There is one positive reference, of sorts, in a jingle sung by the cowardly Lion. The line goes, "What makes the Hottentot hot?" and the answer is "courage."

Stagecoach
1939, AFI's #63 of the Top 100 American Films

Most of the scenes take place on a stagecoach ride across the wild west. Indians attack. Once again, class issues are exposed. Surviving the Indian attack with courage and character intact, a prostitute, a drunken doctor and an escaped convict look more honorable than an Eastern society woman, a former Confederate aristocrat and a bank manager.

Wuthering Heights
1939, AFI's #73 of the Top 100 American Films

An urchin is taken in by a wealthy family. When the head of the family dies, the son takes charge and banishes the orphan to the servant's quarters to do servile work. Nonetheless, the daughter of the house, Kathy, continues to love him.

Continuing with issues of class difference and social prejudice, Heathcliff is referred to as "gypsy scum" and "a roadside beggar giving off airs of equality."

Jamaica Inn
1939, Directed by Alfred Hitchcock

Thieves, who deliberately cause ship wrecks to steal the cargo, occupy an inn. A young woman relative, recently orphaned shows up unexpectedly.

Another of Hitchcock's exposure of the upper crust being just as capable of corruption as everyone else, and that people are not always how they appear from the exterior. Based on a Daphne du Maurier gothic novel, the action takes place entirely in England, so it is not surprising that there are no blacks in the film.

It is the director's final British film before immigrating to America.

Foreign Correspondent
1940, Directed by Alfred Hitchcock

An American newspaper reporter is dispatched to England to find an exciting story to report. He immediately finds himself in the midst of German spies, and in love with a spy's daughter.

Most of the action takes place in Europe right before the outbreak of World War II, so it is not unexpected that no blacks appear in the movie. Hitchcock once again pokes fun at a grinning swarthy man who speaks Latvian, and not English. "Oh, he speaks Latvian. I thought they just rub noses," the main character remarks.

Fantasia
1940, AFI's #58 of the Top 100 American Films
This beautiful and lovely film contains several scenes with a full orchestra, but the lights are too dark to see the race of its members. The remainder of the movie is animated, with characters of all colors.

Rebecca
1940, Best Picture of the Year
Directed by Alfred Hitchcock
A younger woman falls in love with a middle-aged widower. He is withdrawn and depressed much of the time. The housekeeper at his estate, still loyal to his first wife, resents the new one.

The distinctions in economic classes are firmly in place, with the rich being exposed with less character and stamina than the poor. That the story takes place entirely in Europe, even though Hitchcock had moved to the United States, could explain why there are no black characters in the film.

210 Johnpeter Horst Grill and Robert L. Jenkings, "The Nazis and the American South in the 1930s: A Mirror Image?," *supra*, pp. 668-689, 692.

211 Thomas Cripps, *Making Movies Black*, Oxford University Press, 1993, pp. 102, 104.

212 James Oliver North and Lois E. Horton, *Hard Road To Freedom*, *supra*, p. 262.

213 *Id.* at p. 263.

214 *Ibid.*

215 *Id.* at p. 264.

216 *Id.* at p. 265.

217 *Id.* at pp. 264-266.

218 Philip A. Klinkner with Rogers M. Smith, *The Unsteady March, supra*, p. 228.

219 *Los Angeles Times*, Obituaries, June 21, 2003.

220 James Oliver North and Lois E. Horton, *Hard Road To Freedom*, *supra*, pp. 103-104.

221 Marshall Frady, *Martin Luther King, Jr.*, *supra*, p, 15.

222 Nicholas Lemann, *The Promised Land*, *supra*, pp. 3-5.

223 *Ibid.*

224 *Ibid.*

225 *Ibid.*

226 Lisa Aldred, *Thurgood Marshall, Black Americans of Achievement*, *supra*, p. 66.

227 Philip A. Klinkner with Rogers M. Smith, *The Unsteady March, supra*, p. 169.

228 Id. at p. 222.

229 Thomas E. Baker, *The Oxford Guide to United States Supreme Court Decisions*, edited by Kermit L. Hall, 1999, Oxford University Press, p. 290.

230 *Morgan v. Commonwealth of Virginia* (1945) 34 S.E.2d 491, 497; 184 Va. 24, 39

231 Lisa Aldred, *Thurgood Marshall, Black Americans of Achievement*, *supra*, p. 670

232 *Id.*, pp. 64-65.

233 *Shelley v. Kraemer* (1948) 334 U.S. 1. The other three cases were: *McGhee v. Sipes, Hurd v. Hodge* and *Urciolo v. Hodge*.

234 Francis A. Allen, *The Oxford Guide to United States Supreme Court Decisions*, edited by Kermit L. Hall, 1999, Oxford University Press, p. 284.

235 Thomas Cripps, *Slow Fade To Black*, *supra*, p. 3.

236 *Los Angeles Times*, September 29, 2003, from Kazan's front page obituary.

237 The movies in the four categories which are not discussed in the text are:

Suspicion
1941, Directed by Alfred Hitchcock
Self-sufficient woman, on her way to being an old maid, falls in love with jobless Cary Grant. Circumstances make her suspicious that he is a murderer. All of the scenes take place in England, and there are no blacks in the movie. The film provides no information helpful to this work.

How Green Was My Valley

1941, Best Picture of the Year

Idyllic Welsh mining town is the setting for a warm and wonderful family. Both the town and the family are shattered when the mine owner lays off experienced, higher paid, loyal workers. The value of labor is central to the theme of the film. There are no racial issues, but, perhaps signaling a time to change outlook and attitudes, the close-knit family disintegrates and scatters.

Mrs. Miniver

1942, Best Picture of the Year

This film is full of symbolism. World War II shook people—including the middle class family at the center of the story—and their long held values to the core. Everything changed with the war.

The Paradine Case

1947, Directed by Alfred Hitchcock

Lawyer Gregory Peck represents a beautiful woman accused of murdering her husband. He becomes entranced with her, and almost loses his wife. Eventually her guilt becomes obvious, and he snaps back into reality. The entire movie takes place in England. There are no blacks in the film.

Treasure of Sierra Madre

1948, AFI's #30 of the Top 100 American Films

Three men strike off into the Mexican mountains in search of gold. What they find is the depth of each other's souls. The film contains the famous scene where a bandito tells the Americans, "I don't have to show you no stinkin' badges." No black actors appeared in the film.

Rope

1948, Directed by Alfred Hitchcock

Two young men, privileged and snobbish, plan and execute the murder of another young man, just to experience the thrill of danger and the accomplishment of the perfect crime. Afterward they celebrate with champagne. The setting is a high-rise apartment in New York City. There are no black people in the movie. A party following the murder centers around conversation about contempt for humanity and civilization.

Hamlet

1948, Best Picture of the Year

There are three scenes in this movie displaying a man who is outlandishly effeminate, which seems to indicate an intolerance for homosexuals. Gaudily dressed, he limp-wristedly swings his gloves, fans himself with his bonnet, speaks with a lisp, swings his hips and walks on his toes. He looks like a fool when he falls down the steps backward, squealing all the way.

Under Capricorn

1949, Directed by Alfred Hitchcock

The movie is set in mid-nineteenth century Australia where the British rule over a colony founded by convicts. Class distinctions and differences between gentry and ex-convicts become obliterated. Both groups act with honor and dishonor in their activities.

Stage Fright

1950, Directed by Alfred Hitchcock

The film provided no information helpful to this work. It took place entirely in England. Most of the outside shots took place at a garden party. No blacks appear in the film.

238   Thomas Cripps, *Making Movies Black*, supra, p. 104.

239   Neal Gabler, *An Empire of Their Own*, supra, pp. 298-299.

240   Donald Bogle, *Toms, Coons, Mulattoes, Mammies & Bucks*, supra, p. 152.

241   347 U.S. 483, 490.

242   Dudzik, "Desegregation as a Cold War Imperative," 41 Stanford L.Rev. 61, 67, Nov. 1988.

243   *Id.*, p. 62.

244   Brief for the United States as Amicus Curiae, filed in 1952 in 347 U.S. 483.

245   Lee, *Entertainment and Intellectual Property Law* § 12:49, May 2007.

246   Howard Horowitz, "Loyalty Tests For Employment in the Motion Picture Industry," 6 Stanford Law Review 438, FN 48, May 1954.

247   Jeffrey Jacobs, "Comparing Regulatory Models—Self-regulation vs. Government Regulation: The Contrast Between the Regulation of Motion Pictures and Broadcasting May Have Implications For Internet Regulation," 1 Journal of Technology, Law & Policy 4, Spring 1996, p. 4, 16.

248 *Mutual Film Corporation v. Industrial Commission of Ohio* (1915) 236 U.S. 230

249 Reuel E. Schiller, "Free Speech and Expertise," 86 Virginia Law Review 1, Feb. 2000, p. 30.

250 Fox Film Corp. v. Trumbull (1925) 7 F.2d 715.

251 *Department of Education, Division of Film Censorship v. Hissong Classic Pictures* (1953) 112 N.E.2d 311.

252 Neal Gabler, *An Empire of Their Own*, *supra*, pp. 351.

253 Philip A. Klinkner with Rogers M. Smith, *The Unsteady March, supra*, p. 134.

254 Neal Gabler, *An Empire of Their Own*, *supra*, pp. 351-354.

255 Neal Gabler, *An Empire of Their Own*, *Id.*, pp. 356-358.

256 *Id.*, p. 365.

257 Neal Gabler, *An Empire of Their Own*, *Id.*, pp. 354- 355.

258 Nicholas Lemann, "The Long March," *supra*,   pp. 88-90.

259 W.E.B. Du Bois, *Writings*, "The Trial," p. 1071; "The Acquittal," p. 1093, Viking Press, 1984.

260 Mary L. Dudziak, "Desegregation as a Cold War Imperative," 41 Stanford L.Rev. 61, FN-268, Nov. 1988, citing Hearings Regarding Communist Infiltration of Minority Groups, Part I, House Committee on Un-American Activities, 81st Congress, 1st Sess., p. 479.

261 Marshall Frady, *Martin Luther King, Jr., supra*, pp. 30, 36.

262 *Id,* pp. 35-38.

263 *Id,* p. 32.

264 Philip A. Klinkner with Rogers M. Smith, *The Unsteady March, supra*, pp. 241-242.

265 Marshall Frady, *Martin Luther King, Jr., supra*, p. 39.

266 *Id.* p. 37.

267 James Oliver Horton and Lois E. Horton, *Hard Road To Freedom, supra*, pp. 278-279; *Los Angeles Times*, January 20, 2003.

268 Philip A. Klinkner with Rogers M. Smith, *The Unsteady March, supra*, p. 226.

269 See exhibits to case of *Beauharnais v. People of the State of Illinois*, 343 U.S. 250, 276.

270 Nicholas Lemann, *The Promised Land, supra*, pp, 89-95.

271 *Los Angeles Times*, September 29, 2003, from Gibson's front page obituary.

272 James Oliver Horton and Lois E. Horton, *Hard Road To Freedom, supra*, pp. 284-285.

273 *Id.*, pp. 271, 282.

274 *Bolling v. Sharpe*, 347 U.S. 497.The Court in this case came to the same conclusion under the Fifth Amendment, since the District of Columbia is not bound by the Fourteenth Amendment.

275 Lisa Aldred, *Thurgood Marshall, Black Americans of Achievement, supra*, pp. 17-18.

276 Dennis J. Hutchinson, *The Oxford Guide to United States Supreme Court Decisions*, edited by Kermit L. Hall, 1999, Oxford University Press, p. 35.

277 Marshall Frady, *Martin Luther King, Jr., supra*, pp. 33, 35.

278 Marshall Frady, *Martin Luther King, Jr., Id.*, p. 106.

279 J.W. Peltason, *58 Lonely Men: Southern Federal Judges and School Desegregation*, Hartcourt, Brace & World, 1961, p. 15.

280 *Id.*, p. 244.

281 J.W. Peltason, *58 Lonely Men: Southern Federal Judges and School Desegregation, Id.*, p. 38.

282 *Id.*, pp. 81, 109 112, 234.

283 *Id.* pp. 94, 103, 136.

284 *Id.* pp. 58, 64, 65, 69.

285 *Id.* pp. 15-16, 168.

286 Obituary Notice, *Los Angeles Times*, August 10, 2002, p. B-18.

287   *Los Angeles Times*, September 14, 2002

288   Neal Gabler, *An Empire of Their Own*, *supra*,, p. 410.

289   Thomas Cripps, *Making Movies Black*, *supra*, p.4.

290   *Id*. pp. 151-152.

291   Thomas R. Cripps, *The Myth of the Southern Box Office: A Factor in Racial Stereotyping in American Movies, 1920-1940*, *supra*, pp. 116,117, 120, 121, 126, 127, 130.

292   Jack Fischel, "Reds and Radicals in Hollywood," The Virginia Law Quarterly, winter, 2003, p. 177.

293   Jack Fischel, "Reds and Radicals in Hollywood," *Id.*, p. 180.

294   *Id*. p. 370.

295   Jack Fischel, "Reds and Radicals in Hollywood," *Id.*, pp. 178-180.

296   Neal Gabler, *An Empire of Their Own*, *supra*, pp. 383.

297   Neal Gabler, *An Empire of Their Own*, *Id.*, pp. 374, 385.

298   Paul Johnson, *A History of the American People, supra*, pp. 834-837.

299   Nicholas Lemann, "The Long March," The New Yorker, February 10, 2003, pp. 88-90.

300   Jack Fischel, "Reds and Radicals in Hollywood," *supra*, p. 181.

301   Michael J. Klarman, "Brown, Racial Change and the Civil Rights Movement," 80 Va. L. Rev. 7, 26, p. 302

302   Donald Bogle, *Toms, Coons, Mulattoes, Mammies & Bucks*, *supra*, 2001, p. 182.

303   James Baldwin, *The Devil Finds Work, supra*, pp. 61-62.

304   Daniel J. Leab, *From Sambo to Sperspade, supra*, pp. 162-163

305   *Ibid.*

306   Arnold Rose, *Postscript Twenty Years Later,* "Social Change and the Negro Problem," University of Minnesota, June 1962; as a preface to the 1962 publication of Gunnar Myrdal, *An American Dilemma*, Vol. 1, "The Negro Problem and Modern Democracy," Orig. edition published by Harper & Row, 1944, Transaction Publishers, 1999, p. xlviii.

307   See, e.g.; United States of America v. International Longshoremen's Association (1971) 334 F. Supp. 976

308   See Johnpeter Horst Grill and Robert L. Jenkins, "The Nazis and the American South in the 1930s: A Mirror Image?" *supra*, pp. 667-94.

309   Films in four categories not discussed in text are:

All About Eve

1951, AFI's #16 of the Top 100 American Films

The story about the blind ambition of an aspiring actress demonstrates how cruel people can be to others they perceive to be in their way. There are no black actors in this film, which has primarily indoor New York scenes in private homes, theaters and restaurants.

The African Queen

1951, AFI's #17 of the Top 100 American Films

The movie is set in German East Africa in 1914 during World War I. However, most of the actors are white. What interaction there is with the African natives is respectful on the part of both races.

A Place in the Sun

1951, AFI's #92 of the Top 100 American Films

Several scenes take place in a huge bathing suit factory, but the only black employee seen is one janitor. No blacks are shown in numerous street shots and several courtroom scenes. There is a black maid in one of the homes.

An American in Paris

1951, Best Picture of the Year

AFI's #68 of the Top 100 American Films

Gene Kelly and Leslie Caron are lovely as they dance throughout Paris to George and Ira Gershwin's music. In one café, there is a black band, and in a fantasy dance scene, a black man in exotic native costume does a solo.

I Confess

1952, Directed by Alfred Hitchcock

A murderer confesses his crime to a priest in the confessional, and then points to the priest as the suspect.

The priest, bound by his religious duty, must keep silent. The setting is Quebec, and there are no black actors in the film.

High Noon
1952, AFI's #33 of the Top 100 American Films
Within minutes after Grace Kelly and Gary Cooper marry, they find that outlaws are headed for town. Cooper is the marshal and soon finds out the rest of the town will not help him. One character is a Mexican woman who hires a white man to front for her as owner of a store she actually owns. The implication is that her ethnicity would prevent her from success if she tried to run the store herself. There are no blacks in the movie.

Shane
1953, AFI's #69 of the Top 100 American Films
Farmers are being terrorized out of the area by a cattle owner who wants the land to range his herd. A stranger named Shane saves the day. There are no blacks in the movie.

Dial M For Murder
1954, Directed by Alfred Hitchcock
The setting is London. No blacks appear in the film.

The Trouble With Harry
1956, Directed by Alfred Hitchcock
Simple little comedy in unknown tiny American town. Few characters, with no black actors among them.

The Man Who Knew Too Much
1956, Directed by Alfred Hitchcock
Several of the scenes take place in northern Africa. But most of the movie is in London, with no race issues.

The Searchers
1956, AFI's #96 of the Top 100 American Films
The initial setting is Texas, 1868. Almost immediately one of the characters apologetically says his dark skin is explained by his being an eighth Cherokee. When a young white girl's family is killed in a raid, led by a blue-eyed Indian, and she is kidnapped by Indians, two men spend years searching for her.

During the time, an Indian woman mistakenly believes one of them has taken her to be his wife. When he finds her sleeping next to him, he brutally kicks her away, to the delighted laughter of the character played by John Wayne. Later, when it is discovered the white girl, now grown, sleeps with an Indian, there is a discussion about how her mother, were she still alive, would want someone to put a bullet in her head for "sleeping with a buck."

Around the World in 80 Days
1956, Best Picture of the Year
There are no racial issues in the film.

Bridge on the River Kwai
1957, Best Picture of the Year
AFI's #13 of the Top 100 American Films
The entire film takes place in Southeast Asia. There are no black actors in the movie.

Gigi
1958, Best Picture of the Year
The setting is 1900 Paris with beautiful and extravagant song and dance numbers. A teenage girl is taught how to attract and keep male attention. No black actors appear in the film.

Some Like It Hot
1959, AFI's #14 of the Top 100 American Films
The very funny story is about two musicians who join an all-girls band after witnessing a gang massacre. In the train scenes, during travel from Chicago to Florida, there are a few black porters at the Chicago terminal. But during the scenes where the camera stays on a porter for more than a second or two, the train porters are white.

Psycho
1960, AFI's #18 of the Top 100 American Films
Directed by Alfred Hitchcock
The settings are Phoenix, Arizona, the open highway and a few stops on the way from Arizona to California, and a few small towns in the center of California. No black actors appear in the film.

Ben-Hur
1959, Best Picture of the Year
AFI's #72 of the Top 100 American Films
The film takes place primarily in Jerusalem and Rome during the years of Jesus Christ. When the child is

born, one of the wise men is African. Later, when Ben Hur is a slave aboard a Roman galley, a few other slaves are black. In the Rome scenes, black entertainers play African music and perform a native dance.

The Apartment
1960, Best Picture of the Year
AFI's #93 of the Top 100 American Films
Film takes place primarily in a large insurance agency in a Manhattan office building and an apartment. Several well-dressed black workers can be seen in the background of a few scenes in the office building. The janitors in the building are black. The only black actor with a speaking part shines shoes, and states as he catches a coin from a white executive, "Much obliged."

310 Neal Gabler, *An Empire of Their Own*, *supra*, pp. 363.

311 *Los Angeles Times*, September 29, 2003, from Kazan's front page obituary.

312 Cornell Woolrich, "Rear Window," 1942, *The Oxford Book of American Detective Stories*, Oxford University Press, Tony Hillerman and Rosemary Herbert, ed., 1996.

313 Leon Uris, *Topaz,* McGraw-Hill Book Company, 1967, pp. 59-81.

314 Richard Delgado and Jean Stefanic, "Images of the Outsider in American Law and Culture: Can Free Expression Remedy Systemic Social Ills?" 77 Cornell L. Rev., 1258, 1288.

315 Arnold Rose, *Postscript Twenty Years Later,* "Social Change and the Negro Problem, University of Minnesota, June 1962; as a preface to the 1962 publication of Gunnar Myrdal, *An American Dilemma*, Vol. 1, "The Negro Problem and Modern Democracy," *supra*, pp. xxxvii, xliii, liv.

316 Philip A. Klinkner with Rogers M. Smith, *The Unsteady March, supra*, p. 253,

317 *Id*, p. 257.

318 *Id.*, p. 258.

319 *Id.*, pp. 251, 253, 257-258.

320 Robert S. Browne, "The Freedom Movement and the War in Vietnam," No. 4, 1965, *Freedomways Reader*, Westview Press, 2000, p. 160.

321 Lisa Aldred, *Thurgood Marshall, Black Americans of Achievement, supra*, pp. 111-112.

322 James Oliver Horton and Lois E. Horton, *Hard Road To Freedom, supra*, pp. 292-293.

323 Paul Johnson, *A History of the American People, supra*, p. 892.

324 Scott Martelle, *Los Angeles Times* magazine, "A Stain In Alabama," October 27, 2002.

325 Michael J. Klarman, "Brown, Racial Change and the Civil Rights Movement," *supra*, p. 9.

326 Louis E. Burnham, "Not New Ground, but Rights Once Dearly Won," No. 1, 1962, *Freedomways Reader*, Westview Press, 2000, p. 29.

327 Nicholas Lemann, *The Promised Land, supra*, pp, 106-107, 125, 164-165, 200, 227-228,

328 *Ibid.*

329 Philip A. Klinkner with Rogers M. Smith, *The Unsteady March, supra*, 1999, pp. 278, 280-282.

330 Editorial, "Muhammad Ali: The Measure of a Man," No. 2, 1967, *Freedomways Reader*, Westview Press, 2000, pp. 176-177.

331 Louis E. Burnham, "Not New Ground, but Rights Once Dearly Won," *supra*, p. 26.

332 Jimmy McDonald, "A Freedom Rider Speaks His Mind," No. 2, 1961, *Freedomways Reader*, Westview Press, 2000, p. 59.

333 J.W. Peltason, *The Oxford Guide to United States Supreme Court Decisions*, edited by Kermit L. Hall, 1999, Oxford University Press, p. 18.

334 Lawrence M. Friedman, *American Law in the Twentieth Century, supra*, p. 312.

335 Alabama, Mississippi, Texas and Virginia

336 Daniel J. Leab, *From Sambo to Superspade, supra*, p. 234.

337 Thomas Cripps, *Hollywood's High Noon, supra*, pp. 207, 222.

338 Neal Gabler, *An Empire of Their Own, supra*, pp. 394, 431.

339 Ed Guerrero, *Framing Blackness, supra*, p. 29.

340 Melinda Corey and George Ochoa, Editors-in-Chief, *The American Film Institute Desk Reference*, *supra*, p. 98.

341 Daniel J. Leab, *From Sambo to Superspade*, *supra*, p. 233.

342 Melinda Corey and George Ochoa, Editors-in-Chief, *The American Film Institute Desk Reference*, *supra*, p. 94.

343 Donald Bogle, *Toms, Coons, Mulattoes, Mammies & Bucks*, *supra*, pp. 86,88.

344 *Id.* t p. 219.

345 Thomas Cripps, *Hollywood's High Noon*, *supra*, p. 228.

346 Thomas Cripps, *Hollywood's High Noon*, *Id.*, pp. 67, 222.

347 Daniel J. Leab, *From Sambo to Superspade*, *supra*, pp. 233-234.

348 Paul Bergman, Michael Asimow, *Reel Justice, The Courtroom Goes to the Movies*, *supra*, p. 141.

349 Melinda Corey and George Ochoa, Editors-in-Chief, *The American Film Institute Desk Reference*, *supra*, p. 98.

350 Ed Guerrero, *Framing Blackness*, *supra*, p. 73.

351 James Baldwin, *The Devil Finds Work, supra*, pp. 44, 51, 55-56, 57.

352 *Id.* p. 124.

353 Philip A. Klinkner with Rogers M. Smith, *The Unsteady March*, *supra*, pp. 251, 253, 240-241.

354 Donald Bogle, *Toms, Coons, Mulattoes, Mammies & Bucks*, *supra*, p. 219.

355 Ed Guerrero, *Framing Blackness*, *supra*, p. 30.

356 Donald Bogle, *Toms, Coons, Mulattoes, Mammies & Bucks*, *supra*, p. 219.

357 Ed Guerrero, *Framing Blackness*, *supra*, p. 76.

358 Daniel J. Leab, *From Sambo to Sperspade*, *supra*, p. 230.

359 James Baldwin, *The Devil Finds Work, supra*, p. 68.

360 Films in four categories not discussed in text are:

The Birds
1963, Directed by Alfred Hitchcock
Some scenes are in a store and outdoors in San Francisco, and others in a small town sixty miles north of the city where there is an episode in a grammar school classroom. No blacks appear in the film.

Tom Jones
1963, Best Picture of the Year
Most the story takes place in and around London in 1745 with an all-white cast. Yet, out of the blue, a little black boy foppishly dressed in upper class garb, with a turban on his head and a jewel dangling across his forehead, appears as a house servant. He is cast as a buffoon in his few scenes. Later, when Tom Jones escapes the hangman, a unexplained, bare-chested black man gives chase.

Marnie
1964, Directed by Alfred Hitchcock
The entire story about a psychopathic misogynist takes place in England. There are no racial issues in the film.

My Fair Lady
1964, Best Picture of the Year
AFI's #91 of the Top 100 American Films
Story takes place entirely in England, and has no racial issues.

Doctor Zhivago
1965, AFI's #39 of the Top 100 American Films
Set in Russia during the revolution, there are no blacks or racial issues.

The Sound of Music
1965, Best Picture of the Year
AFI's #55 of the Top 100 American Films
Set in Austria immediately before and at the beginning of World War II, there are no racial issues.

Torn Curtain
1966, Directed by Alfred Hitchcock
Scenes are aboard ships and in Scandinavia and Eastern Europe. No black actors in film, and no issues relevant to this work.

A Man for All Seasons
1966, Best Picture of the Year
The story takes place in ancient England when Sir Thomas More and King Henry VIII differ about religion.
The Graduate
1967, AFI's #7 of the Top 100 American Films
No black actors appear in this very funny movie about a recent college graduate who has an affair with a friend of his parents, even though there are outdoor scenes in northern and southern California.
Bonnie and Clyde
1967, AFI's#27 of the Top 100 American Films
Several black men are in the background of a few scenes in film about bank robbers in the South during the Depression.
2001: A Space Odyssey
1968, AFI's #22 of the Top 100 American Films
Film about outer space contains no significant racial scenes.
Oliver
1968, Best Picture of the Year
Eighteenth century London is the scene for this movie, and it has no racial issues.
Butch Cassidy and the Sundance Kid
1969, AFI's #50 of the Top 100 American Films
Story is about train robbers and has no racial issues.
The Wild Bunch
1969, AFI's #80 of the Top 100 American Films
Violent film in the old West; has no significant racial issues.
Easy Rider
1969, AFI's #88 of the Top 100 American Films
Two drug dealers ride their motorcycles throughout the Southwest. In one hick town they ask a lawyer if he can help them get out of jail, where they have been charged with parading without a license. He tells them, "I imagine I can if you haven't killed anybody, at least nobody white."
Midnight Cowboy
1969, Best Picture of the Year
AFI's #70 of the Top 100 American Films
Film takes place primarily in New York City and has no significant racial issues.

361 Neal Gabler, *An Empire of Their Own*, Neal Gabler, *supra*, p. 432.

362 James Baldwin, *The Devil Finds Work, supra*, p. 72.

363 James Oliver Horton and Lois E. Horton, *Hard Road To Freedom, supra*, pp. 329-330.

364 *Id.*, 330.

365 Philip A. Klinkner with Rogers M. Smith, *The Unsteady March, supra*, pp. 295-296.

366 James Oliver Horton and Lois E. Horton, *Hard Road To Freedom, supra*, p. 330.

367 Philip A. Klinkner with Rogers M. Smith, *The Unsteady March, supra*, pp. 295-292.

368 James Oliver Horton and Lois E. Horton, *Hard Road To Freedom, supra*, p. 334.

369 *Id.*, 333-334.

370 Derrick A. Bell, *School Desegregation: Seeking New Victories Among the Ashes*, No. 1, 1977, "Freedomways Reader," Westview Press, 2000, p. 230.

371 Nicholas Lemann, *The Promised Land, supra*, p. 218.

372 Thomas Cripps, *Black Film As Genre, supra*, pp. 60-61.

373 *Id.*, 324.

374 Lennox H. Hinds, *The Death Penalty: Continuing Threat to America's Poor*, No. 1, 1971, "Freedomways Reader," Westview Press, 2000, pp. 262, 265.

375 Bruce McM. Wright, *Bangs and Whimpers: Black Youth and the Court*, No. 3, 1975, "Freedomways Reader," Westview Press, 2000, pp. 254, 257.

376 Philip A. Klinkner with Rogers M. Smith, *The Unsteady March, supra*, pp. 293, 295.

377 *Id.*, pp. 295, 293.

378   *Id.*, 296.

379   *Id.*, 296.

380   Haywood Burns, *The Bakke Case and Affirmative Action: Some Implications for the Future*, No. 1, 1978, "Freedomways Reader," Westview Press, 2000, pp. 233-236.

381   Paul Johnson, *A History of the American People, supra*, pp. 953-954.

382   Philip A. Klinkner with Rogers M. Smith, *The Unsteady March, supra*, p. 299.

383   Paul Johnson, *A History of the American People supra*, p. 955.

384   Melinda Corey and George Ochoa, Editors-in-Chief, *The American Film Institute Desk Reference, supra*, p. 97.

385   *Ibid.*

386   Ed Guerrero, *Framing Blackness, supra*, p. 83.

387   *Id.*, 83.

388   *Id.*, 84.

389   *Id.*, 86.

390   Daniel J. Leab, *From Sambo to Superspade, supra*, p. 254.

391   *Id.*

392   Thomas Cripps, *Black Films As Genre,supra*, p. 53.

393   Ed Guerrero, *Framing Blackness, supra*, p. 81.

394   Donald Bogle, *Toms, Coons, Mulattoes, Mammies & Bucks, supra*, pp. 233-234.

395   Daniel J. Leab, *From Sambo to Sperspade, supra*, p. 239.

396   Donald Bogle, *Toms, Coons, Mulattoes, Mammies & Bucks, supra*, p. 234.

397   Daniel J. Leab, *From Sambo to Sperspade, supra*, p. 241.

398   Donald Bogle, *Toms, Coons, Mulattoes, Mammies & Bucks, supra*, p. 234.

399   Daniel J. Leab, *From Sambo to Sperspade, supra*, p. 249.

400   Donald Bogle, *Toms, Coons, Mulattoes, Mammies & Bucks, supra*, p. 238.

401   Darius James, a.k.a. Dr. Snakeskin, *That's Blaxploitation!, supra*, p. 15.

402   *Id.*, 126.

403   Ed Guerrero, *Framing Blackness, supra*, p. 104.

404   *Id.*, 104-105.

405   Ed Guerrero, *Framing Blackness, Id.*, p. 104.

406   Ed Guerrero, *Framing Blackness, Id*, p 60.

407   *Id.*, 121-122.

408   Ed Guerrero, *Framing Blackness, Id.*, p. 113.

409   *Ibid.*

410   *Id.*, 117-118.

411   *Id.*, 117.

412   W.E.B.Du Bois, *The Souls Of Black Folk, supra*, p. 486.

413   Melinda Corey and George Ochoa, Editors-in-Chief, *The American Film Institute Desk Reference, supra*, p. 98.

414   Donald Bogle, *Toms, Coons, Mulattoes, Mammies & Bucks, supra*, p. 303.

415   *Frenzy*
1972, Directed by Alfred Hitchcock
The entire film takes place in England, and has no racial issues.

416   Ed Guerrero, *Framing Blackness, supra*, p. 94.

417   Paul Johnson, *A History of the American People, supra*, pp. 941, 950.

418   Donald Bogle, *Toms, Coons, Mulattoes, Mammies & Bucks, supra*, p. 268.

[419] James Oliver Horton and Lois E. Horton, *Hard Road To Freedom, supra*, pp. 336-337.

[420] *Id.*, p. 337.

[421] *Ketchum v. Byrne* - The federal trial court's ruling was appealed to the federal Court of Appeals at 740 F.2d 1398 (7th Cir.(Ill.) May 17, 1984); Certiorari to the U.S. Supreme Court denied at 471 U.S. 1135: on remand to the trial court at 630 F.Supp. 551 (N.D.Ill. Dec 27, 1985) (NO. 82 C 4085, 82 C 4431, 82 C 4820).

[422] James Oliver Horton and Lois E. Horton, *Hard Road To Freedom, supra*, p. 334.

[423] Philip A. Klinkner with Rogers M. Smith, *The Unsteady March, supra*, pp. 300, 303.

[424] Paul Johnson, *A History of the American People, supra*, pp. 953-954, 956, 958, 963.

[425] Philip A. Klinkner with Rogers M. Smith, *The Unsteady March, supra*, pp. 304-305.

[426] James Oliver Horton and Lois E. Horton, *Hard Road To Freedom, supra*, p. 334.

[427] Philip A. Klinkner with Rogers M. Smith, *The Unsteady March, supra*, pp. 306-307.

[428] James Oliver Horton and Lois E. Horton, *Hard Road To Freedom, supra*, p. 342.

[429] Philip A. Klinkner with Rogers M. Smith, *The Unsteady March, supra*, pp. 301-303.

[430] Lisa Alred, *Thurgood Marshall, Black Americans of Achievement, supra*, p. 120.

[431] Paul Johnson, *A History of the American People, supra*, pp. 926, 928, 930.

[432] James Oliver Horton and Lois E. Horton, *Hard Road To Freedom, supra*, p. 341.

[433] Philip A. Klinkner with Rogers M. Smith, *The Unsteady March, supra*, 1999, p. 305.

[434] *Ibid.*

[435] Paul Johnson, *A History of the American People, supra*, p. 959.

[436] *Ibid*

[437] James Oliver Horton and Lois E. Horton, *Hard Road To Freedom, supra*, p. 335.

[438] *Id.*, p. 338.

[439] Philip A. Klinkner with Rogers M. Smith, *The Unsteady March, supra*, p. 321.

[440] Donald Bogle, *Toms, Coons, Mulattoes, Mammies & Bucks, supra*, 2001, p. 268.

[441] Theodore Eisenberg, *The Oxford Guide to United States Supreme Court Decisions*, Oxford University Press, 1999, Ed. by Kermit L. Hall, p. 143.

[442] Melinda Corey and George Ochoa, Editors-in-Chief, *The American Film Institute Desk Reference, supra*, pp. 146-147.

[443] Donald Bogle, *Toms, Coons, Mulattoes, Mammies & Bucks, supra*, p. 268.

[444] Melinda Corey and George Ochoa, Editors-in-Chief, *The American Film Institute Desk Reference, supra*, pp. 144, 164, 168, 172-173.

[445] Ed Guerrero, *Framing Blackness, supra*, pp. 138, 140.

[446] Melinda Corey and George Ochoa, Editors-in-Chief, *The American Film Institute Desk Reference, supra*, pp. 105, 112, 113, 118, 140.

[447] *Id.*, p. 146.

[448] Ed Guerrero, *Framing Blackness, supra*, pp. 115-116.

[449] Melinda Corey and George Ochoa, Editors-in-Chief, *The American Film Institute Desk Reference, supra*, pp. 141, 146.

[450] Donald Bogle, *Toms, Coons, Mulattoes, Mammies & Bucks, supra*, p. 268.

[451] *Id.*, p. 285.

[452] *Id.*, p. 283.

[453] Ed Guerrero, *Framing Blackness, supra*, p. 144.

[454] Donald Bogle, *Toms, Coons, Mulattoes, Mammies & Bucks, supra*, pp. 297-298.

[455] *Id.*, p. 292.

[456] *Id.*, p. 298.

[457] Ed Guerrero, *Framing Blackness, supra*, p. 121.

458 Donald Bogle, *Toms, Coons, Mulattoes, Mammies & Bucks, supra*, p. 269.

459 Melinda Corey and George Ochoa, Editors-in-Chief, *The American Film Institute Desk Reference, supra*, 2002, p. 109.

460 Donald Bogle, *Toms, Coons, Mulattoes, Mammies & Bucks, supra*, p. 299

461 *Id.*, p.322.

462 Ed Guerrero, *Framing Blackness, supra*, p. 115, 116.

463 Donald Bogle, *Toms, Coons, Mulattoes, Mammies & Bucks, supra*, p. 302.

464 Ed Guerrero, *Framing Blackness, supra*, 1993, p. 114.

465 Donald Bogle, *Toms, Coons, Mulattoes, Mammies & Bucks, supra*, pp. 269-270.

466 Ed Guerrero, *Framing Blackness, supra*, p. 58.

467 Films in four categories not discussed in text are:
Amadeus
1984, Best Picture of the Year and AFI's #53
There are no black people or racial issues in the film.
The Last Emperor
1987, Best Picture of the Year
There are no black people or racial issues in the film.

468 Ed Guerrero, *Framing Blackness, supra*, p. 127.

469 Donald Bogle, *Toms, Coons, Mulattoes, Mammies & Bucks, supra*, p. 284.

470 *Id.*, p. 285.

471 Ed Guerrero, *Framing Blackness*, Temple University Press, 1993, pp. 122, 123.

472 *Id.*, p. 126.

473 *Id.*, p. 131.

474 "Violence as a way of achieving racial justice is both impractical and immoral. It is impractical because it is a descending spiral ending in destruction for all. The old law of an eye for an eye leaves everybody blind. It is immoral because it seeks to humiliate the opponent rather than win his understanding; it seeks to annihilate rather than to convert. Violence is immoral because it thrives on hatred rather than love. It destroys community and makes brotherhood impossible. It leaves society in monologue rather than dialogue. Violence ends by defeating itself. It creates bitterness in the survivors and brutality in the destroyers.' Martin Luther King, Jr. 475   Ed Guerrero, *Framing Blackness, supra*, p. 147.

476 *Id.*, p. 160.

477 James Oliver Horton and Lois E. Horton, *Hard Road To Freedom, supra*, p. 335.

478 W. Lewis Burke, South Carolina Law Review, "Killing, Cheating, Legislating, and Lying: A History of Voting Rights, Summer 2006, pp. 864-865.

479 Smith, Catherine E., "(Un)Masking Race-Based Intracorporate Conspiricies Under the Ku Klux Klan Act," Virginia Journal of Social Policy, Winter, 2004, p. 137.

480 Du Bois, W.E.B., "The Souls of Black Men," Du Bois Writings, Viking Press, 1984, p. 486.

481 Michael J. Klarman, *The Racial Origins of Modern Criminal Procedure, supra*, p. 50.

482 *Id.*, p. 52.

483 *Moore v. Dempsey* (1923) 261 U.S. 86

484 Friedman, Lawrence M., *American Law in the 20th Century* , *supra*, p. 290.

485 Lemann, Nicholas, *The Promised Land,, supra*, pp. 283, 285-286.

486 Butler, Paul, "Racially Based Jury Nullification: Black Power in the Criminal Justice System," 105 Yale Law Journal 677, 1995, p. 678.

487 *Id.*, pp. 678, 679.

488 *Id.,* pp. 679, 695-696.

489 Pittsburgh Post-Gazette, "Stop Snitchin' shirts stopping criminal trials," October 18, 2005, Local News.

490 The Boston Globe, "No Honor in Silence," December 19, 2005, B1.

491 *The Baltimore Sun*, "Stop Snitchin' Shirts Have People Talking For Different Reasons," April 30, 2005, 1A.

492 Hyman, David A., "Rescue Without Law: An Empirical Perspective on the Duty to Rescue," 84 Texas Law Review 653, 2006, fn. 144.

493 Steinbuch, Robert, "Reforming Federal Death Penalty Procedures: Four Modest Proposals To Improve the Administration of the Ultimate Penalty," 40 Indiana Law Review 97, 2007, fn. 66.

494 Sherwin, Richard K., "Law in the Digital Age: How Visual Communication Technologies Are Transforming the Practice, Theory and Teaching of Law," Boston University Journal of Science and Technology Law, Summer 2006, 227, fn. 115.

495 US Sentencing Commission, Special Report to the Congress: Cocaine and Federal Sentencing Policy (Washington, DC: US Sentencing Commission, April 1997), p. 8.

496 Report to the Legislature Pursuant to Penal Code Section 1170.45, "2006 Report on the Disposition of Criminal Cases According to the Race and Ethnicity of the Defendant," Judicial Council of California, 2007, pp. 7, 11 12.

497 American Civil Liberties Union, "Sanctioned Bias: Racial Profiling Since 9/11, 2004, p. 11.

498 American Civil Liberties Union, "A Bond Forged in Struggle," 2006, p. 28.

499 American Civil Liberties Union, "Sanctioned Bias: Racial Profiling Since 9/11, 2004, p. 18.

500 *Whren v. U.S.* (1996) 517 U.S. 806

501 *Terry v. Ohio* (1968) 392 U.S. 1; *Illinois v. Wardlow* (2000) 528 U.S. 119.

502 *Brown v. Texas* (1979) 443 U.S. 47

503 *Whren v. U.S.* (1996) 517 U.S. 806

504 James Oliver Horton and Lois E. Horton, *Hard Road To Freedom*, *supra*, p. 346.

505 *Id.*, p. 341.

506 Ed Guerrero, *Framing Blackness*, *supra*, p. 162.

507 James Oliver Horton and Lois E. Horton, *Hard Road To Freedom*, *supra*, p. 346.

508 *Id.*, pp. 347-348.

509 Paul Johnson, *A History of the American People, supra*, p. 958.

510 James Oliver Horton and Lois E. Horton, *Hard Road To Freedom*, *supra*, p. 349.

511 Ed Guerrero, *Framing Blackness*, *supra*, p. 162.

512 James Oliver Horton and Lois E. Horton, *Hard Road To Freedom*, *supra*, p. 346.

513 Paul Johnson, *A History of the American People, supra*, p. 934.

514 James Oliver Horton and Lois E. Horton, *Hard Road To Freedom*, *supra*, p. 347.

515 *Ibid.*

516 Paul Johnson, *A History of the American People, supra*, pp. 966-967.

517 James Oliver Horton and Lois E. Horton, *Hard Road To Freedom*, *supra*, p. 354.

518 *Id.* , p. 344.

519 Philip A. Klinkner with Rogers M. Smith, *The Unsteady March, supra*, p. 306.

520 Paul Johnson, *A History of the American People, supra*, pp. 939, 971-972.

521 *Id.*, p. 956.

522 James Oliver Horton and Lois E. Horton, *Hard Road To Freedom*, *supra*, pp. 349-350.

523 Paul Johnson, *A History of the American People, supra*, p. 962.

524 Barry Glassner, *The Culture of Fear*, Basic Books, 1999, p. 109.

525 James Oliver Horton and Lois E. Horton, *Hard Road To Freedom*, *supra*, pp. 350-351.

526 *Id.*, pp. 353-354

527 Philip A. Klinkner with Rogers M. Smith, *The Unsteady March, supra*, p. 306.

528 *Id.*, p. 313.

529 Melinda Corey and George Ochoa, Editors-in-Chief, *The American Film Institute Desk Reference, supra*, p. 147.

530   James Oliver Horton and Lois E. Horton, *Hard Road To Freedom, supra*, p. 52.

531   Donald Bogle, *Toms, Coons, Mulattoes, Mammies & Bucks, supra,,* p. 369.

532   Films in four categories not discussed in text are:
Dances With Wolves
1990, Best Picture of the Year
AFI's #75 of the Top 100 American Films
There are no racial issues relevant to this work in the film.
The Silence of the Lambs
1991, Best Picture of the Year
AFI's #65 of the Top 100 American Films
There are no racial issues in film.
Schindler's List
1993, Best Picture of the Year
AFI's #9 of the Top 100 American Films
While there are significant racial issues in the film, there are none that directly apply to this work.
Braveheart
1995, Best Picture of the Year
There are no racial issues in the film that are relevant to this work.
Fargo
1996, AFI's #84 of the Top 100 American Films
There are no racial issues in film.
The English Patient
1996, Best Picture of the Year
There are no racial issues in the film relevant to this work.
Titanic
1997, Best Picture of the Year
There are no racial issues in film.
Shakespeare in Love
1998, Best Picture of the Year
There are no racial issues in film.
American Beauty
1999, Best Picture of the Year
There are no significant racial issues in film, although the few black high school students shown 46 years after *Brown* is worthy of note.

533   781 F.2d 993

534   484 U.S. 1011

535   Thomas Cripps, *Slow Fade To Black, supra*, pp. 150, 152.

536   Harriet Beecher Stowe, *Uncle Tom's Cabin*, Signet Classic, Penguin Putnam, Inc., 1998, p. 12.

537   Mrs. Stowe merely wrote that Eliza and Harry stayed in "a neat little apartment." p. 19.

538   Harriet Beecher Stowe, *Uncle Tom's Cabin*, Signet Classic, Penguin Putnam, Inc., 1998, pp. 259, 265.

539   Thomas Cripps, *Slow Fade To Black, supra*, pp. 150, 152.

540   *Id.*, pp. 416, 419.

541   Richard M. Dalfiume, *Desegregation of the U.S. Armed Forces,* University of Missouri Press, 1969, pp. 159, 161, 171, 220.

542   Executive Order 9981 reads: "1. It is hereby declared to be the policy of the President that there shall be equality of treatment and opportunity for all persons in the armed services without regard to race, color, religion, or national origin. This policy shall be put into effect as rapidly as possible, having due regard to the time required to effectuate any necessary changes without impairing efficiency or morale. [¶] 2. There shall be created in the National Military Establishment an advisory committee to be known as the President's Committee on Equality of Treatment and Opportunity in the Armed Services, which shall be composed of seven members to be designated by the President."

543   Donald Bogle, *Toms, Coons, Mulattoes, Mammies & Bucks, supra*, p. 152.

544 Daniel J. Leab, *From Sambo to Sperspade, supra*, 1975, pp. 162-163.

545 Sherrie Armstrong Tomlinson, "No New Orleanians Left Behind: An Examination of the Disparate Impact of Hurricane Katrina on Minorities," 38 Connecticut Law Review 1153, July 2006, p. 1174, 1176.

546 William P. Quigley, "Thirteen Ways of Looking at Katrina: Human and Civil Rights Left Behind Again," Tulane Law Review, March, 2007, 955, p. 1009.

547 Sherrie Armstrong Tomlinson, "No New Orleanians Left Behind: An Examination of the Disparate Impact of Hurricane Katrina on Minorities," 38 Connecticut Law Review 1153, July 2006, p. 1176.

548 Los Angeles Times, *Unfinished Business*, Opinion, July 8, 2007.

549 Diane J. Klein, Associate Professor of Law at the University of La Verne College of Law, Los Angeles Daily Journal, Forum, July 9, 2007.

550 Derrick A. Bell, "Who's Afraid of the Critical Race Theory," University of Illinois Law Review, 1995, pp. 901-902.

551 *Id.*, pp. 899-902.

552 *Id.*, pp. 899-903.

553 Editor's Foreward, "Symposium: New Dimensions of Citizenship,"75 Fordham Law Review 2373, April 2007, p. 2373.

554 Patrick M. Garry, "Liberty From on High: The Growing Reliance on a Centralized Judiciary to Protect Individual Liberty," 95 Kentucky Law Review 385, 2006-2007, p. 402.

555 James Forman, Jr., "The Rise and Fall of School Vouchers: A Story of Religion, Race, and Politics," 54 UCLA Law Review 547, February 2007, pp. 550-551.

556 127 S.Ct. 2738; WL 3342258 (U.S.), Nov. 9, 2007

ABOUT THE AUTHOR

Author Eileen Comerford Moore was born and raised in Philadelphia, Pennsylvania. She worked as a registered nurse for seven years, including serving as a combat nurse in Vietnam. She is a life member of Vietnam Veterans of America and has kept her nursing license active so she doesn't forget her roots. She graduated Cum Laude from the University of California Irvine in 1975, then pursued the study of law and graduated from Pepperdine University School of Law in 1978. She received a Masters degree from the University of Virginia in 2004. Moore has been a Justice on the California Courts of Appeal since 2000. From 1989 to 2000, she was a trial judge on the California Superior Court.